MATT PRESTON'S
100 BEST RECIPES

Simple and delicious recipes everyone should know

plum.

Pan Macmillan Australia

CONTENTS

INTRODUCTION

There is a small, flat, white and yellow enamel bowl in my mum's kitchen; its edges have always been chipped so the black metal underneath shows through. It's the sort of cheap, crocked thing that should have been thrown away years ago, but I've always insisted my mother keep it. She doesn't know why, but being a mother she doesn't question, just does it. Well, at least this time.

This is my favourite piece of kitchen kit because it is the only pan that's perfect for making the first recipe I ever 'invented'. I must have been about seven. It started out as a sort of eggs in butter baked under the grill (ooh, see how early a theme starts to emerge here); the metal pan was vital for heat transference so the bottom of the eggs cooked even though only the top was exposed to the direct heat. This simple dish morphed into something with curry powder and currants. As there are only so many glassy-topped eggs you can eat, I then moved on to customising baked beans. First with curry powder and sultanas – perhaps then with an egg cooked in it, all cooked in this pan under the grill of course – or with chunks of frankfurter sausages. This was long before you could buy cans of Franks 'n' Beans, or before I even understood what the euphemism 'frank and beans' actually meant.

It is perhaps a little worrying that my earliest vivid memories all seem to involve food – albeit often inextricably linked to football. I grew up in a basement flat behind the old Watney's bottling plant in the King's Road in London. Mick and Keef from the Stones lived in the next street and with the ever-so-groovy Granny Takes a Trip boutique round the corner, the area was a centre of 1960s counterculture. I remember nothing of this – but I do clearly remember the summer of 1966 and stepping out of the local newsagent with a World Cup Willy nougat bar clutched in my hot little hand. I'd saved up the pennies to buy it for weeks. I can still clearly remember the waxy feel of the paper and the white sticky pully chewiness beneath. Can't remember Geoff Hurst's goal in the final, but.

The flat was a beer bottle's throw from Stamford Bridge, home of the mighty Chelsea Football Club. That was back in the days when the players all lived around the area and you'd see them on Sundays tinkering under the bonnet of their Ford Anglias – even though Chelsea were then (as they are again) a playboy glamour team of flash-dressing players like Peter Osgood and Alan Hudson. Every other Saturday the whole area would ring with the chants of the Shed boot boys and reek with the stench of stewing rehydrated onions and grey burgers bobbing in brine from the burger carts that coralled the ground; all somewhat different from the Marco Pierre White restaurant and oyster bars at the Bridge today.

These burgers weren't the only food I had a massive aversion to. I must have been about four when I started to refuse to eat the whites of eggs – especially if they were still runny. This caused a number of Mexican stand-offs with my mother that would result in me having to sit on the back step with my dinner plate, usually in tears and with a burning sense of indignation, until I'd 'finished'. This stopped when she noticed how the cat and dog were putting on weight. Later at school my horror at scotch eggs, or more importantly my refusal to eat their whites, landed me in similar strife. The line 'Well send it to the starving Biafrans, then!' didn't endear me to the dinner ladies; I would have been eight or so, and already quite lippy. I still don't like egg whites that are translucent – too much like the start of a bad head cold for me – but now I can professionally blame the incompetence of the cook for why I am not eating them! Good times!

Most of my food aversions as a kid, I now realise, were totally defensible. I hated gristly stews and fish pies made with stinky old fish, which were pretty much all you seemed to be able to get in London those days. Only while writing this now do I realise that all four of these – the burger, egg whites in many forms, stews and fish pie – make an appearance in this book but in a far, far more appetising guise. I see this as proof that cooking is a far better way to overcome aversions than expensive therapy!

There was, however, much that I loved to eat. I remember my mother as a good cook. She had a roster of a dozen or so recipes rotated weekly. Spag bol, stuffed cabbage leaves and meatloaf were highlights; packet chicken noodle soup, canned tomato soup or eggy bread on Sunday less so. She'd studied in France and Italy, first at the Sorbonne in Paris and then in the Eternal City, although from what I can gather her chosen subject there seemed to be 'young Australian artists in residence'. The spag bol she learnt was great, however, and it underpins my one that follows. She also made a great risotto with chicken livers, which was more like a pilaf – she'd apparently learnt it from her stepmother, who'd learnt it from the UK's first celebrity cook, Elizabeth David, back in her dissolute Cairo days. This was my first understanding of how far a recipe could travel, how influential it could be, and that back then cooks and food writers like David were always far cooler (and having far more fun) than the scary grumpy blokes in the tall white hats shouting at people in hotel kitchens.

My father seldom cooked but when he did it would be curries that would take two days to prepare and two weeks to clean up after (Apple? Tree?), or better yet a sort of chocolate malted milk shake that tasted like icy-cold liquid Maltesers. That's one that I'll have to develop for the next book, as it's right in line with those trendy 'dude food' principles of excess that lure me!

It was Dad who would make us eat out: thin-crust pizza at the original Pizza Express, an authentic burger at the Great American Disaster, tripe in a little French place, a dinner of 19 little courses at a Sichuan restaurant, and jugged hare at the very hip Hungry Horse, which was the first real restaurant in London to re-celebrate traditional English food. Each was a watershed moment in London dining, I realise now. I can also remember each of these pre-teen memories so very clearly – the room, the atmosphere and even the taste and texture the food. In light of this, perhaps I shouldn't have waited until I was over 30 to start writing about food!

It is, of course, illegal to write about early food memories without crediting your grandmother – even if now, in your own so-modern restaurant, you only put up plates of flavoured dust and gels that she'd never recognise as food.

My maternal grandmother was a wonderful woman, a skilled punter but a terrible cook. She did, however, grow her own white asparagus and take me picking blackberries from jumbled barbed-wire briars to make a bramble jelly so dark that it shimmered like liquid jet. Besides these – oh, and having a mouse-y pantry famous for its very out-of-date use-by-dates – she was famous for three things: her lemon mousse, her mayonnaise salads loaded with cheese or egg, and the way she ate her apple with salt. We put this last one down to her being half American, but nowadays salt with sweet is all the rage and maybe she was just ahead of her time. You'll find salty desserts and a certain number of cheese- and egg-based salads served with mayo in the following pages, so her fingerprints are definitely on how I cook today.

That's the weird thing about the food you loved as a child. It doesn't need to be great to be remembered fondly. It is also a reminder to me that too often, great home cooking is about clearing a path down a previously trodden but now overgrown track rather than blazing a whole new trail.

My other grandmother was a magnificent cook but came from a family of shocking punters. She'd come to cooking late, in a post-war era when a whole class of army wives found themselves at the stoves where once there used to be 'cook'. She had a wonderful natural aptitude for re-creating dishes she'd tried before and an appreciation of flavours. Hers was an old-fashioned farmhouse kitchen with a split stable door and a large, wood-fired Aga stove which always had something warm and meaty slowly cooking in its depths. When I arrived in Australia I saw so much of her cooking and baking out in the countryside here. It's just that the battered old fifties biscuits tins here had fading pictures of long-forgotten surf carnivals on them rather than a Clydesdale straining at the plough against a Constable landscape.

She loved to make big meaty soups. I loved to eat them – until she shocked my little six-year-old self by revealing it was oxtail. I promptly burst into tears and demanded to know what other horrors she had done to Ferdie, my favourite bull down on Mr Ticehurst's farm. I wouldn't eat until I walked down to his stall to check that Ferdie was unmaimed. He was fine, but you still won't find oxtail in any of the recipes that follow.

She also loved to spoil me with food and didn't really 'get' some of the then-modern fads like cereal. Hence her decision that Coco Pops should be served with whipped cream, as serving them with milk was common. I was never going to correct her on that one. This might explain why you'll find, among all the seasonal and local ingredients, the occasional addition of Coco Pops, instant coffee, tinned peaches or pineapple, cola and tomato sauce in the recipes that follow.

At her instruction, my grandfather tended a large vegetable plot where we'd cut lettuces, pick strawberries that tasted extra sweet on the sun-warmed side, and endlessly water the tangled fruit-laden jungle of tomato plants in a greenhouse heady with their scent. He didn't cook apart from magnificent scrambled eggs which he claimed he'd learnt from President Kennedy. As both my grandfathers appeared to have some quite serious connections to the intelligence community, you could never be sure if he was joking or not.

My earliest summer holidays were months in the country with my grandparents, but then came the cheap package holidays. Suddenly the mussels of Brittany, the cheese- and custard-filled pastry 'nuns' of Normandy, the grills and paellas of the Costa Brava and a whole kaleidoscope of pizza and pastas were opened up to me. The food was often basic (we weren't rich – my father was a perpetually struggling naval historian who was a far better writer than businessman) but even back then I realised that the best food didn't always come in the flashiest places or on fancy plates. Like the damp campsites where the squidgy dark porkiness of local dried sausages and dry local bread sodden into sweet tangy juicy submission by impossibly ripe tomatoes would keep our spirits up between the inflammatory games of Monopoly and Racing Demon that would always dissolve into internecine sibling rivalry.

Older and wiser, next the rows were with girlfriends, but punctuated with mushroom-picking on Italian hillsides and afternoons spent drinking moonshine with the local farmers who kept their cows under the bedrooms for warmth in winter. By now I'd always be the one who ended up cooking. I'm not sure why, but recently another old girlfriend did reveal that she was actually a pretty good cook but just couldn't be bothered doing it during the five years of our relationship. I should probably thank her for this, as there is nothing like cooking every day to improve your skills in the kitchen! A Melbourne girl, she was also the first really obsessive foodie I'd ever dated and that led to some amazing culinary adventures which helped set me on the path that I am on now. We are still friends, which is a testament to the power of the love of food.

These are all the foundations of who I am as a cook as much as they are of who I am as a man. Much more so than those years of school lunches, when what was on the plate was just a carb hurdle to clear before getting down behind the bike sheds, or that decade of corporate entertaining when I come to realise that memorable food is usually memorable because of your love of the people you share it with. Take that away and it runs the risk of being no more than fuel or, worse than that, ostentation.

Much of the food in this book reflects these roots – not because it's some homage to the past, but because it's the food I eat at home today with my family or with my friends. It is simple, honest food that doesn't bust the bank and doesn't take two days to make. With the swimming squad, footy training, school drop-offs, band practice, netball, dishwasher unstacking, washing folding, dog walking and soccer regime that comes with three children under 12, it has to be! Australian figures show that we tend to spend about 20 minutes in the kitchen making dinner, which conveniently is also reflected by the time it takes to prepare so many of my recipes here.

There are also some recipes here for meals that my kids, Sadie, William and Jonathan, would now like to call their own and regularly demand to make. The sort of stuff they cook now, and will undoubtedly cook for their own children – pasta, pizza dough, meringue, pastry, biscuits. Interestingly these all revolve around sugar, eggs or flour, which I suspect is just so they can ensure maximum mess in the kitchen for me to clean up! When it comes to favourite dishes, apart from this DIY food, there's usually a clamour for chicken wings, pretty much any meat that's been barbecued or roasted, and anything sweet.

Jonathan (12) loves his soups (pumpkin, minestrone, pea and ham) and pretty much all the braises in this book. He's also the most adventurous eater, so he's the one who'll demand I dust off my recipe for mussels or for salmon with a honey, dill and mustard sauce. William (9) is the fussiest and hates both mashed potato and mushrooms, but he's also the most likely to take ownership of a recipe. Like a Genovese nonna, he is convinced that his pesto is the best and that mine is too cheesy and too oily. I fear he might be right, which is why it's his recipe for pesto that appears here. Sadie (7) is our contrary eater. She loves fresh tomatoes but is one of only ten children in Australia who hates lasagne. She is also the most dismissive and critical of my cooking – I don't know how those chefs put up with it! She also loves the social experience of eating out and the dressing up that goes with it. She is undoubtedly my daughter!

While we are on family meals, yes, I do think it is important to sit down and eat together around the table or at the kitchen bench with the video games away and the TV off – and we do, less, it is important that everyone waits until the cook is seated before starting. And yes, it is also important that the kids say thanks for dinner, don't eat like barbarians, and help lay the table and clear afterwards. These are the rituals that maintain civilisation. Having said that, and before I start sounding like my severe grandmother, I am a firm believer that the table should also always be a place for laughter and joy; somewhere to celebrate both life and food.

To be able to eat with the ones you love is such a joyous thing and provides the memories on which your future will be built. So please, cherish each meal, no matter how humble. Be conscious when you eat and always remember it is the people round the table rather than the food on the table that truly matter – but it doesn't hurt if the food is beautiful too, right!

At home it tends to be my wife Emma who cooks for the kids and I cook for her, so I suppose this recipe book is as much about her cooking as mine. One of the greatest things about a new family's food is the cross-pollination of two different families' kitchens. This can also occasionally cause issues, such as the constant debate that rages in our house over the correct way to make a pea and ham soup or a spag bol. Just for the record <u>mine is better</u> and that's why it's <u>my</u> recipe in <u>my</u> recipe book! Don't worry, she wins more than her fair share in the following pages!

Emma loves great food as much as I do but she remains refreshingly undazzled by fancy restaurants, where I can get a little over-excited and skittish. She remains constantly unimpressed by some new fancy technique or ingredient that I've picked up from a chef mate unless it tastes really good. We are a good match and I promise that these recipes are free of any cheffy trickery unless it's a wheeze or tip that will help you do something far quicker, a lot better or much more easily.

One thing that working for *delicious.* and for the 'Taste' section in your favourite metro newspaper has taught me is that if a recipe isn't easily achievable, affordable and minimum fuss, then neither you nor I will bother to make it. So again that's what you'll find here – dozens of recipes that I love to cook at home for family or friends using such much-loved staples such as mince, salmon, chicken wings, lamb chops or veg. You'll also find great suggestions on how to lift everything from your chocolate brownies or banana bread to your bolognese, salads or favourite soup to new levels of flavour and texture with regular tips on how to accessorise or improve a familiar dish.

These are affordable, easily achievable and delicious dishes that I hope you'll want to try – and then cook again and again. It is the food that I cook when the cameras aren't rolling, when friends are due over for dinner or the kids are screaming for their tea. It is unapologetically simple food using everyday ingredients that you'll also be able to get your hands on easily. Let's face it, life's too short to spend hours in the car gathering the obscure elements for some equally obscure Bavarian dish that might be ruthlessly authentic but also not very tasty.

The recipes here might be generally easy and quick to make, but they have been designed to deliver maximum flavour. For me, flavour is the Holy Grail when cooking. Also, because these recipes are largely by a home cook (me!) and made in a home kitchen (mine!) there are no $30K blast chillers or immersion circulators in use here. A pot, a knife, a wooden spoon and a blender or sieve are about all you'll need. Even the majority of the ice-cream recipes here are made without an ice-cream machine! I will nag you to buy a $20 kitchen thermometer, though, so do it next time you are at the shops and you can feel a little smug when I bring it up for the first of many times on page 80. Over its life it will save you hundreds of dollars in overcooked or undercooked food.

So there we have it. This is the food that I've loved since childhood; the things I cook on a Friday night or Sunday lunch or Tuesday evening at home; the dishes that came with my relationships and stayed like the best sort of out-of-court settlement; the recipes that were the best dowry ever paid; and the meals that I cook my children and my wife to tell them, without words, that I love them. This is everyday food that should never be taken for granted because the very act of cooking it for the ones you love ennobles it – no matter how quick and easy it was to make.

… and none of it requires you to have a small, flat, yellow and white enamel bowl to make it!

SOUP

Great soup is simple soup. Chunky, creamy, thick or crystal clear, great soup is made up of four key elements: the stock, the flavourings, the hero ingredient and any garnishes. First up, make sure you use the best stock you can find.

Good stock is easy, cheap and very satisfying to make, which is why you'll find a great chicken stock recipe in this chapter! While homemade stock is wonderful and frugal, shop-bought stock is fine too. Just make sure you buy the salt-reduced varieties, as stocks reduce during the cooking of your soup and you want to be able to control the saltiness.

My favourite soups revolve around puréeing cooked vegetables with stock and adding some milk for extra creaminess. These are crazy-simple to make. I usually start with a flavour base of diced carrot, celery and onion, which I fry. Add some bacon or speck if you want an oomphier soup! A mashed anchovy will give your bigger, red-meatier soups an added savouriness, while frying your onions with a blade or two of star anise will make them taste almost meaty.

Next I'll deglaze the pan with sherry or white wine and throw in the hero of my soup, whether it's a kilo of parsnips or sweet potatoes roasted until soft in a 160°C oven; cubes of celeriac that have been simmered in milk until soft; peeled and sliced Jerusalem artichokes that have been sautéed in butter until tender; or simple steamed broccoli. Cooking veg for soup in these ways ensures their flavour goes into the soup and not into any cooking water.

Now blitz your base with your chosen veg and a cup of stock until smooth with a stick blender or in a food processor. Add more stock (or some milk for creamier soups) until you get the desired consistency. If you want your soup even smoother, pass it through a fine sieve to remove fibres and any lumps. This will give you a satiny-textured soup.

Many soup recipes suggest adding potatoes. This is as much for the smooth texture they add to soups as for their cheap bulking properties. I'd rather use more of the soup's core vegetable as I find the potato inevitably dilutes the intensity of the soup. In Spain and Italy, bread can serve the same purpose. Break up stale bread and let it soak and soften in your soup before serving. This works best with looser, clear or broth-ier style soups.

Now, time for more flavourings: a little curry powder or a spoon of Thai green curry paste goes great with that sweet potato, while roasting unpeeled cloves of garlic with your parsnips will add a welcome extra sweetness and interest to that soup. Just squeeze the roasted garlic out of their papery skins into the soup when you process it.

The final touch is to garnish the soup. Soups crave garnishes the way a dictator's wife craves designer shoes, $10,000 handbags and a trip to Rodeo Drive. The right garnish on a soup can add wonderfully delicious twists and contrasts in taste, texture and even temperature.

It can be something as simple and classic as swirling a little comma of cream on the top of your tomato soup, or just some chopped fresh herbs. Basil and marjoram both work wonderfully on tomato soup, while a thyme-infused cream is perfect added to your chicken or leek and potato soup. Your garnish can be very simple, such as butter-fried leeks, or as intricate as croutons dolloped with garlicky rouille (a sauce made from olive oil, breadcrumbs, garlic, saffron and chilli) on a bouillabaisse, or a raft of toasty bread all bubbly with melted gruyere cheese on top of a classic Parisian onion soup.

Saltiness and crunch are also perfect additions to most puréed soups, whether this comes from a crumble of crushed salty nuts with nubs of nicely browned bacon or even smashed corn chips or strips of tortillas on any soup with Mexican flavourings.

You won't be surprised to discover that for me there are few more important garnishes than pork. Sizzly, crispy strips of bacon, shards of toasted prosciutto or cubes of fried speck will meet all three of those garnish aims, providing contrasts in texture, taste and temperature. That celeriac soup loves the addition of fried pancetta and Brussels sprouts, while a Jerusalem artichoke soup sings with a crumble of hazelnuts, bacon, chestnuts and thyme piled in its centre. Porky goodness is ace on every soup but especially those made with veg from the cabbage family, such as broccoli.

To prove how soup can be a canvas for so many great flavours, let's look at a test case:

CAULIFLOWER SOUP

To make the perfect cauliflower soup, first soften diced onion and a couple of crushed garlic cloves in a little olive oil in a large pot. Throw in a large (1 kg) head of cauliflower chopped into florets. Cover with 1 litre (4 cups) of chicken stock, bring to the boil and then reduce to a simmer. Cook until the cauliflower is tender. Blitz, stir in 100 ml of cream and season.

To garnish it . . . Oh, where do we start? Cauliflower soup is a wonderful canvas for myriad flavours. A dollop of crème fraîche or a swirl of sour cream are classic, especially if you sprinkle on some thyme as well – but why not try floating some pan-seared scallops on the top of your cauliflower soup instead. These can then be topped with a golden crumble of fried diced bacon, garlic and large breadcrumbs. Alternatively, crumble on a salty blue cheese like stilton or roquefort. They are expensive but you don't need much because the blue flavour and saltiness are so strong. Add some toasted or candied walnuts if you want some crunch and a perfect flavour counterpoint.

For a rather more Sicilian approach, make a mix of capers, raisins and pine nuts tossed with a little vinegar and sugar, and spoon into the middle of each bowl. A more texturally interesting version of this would be to reduce the vinegar and sugar to a sweet-sour syrup and leave the raisins to plump in this hot syrup. Toast the pine nuts and fry the capers in a little oil until they are bursting and crispy. Then dot the surface of the soup with these explosions of flavour and a final drizzle of the syrup.

Cauliflower also loves Middle Eastern flavours, so think about making a rough chop of parsley, almonds, currants, roast garlic, crushed cumin and coriander seeds moistened with a little lemon juice. Spoon this into the middle of each full bowl.

7 ways with...
CHICKEN STOCK

Great stock is the foundation of great cuisine, whether you are in China or France.

A great chicken stock is at the heart of so many Australian soups and its clean simplicity makes it the perfect chameleon, able to take on more personalities than the most pugilistic celebrity gossip columnist.

- Adding fine noodles and some finely chopped parsley to your chicken broth is a classic, which recalls that Eastern European chicken soup often called 'Jewish penicillin'. At Passover time, Ashkenazic communities will make *knaidlach*, which are dumplings made from a dough of matzo meal bound with eggs and cooked in the soup.

  To make these dumplings, whisk the whites of 2 eggs until frothy, then whisk in the yolks and 2 tablespoons of vegetable oil – or better yet, chicken fat (if you have it from the stock). Fold in a cup of matzo meal and bring together with about 2 tablespoons of sparkling mineral water. Season and add chopped parsley or dill if you like. For lighter, nuttier dumplings, form them now with wet hands and drop them into the soup, but for 'sinkers' leave the meal in the fridge for half an hour or so to soak up the liquid. Then form and cook them. Matzo balls can be poached in a separate pan of water if you want to help maintain the clarity of your broth. For another European spin, why not add orzo pasta, risoni or cooked rice instead and add some fresh dill, lemon juice and small meaty balls made from minced chicken. Or throw in some fresh Italian stuffed pasta such as cappelletti or tortellini to cook in the broth.

- You can give your chicken broth a Chinese spin by adding a couple of slices of ginger to the soup and a splash of soy sauce. Even better, add some homemade wontons. Buy some cheap wonton skins and make little purses of these pasta sheets filled with a mix of pork mince, spring onions and a fine dice of canned water chestnuts for crunch, all bound with a little cornflour. These can be gently cooked in the broth.

- There are three other great Chinese soups you can make with chicken broth. For a homemade chicken and sweetcorn soup, add some shreds of cooked chicken, a can of creamed corn, a cup of frozen corn plus some sliced spring onions and iceberg lettuce.

- For a Chinese egg drop soup, cook some frozen peas in the broth and slice some spring onions to drop into the soup. When the peas are cooked, whisk an egg and set it aside. Remove the soup from the heat and flavour with sesame oil and lots of white pepper. Give the soup a stir so it is whirling around. Now, little by little, drizzle the whisked egg into the whirling soup, using the end of the tines of a fork. This should give you silky strands of egg through your soup! Garnish with the spring onions. The Italians make a similar soup called stracciatella, where the broth is flavoured with saffron, parmesan and nutmeg, and then an egg is stirred through.

- For a Chinese hot and sour soup, add bean shoots, a splash of rice wine vinegar, some sliced fresh red chillies, some finely sliced mushrooms and asparagus, plus a splash of soy. Replacing these ingredients with crushed lemongrass, finely sliced lime leaves, a little palm sugar, a splash of fish sauce and a handful of Thai basil will give your broth distinctly South East Asian flavours. Add fresh lime, chilli, sliced capsicum and roasted corn kernels for a Mexican flavour; garnish this with fresh coriander and strips of fresh tortillas.

- If that is all too exotic, then how about just mixing in those finely sliced asparagus and button mushrooms by themselves. Throw in a bay leaf for good measure and garnish with fresh herbs and a little crumbled goat's cheese.

RICH CHICKEN STOCK

I cook my chicken stock in the oven because I find it easier to keep the temperature at a gentle level that way, but this stock can be made on the stovetop in a saucepan, or even in a pressure cooker once you've browned the wings.

olive oil, for frying

2 kg chicken wings, chopped in pieces

2 large brown onions, quartered with skins left on

50 g (1½ cup) skimmed milk powder

2.5 litres hot water

carcass of today's roast chook, chopped into pieces (optional)

2 carrots, chopped

2 celery stalks, chopped

5 black peppercorns

2 garlic cloves, peeled and crushed

parsley stalks, bruised along their length with the back of a knife

Preheat the oven to 90°C.

To brown the chook, pour a little oil in a large, high-sided roasting pan and place on the stovetop over high heat. When the oil is hot, throw in the chicken wings. Cook until they start to brown and give them a toss. Now throw in the onions and sprinkle over the skimmed milk powder. Cook some more until the wings are well browned. Remove the wings and drain the fat from the wings and from the pan.

To cook the stock, start by splashing a little water in the pan and working off any delicious burnt bits. Replace the wings in the pan and cover with hot water – about 2.5 litres. Place the chook carcass into the pan (if you are using it), carefully pop the pan in the oven and cook for 3 hours very slowly. This is a stage you can also do in a pressure cooker or in a saucepan on top of the stove over low heat.

Check after 2 hours and, if required, top up with water to cover the chook bits. After 2½ hours throw in the chopped carrots, celery, black peppercorns, garlic and parsley stalks for a further 30 minutes. This is so the veg give their flavour but don't soak up too much of the stock while cooking to a mushy stage.

To finish the stock, drain it and clarify if you want (see the following instructions for clarifying chicken stock).

Chill the stock in the fridge and remove the fat that will collect and solidify on the top. This can be used to make *knaidlach* for Jewish chicken soup if you want. Now you have a rich chicken stock to use for a whole range of soups and broths. The stock can be frozen for later use.

TIPS & TRICKS

- Really, a stock can be the repository of loads of kitchen discards, such as corn cobs that have had the kernels cut off, onion skins, carrot peelings, leek tops, herb stalks – anything, just so long as it is clean and of good quality. The water will suck the flavour out of all of it.

- Using skimmed milk powder is one of my great discoveries of the last year or so. First I read Aki Kamozawa and H Alexander Talbot's *Ideas in Food,* and they suggested making burnt butter by adding extra milk solids in the form of 100 g of skimmed milk powder to every 250 g of butter used. What makes burnt butter so deliciously nutty and toasty is the browning of the milk solids in the butter – and that's basically what's in the skimmed milk powder. I used the resulting toasty sludge to make a delicious burnt butter ice cream to serve with French toast. It was Heston Blumenthal's bright idea to add skimmed milk powder to his roast wings for chicken stock for the very same reason of adding an extra delicious nutty roasty element!

If you want to make a perfectly clear stock for something very fancy and very simple, then follow the instructions below. But honestly, unless you want to make a consommé, it's not necessary.

CLARIFYING CHICKEN STOCK

I think that the classic method of clarification of adding mince, egg whites, onions, carrots and celery to the basic stock is a palaver. It's far better to use the ice filtration method. First, freeze the stock. Then line a strainer with a coffee filter (or muslin) and place over a clean pot. Drop the frozen stock in the filter and let it thaw. As it thaws the pure stock will run out and the impurities that make it cloudy will be left behind. But honestly, I never clarify – anything, apparently.

Sure, fresh is usually best but unless you are picking peas yourself much of the sugar will have turned to starch by the time they've made it to your kitchen. That's why I rather like frozen peas! Oh and they're also so sweet and so convenient – like dating the cute girl next door. This soup is a play on a Parisian 'potage Saint Germain' but replaces leeks with spring onions for added freshness and uses the lettuce as a garnish so it retains some texture in the soup. Think of this as the summer or spring equivalent of the pea and ham soup! It is also stupidly simple to make and can be served chilled as well.

PEA SOUP WITH RICOTTA AND MINT

1 litre (4 cups) chicken stock
4 spring onions, sliced
1 kg frozen peas
½ cup mint leaves
3 rashers of middle bacon

4 inner cos lettuce leaves, finely shredded
200 g fresh ricotta
freshly ground black pepper
50 g butter, melted

Warm the chicken stock with the spring onions over medium heat until they soften. Add the peas and heat.

When the peas have softened after around 3 minutes, pour the mixture into a processor and blitz it with most of the mint (leave a little aside for garnish).

Grill or microwave the bacon to crisp it up, and cut it into thin strips.

Serve the pea soup warm and garnish with a little pile of shredded lettuce mixed with the bacon and topped with a nugget of fresh ricotta, some more (small) fresh mint leaves and a good grind of fresh black pepper. Spot with little streams of melted butter.

Serves 4

Minestrone is an Italian soup that welcomes any random left-overs or seasonal veg you might have. This one is made special by cooking it with old parmesan crusts which is like adding an umami flavor bomb to the soup. Save your old parmesan crusts in the freezer until you need them for minestrone or bolognese.

EMMA'S MINESTRONE

2 tablespoons olive oil

2 garlic cloves, finely chopped

1 brown onion, sliced

2 carrots, cut into
2 cm chunks

½ bunch silverbeet, white stalk separated and reserved, thinly sliced; or 2 cups shredded savoy cabbage

2 celery stalks, cut into
2 cm chunks

1.5 litres vegetable stock

400 g can crushed tomatoes

1 parmesan rind (optional)

75 g small macaroni pasta

400 g can cannellini beans, drained and rinsed

olive oil and grated parmesan, to garnish

Heat the oil in a large pot, add the garlic, onion, carrots, celery and silverbeet stalks, and sauté for a few minutes over medium heat. Add the stock, tomatoes and parmesan rind, if using, and bring to the boil. Turn down the heat and simmer gently for at least 20 minutes.

Add the macaroni and cook for around 5 minutes or until al dente, stirring to ensure it doesn't stick. Add the silverbeet greens and beans, stirring to heat through until the silverbeet is wilted.

Remove from the heat, remove the parmesan crust (if using) and ladle the soup into deep bowls. Drizzle with olive oil and grated parmesan.

Serves 4–6

VEGETABLE STOCK

2 kg vegetables (such as 1 leek, 2 brown onions, 1 fennel bulb, 4 large carrots, 4 celery stalks), roughly chopped

1 garlic clove, chopped

mushroom trimmings

2 bay leaves

2 litres vegetable water (the cooking liquid from boiling vegetables, but not potatoes); use plain water if you haven't got any saved vegetable water on hand

salt and pepper

Mix the vegies with the garlic, mushroom trimmings, parsley stems and bay leaves in a large pot with a lid. Add the water to cover the vegies.

Simmer for at least 45 minutes over medium-low heat. Remove the pot from the heat, allow to stand for 5 minutes, then strain through a fine sieve, reserving the vegies.

Makes 2 litres

Paris is the city of love. The first time I took my wife there for a bit of hand-swinging, the love she developed was a fearsome obsession with French onion soup. Trouble was the only places selling it were the sort of cheapo tourist joints loved by polyester-pantsuit-wearing tour groups from Des Moines. Every night we'd eat in places like this and I'd hint at the gastro temples I craved to visit. She'd ask if they had French onion soup on the menu. Each time she did, I knew my argument was lost and we'd be back to discussing Rodin and Monet over an 18 euro prix fixe menu. It could have caused an argument but I was in Paris, I was with the woman I love, and this sweet, earthy winter soup loaded with rafts of melty cheese is one of the world's most delicious! My mum used to eat this soup from Les Halles market, where it originated, after she went out clubbing as a girl. So it must be in my DNA.

FRENCH ONION SOUP THAT
ALMOST CAUSED AN ARGUMENT

100 g butter
1 tablespoon olive oil
1.5 kg brown onions, finely sliced
500 g shallots
250 ml (1 cup) white wine
1 litre (4 cups) beef stock
salt and pepper, to taste

Gruyere croutons
1 baguette or French stick
1 garlic clove, halved
125 g (1 cup) grated Swiss-style cheese (Comte or gruyere, not holey Swiss cheese, but bitey tasty will do)

In a large heavy-based saucepan, melt the butter and oil. Cook the onions on low heat for an hour, or until they start to darken. Stir regularly until they are dark brown.

Turn up the heat and get it singing. As the onions start to stick and almost burn, pour in a ½ cup of wine. It will sizzle and steam as the alcohol burns off. Stir in the remaining wine and scrub away those burny bits. Deglazing your pan like this will give the soup loads of extra flavour. When the wine has evaporated, reduce the heat.

Pour the stock into the pan in four batches, stirring and cooking for 3 minutes between each batch. Simmer for 20 minutes then season to taste. Leave the soup on a gentle simmer.

To prepare the croutons, cut a dozen 1 cm bread slices and rub garlic on both sides of each slice. Grill one side to golden, the other side to pale golden.

To serve, pour soup into four ovenproof bowls. Put three toast rafts on the surface of each soup, pale golden side up, and top each with a mound of cheese. Grill until the cheese melts and bubbles and shows little burnt patches. Top with a good grind of fresh black pepper and serve immediately, but take care – the bowls will be hot.

Serves 4

TIPS & TRICKS

• If you want a Lyonnaise touch, mix 60 ml (¼ cup) port and 1 egg yolk together and stir into the soup before garnishing to make it even more rich and silky (that's what they do in Lyon!).

A Canadian-inspired garnish of maple syrup and bacon is the secret to taking this deliciously homely pumpkin soup to new and rather deliciously sweet 'n' salty heights. Good times!

PUMPKIN SOUP

1.5 kg pumpkin, seeds removed and cut into chunks. You can leave the skin on
4 tablespoons olive oil
1 teaspoon paprika
salt
125 ml (½ cup) maple syrup
40 g butter
1 bay leaf
175 g bacon, cut into little squares
2 onions, chopped
3 garlic cloves, chopped
1 leek, washed and sliced
1 celery stalk, chopped
250 ml (1 cup) sherry
2 litres chicken stock
freshly ground black pepper
½ teaspoon cinnamon

Garnish
2 rashers of back bacon
20 g butter
small sage leaves
80 ml (⅓ cup) maple syrup
zest of ½ lemon
sea salt

Preheat the oven to 200°C.

Place the pumpkin chunks in about 2 tablespoons of olive oil on a baking tray. Sprinkle the pumpkin with the paprika and a couple of pinches of salt, and pop the tray into the oven.

Bake for about an hour, or until soft and browning slightly at the edges. When the pumpkin is cooked, toss it in maple syrup. Return to the oven for five minutes. Turn off the heat.

While the pumpkin is cooking, melt the butter in 2 tablespoons of olive oil in a large, heavy pot. Throw in the bay leaf and fry the bacon, onions, garlic, leek and celery over medium heat until softened, stirring regularly. This will take about 10 minutes.

Deglaze the pan with half of the sherry and let the alcohol burn off. When the onion and leek start looking syrupy, pour in another slug of sherry and reduce. Continue until there's one splash of sherry left. With this last bit of sherry, add the roast pumpkin, stock, a couple of big twists of black pepper and the cinnamon. Cook for a couple of minutes to combine the flavours and then remove the bay leaf and any pumpkin skin.

Now, liquefy this soup using a blender or a food processor until smooth. If using a blender, leave the air vent open and cover with a tea towel to stop the pressure and heat blowing the blender lid off. No one wants pumpkin soup all over the kitchen.

To make the garnish, heat the bacon strips in a small frying pan over high heat until crispy and set aside. Wipe the pan clean, then add the butter to the pan and heat. When the butter starts to froth, drop in the sage leaves. The sage will curl up at the edges slightly and go crisp. At this stage, remove the pan from the heat, remove the sage leaves and set them aside. The butter will be brown and nutty. Stir the maple syrup for the garnish into the browned butter in the pan and reheat. Once it has started to froth, count to 10 and remove from the heat.

To serve, warm four bowls. Pour the pumpkin soup into each bowl and spoon drips of the maple butter over the soup. Sprinkle the crisp sage leaves and bacon pieces on top of each bowl of soup. Grate on a few tendrils of lemon zest and add a few flakes of salt.

Serves 8–10

My wife has only very occasionally been wrong. The first time, she will tell you, was when she foolishly married me. The only other times are when she makes pea and ham soup with lumps of carrot and yellow split peas in it. SO WRONG! My classic version of pea and ham soup needs no such aberrations detracting from its almost creamy richness. In fact it is so loaded with meaty goodness that it will even jellify when it cools. Yum!

A PROPER PEA AND HAM SOUP

2 tablespoons olive oil
2 onions, diced
3 garlic cloves, peeled
4 celery stalks, sliced
2 x 750 g ham hocks, skin on
375 g (2 cups) green split peas

3 litres cold water
bay leaf
sprig fresh thyme
sea salt and freshly ground pepper
butter, to garnish
dash of malt vinegar

Heat the oil in a large heavy-based pot, add the onions, garlic and celery, and cook these over low heat for 10 minutes until a little mushy. Add the ham hocks, split peas, water and herbs. Bring these ingredients to the boil, reduce the heat and simmer for 1½ hours.

Remove the hocks, discard the skin and bone, then shred the meat and set aside.

Now purée the soup thoroughly so it becomes as green and silky as Peter Pan's stocking. Return the ham to the pot, heat the soup to serve and season well with salt and pepper.

To serve, ladle the pea and ham soup into deep soup bowls, and garnish with a dollop of butter and a drizzle of malt vinegar. Serve with warm crusty bread.

Serves 8

SALADS

Which food group do you love the most? Meat, seafood, dairy or fruit and veg? Which of these four would be the last you'd surrender? For me, it's fruit and veg because between them they offer an almost infinite variation of flavours and textures. That's why this chapter on salads is one of my favourites!

Forget the old idea of a salad being limp green leaves, leathery rounds of drying cucumber and wedges of floury tomato. These are salads that stand proudly on their own for a light lunch but are also happy to welcome a bit of meat or the sweet salty flash of seafood.

Here you'll find classic dressings and simple ideas, not just for summer but also to use through winter too. For me that perfect salad is about using balance and contrasts of flavours and textures – and salad certainly isn't limited to the warmer months.

In winter think of partnering the sweetness of ripe pear with the bitter wet snap of witlof, the crunch of walnuts and the salty creaminess of blue cheese. Even simpler is covering witlof leaves with shavings of parmesan and balancing with the sweetness of balsamic vinaigrette. If you like bitterness and crunch like that, then why not make the classic Italian combination of radicchio leaves with finely sliced fennel and pith-free segments of blood orange. Dress this with olive oil, a little vinegar and a good sprinkling of flake salt.

Roasting veg makes them sweeter, so how about throwing in extra root vegetables like carrots, parsnips, beetroots and pumpkin when doing the Sunday roast. These can be served the next day as a root veg salad dressed in olive oil, a good splash of sherry vinegar and some toasted pine nuts for crunch. Sprinkle over fresh thyme leaves or some finely snipped rosemary to finish. Or just roast beetroots and serve these with the classic combination of goat's cheese and hazelnuts. Snip over some fronds of dill and a dusting of orange zest to finish.

Winter opens itself up to some of the world's most classic salads without having to break the rules of seasonality or break the bank. Of course some of these winter salads do involve slathering everything with mayonnaise, such as the classic crunchy Waldorf salad combination of a diced crunchy red apple, crunchier green apple, two celery stalks and a big handful of walnuts. The Waldorf salad was created back in 1894 by Swiss maître d' and amateur chef Oscar Tschirk, newly arrived at the flash New York hotel. It's no surprise that they called the salad after the hotel rather than the creator. The Tschirky salad doesn't quite have the same ring to it!

Oh, and while we are getting all 'food history nerd' can I point out that the first Waldorf salad was actually only a mix of apple, lettuce and mayo. Before the 'tsk, tsk, tsking' echoes down from the desirably svelte pedestal that *The Biggest Loser*'s Michelle Bridges perches on, please note that a modern take on Waldorf is keeping the use of mayo (low fat, even) to a very bare minimum and replacing the apple with hunks of very ripe pear, which will give the salad the impression of juiciness without all those mayo calories and fat. Whether pear or apple is your choice, I'd always suggest adding a sprinkling of plump sultanas for some extra chewy sweetness and a squeeze of lemon juice to balance this.

So much, of course, revolves around the dressing…

MAYONNAISE

Shhh...don't tell anyone but the secret to a good mayo is not the egg yolk but the water. What makes mayo is the emulsification of oil with egg yolk to create a rich, creamy, spoonable dressing, but it is actually the use of enough water and/or lemon juice that makes this magic trick hold. Mayo works best with warm or room temperature ingredients.

Whisk the yolk in the bowl with 2 teaspoons of water until it's pale and foamy. Keep whisking and very slowly drip in up to 200 ml of a neutral oil such as grapeseed. The oil will incorporate and a thick glossy mayo will develop. If the mayo is getting too thick just add a little water to loosen it before it splits. Season to taste with salt and lemon juice. If it splits, whisk in a spoon of warm water – this may help pull it back together.

You can add powdered English mustard in the beginning, or finely chopped herbs or a purée of roast garlic at the end for an edgier mayonnaise.

FRENCH VINAIGRETTE

Three parts oil to one part vinegar (or other acid such as lemon juice) is the basic rule of this classic salad dressing, which is also great to use to dress steaks or fish. The only rule is to be prepared to deviate from this ratio, depending on the acidity level of the vinegar and what other sweet ingredients (such as honey) or tart ingredients (such as Dijon mustard) might be added.

ITALIAN DRESSING

As in salad dressings, so in life! While the French are very exact about their dressings, the classic Italian dressing is far more intuitive – just splash on lots of olive oil, a little vinegar and then sprinkle on flake salt. Always add in this order so the elements adhere to your leaves properly… 'What leaves?' you may ask. Any you like, I say, but adding something bitter like red Treviso and something peppery like rocket is a great place to start.

BALSAMIC SYRUP

Yes, we'd all like to use really expensive 50-year-old balsamic that has reduced over the years to a dark syrupy deliciousness. But far cheaper and almost as effective is this cheat balsamic syrup. Combine 125 ml (½ cup) of balsamic vinegar with 125 ml (1 cup) of cider vinegar and 110 g (½ cup) of sugar in a pan over the heat. Simmer until it starts to get syrupy. Pour in a jug and use to drizzle over such classic fruit and meat salad combinations as prosciutto and melon, or prosciutto in a rocket salad with grilled peaches or figs.

Also check out the yoghurt dressings on the iceberg salad (page 17) and the potato salad (page 24), which can both be used as other dressing options.

This wonderfully refreshing salad was specifically designed so I could be caught eating it and then point out how very virtuous I was. It uses no oil and just a little bit of Greek yoghurt and feta to add creaminess to the wet crunch of iceberg and cucumber. Just don't tell anybody that you can also hide extra feta <u>under</u> the lettuce leaves!

ICEBERG SALAD

1 iceberg lettuce, torn into bite-sized pieces
1 Lebanese cucumber, peeled and diced into 5 mm pieces
1 tablespoon fresh thyme leaves

200 g feta, crumbled
60 g (¼ cup) Greek yoghurt
squeeze of lemon
salt and pepper, to taste

Scatter the lettuce on a plate, and cover with cucumber, thyme leaves and feta. Mix the yoghurt with a squeeze of lemon, season with salt and pepper and combine. Dot frugally over the salad.

Serves 4

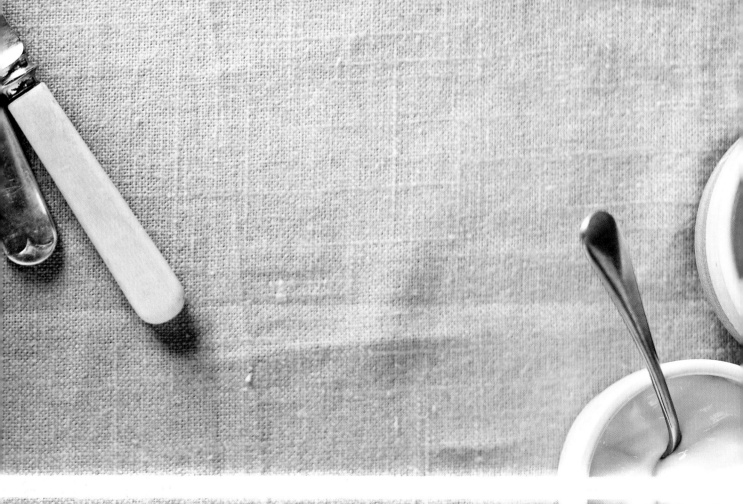

You find that an awful lot of my recipes revolve around ingredients that you'll probably already have in the kitchen – olives, capers, tinned tuna, frozen peas or corn. This simple store cupboard salad is another such example but the presence of soft-yolked eggs, the bite of fresh lemon juice in the tuna dressing and the wonderful vitality of iceberg lettuce gives it a real vibrancy.

CANNED TUNA SALAD

1 x 425 g can of tuna in oil, drained

470 g (2 cups) good-quality egg mayonnaise

zest and juice of 1 lemon

½ red onion, finely chopped

1 tablespoon capers in brine, rinsed and drained

1 iceberg lettuce, cut into 8 equal wedges

4 eggs, soft boiled, halved

12 thin curls of good Italian parmesan (use peeler)

8 good-quality sweet anchovies

4 small gherkins, halved

There really isn't a lot of method to this salad which is why I have added this totally superfluous first paragraph just so you feel like you are getting value for money. After all you – or someone dear to you – has paid good cash for this book and I'd afraid you might feel gypped when you read the scant two paragraphs of method that basically say 'open some jars, mix stuff together and scatter on a plate'. Trouble is that sometimes good things come together easily – and this salad is one of those good things.

To make the dressing, blend the tuna, mayo and lemon juice until smooth, with a fork. Then fold in the zest, onion and capers. If it gets runny add some more mayo. Season to taste.

Arrange the lettuce on a plate and top with some of the tuna mayo, eggs, parmesan, ancovies and gherkins.

Serves 4

TIPS & TRICKS

- For a salty crunch, fry 1 tablespoon of capers in 1 tablespoon of olive oil until they start to flower and the buds open slightly. Now take these crispy capers, drain them on a kitchen towel and scatter over the top of your salad.

I once lived for the summer in a little stone hut in an olive grove on the Greek island of Sifnos. The cold water for my morning shower was pulled by bucket from a concrete cistern, my bed was a straw mattress on stone shelf, I cooked in a small fire place and my walk home from the local tavern was along a dry river bed fragrant with wild oregano. Looking back it was as impossibly romantic as it sounds which is probably why, in all the pictures of me with my girlfriend (who arrived at the end of summer to visit) I look so tanned and happy and she is so pale and sour.

In the local bay of two tavernas and a handful of houses, they made the classic Hellenic 'village' salad using a dollop of their oozy local fresh goat's curd from the hillside rather than cubes of feta, which is a fine variation.

I also felt the tomatoes messed up the clarity of the salad and so I'd rather serve them in a separate bowl. This might also have something to do with the fact that I once saw Nigella Lawson saying that putting tomatoes in your salad was very common (and I am quite easily led). Interestingly, after shooting this picture it was pointed out that Nigella uses tomatoes in her Greek salad which means she must be fickle – as I can't countenance that she has a common side.

GREEK SALAD – VATHI STYLE

1 punnet ripe cherry tomatoes, cut in half

1 Lebanese cucumber, cut into thick rounds

1 red onion, peeled and cut into thin wedges

1 cup kalamata olives, pitted

3 tablespoons olive oil

1 tablespoon lemon juice

sea salt and ground black pepper, to taste

200 g Greek feta

250 g (1 cup) Greek yoghurt

½ cup fresh dill sprigs (optional)

Place the thick cucumber rounds, ⅔ of the red onion and the kalamata olives in a salad bowl and toss.

Place the cherry tomatoes in a bowl with the remaining onion.

Make a simple dressing by combining olive oil and lemon juice. Season with salt and pepper. Drizzle over both the salads.

Use a stick blender to whip the feta, yoghurt and dill (if using). Dollop on top of the cucumber salad.

Serves 4

TIPS & TRICKS

- This salad is great without the dill – or you can use any herb if you want a change from the dill. Feel free to sprinkle over shredded oregano or mint, or both.

The Caesar is the deep-fried Mars bar of the salad world. Here we take this US classic, invented as an emergency stopgap by a Tijuana restaurateur, further into the world of wrong. Now the toasty crunch comes from browned corn not dull croutons and Aussie supermarket cheese replaces the usual heel-peelings Italian. Instead of a tangy anchovy mayo, this trip to the dark side is completed by a trendy New York mayo taught to me by the king of all things tasty, David Chang. Quite frankly, this is the world's only Caesar salad which is actually improved by the addition of chicken – smoked or not!

NEW CAESAR SALAD

1½ tablespoons mayonnaise

3 drops Maggi liquid seasoning

200 g sweetcorn kernels, drained canned or thawed frozen

2 tablespoons olive oil

175 g smoked bacon, unsliced

1 cos lettuce

100 g vintage tasty cheese, cut into ½ cm cubes

2 soft-boiled eggs, halved

Mix the mayonnaise with the liquid seasoning. Heat a little oil in a saucepan to a high heat and add the drained corn. Put on the lid. The corn will react quite violently and ping around the pan. Do not be frightened – just give the pan an occasional shake to keep the corn moving. When you smell toastiness, the corn is ready. We want brown scorch marks on our kernels.

Microwave the bacon between two sheets of paper towel somewhere between 90 seconds and 2 minutes, depending on the power of your microwave. We want the bacon crispy, but not desiccated like a 90-year old dowager. Chop the bacon into 1 cm batons.

Wash the lettuce and remove any dodgy or overly dark leaves. Arrange the lettuce leaves on a plate. Sprinkle on the corn, the cheese and the bits of bacon, add the eggs and splatter the whole lot with dollops of your New York mayo.

Serves 2

TIPS & TRICKS

- This mayo gets even better if you add a couple of drops of liquid smoke to it. This can be found at camping shops and anywhere that large groups of barbecues gather. It's dead cheap and makes it taste like your mayo has spent a couple of hours in the smokehouse.

- You can also use dried or canned smoky chipotle chillies to flavour this mayo wonderfully. Buy the dried ones online at www.montereyfoods.com.au. Soak one dried chipotle, remove stem and seeds, chop finely and add to the mayo. Leave for at least 15 minutes for the flavours to infuse, then use.

- Add 300 g of sliced smoked chicken breast to your salad for a delicious Australian take on a Caesar salad.

It wasn't just her scowl in my Greek holiday snaps that that ex left me with. She also taught me this delicious German take on a classic potato salad. The tang of yoghurt makes the salad seem lighter and the profusion of egg and bacony goodness ensures that this is never the salad that is left forlornly unfinished at the end of the BBQ! Oops, think that turn of phrase might have given away more than I wanted to!

THAT EX-GIRLFRIEND'S POTATO SALAD

10 large waxy potatoes, washed (Nicola or Desiree are good alternatives)
4 large eggs
6 rashers bacon, finely sliced
185 g (¾ cup) yoghurt

185 g (¾ cup) good-quality egg mayonnaise
1 teaspoon caster sugar
6 spring onions, thinly sliced
1 bunch chives, finely chopped
sea salt and black pepper

Place the potatoes in a saucepan of cold water. Bring to the boil, then cook for 15 minutes or until potatoes are tender when pierced with a knife. When cooked, drain into a colander and set aside for a few minutes. Peel and cut into quarters.

Meanwhile, place the eggs in a small saucepan of cold water, bring to the boil and cook for 8 minutes. Pour off the water and run plenty of cold water over the eggs to prevent a grey ring forming around the yolk. Peel the eggs and set aside.

Cook the bacon in a non-stick frying pan over medium heat until crisp. Drain on paper towel.

Mix the yoghurt and mayonnaise together and a little sugar to balance the flavour, but not so that it becomes sweet. Roughly chop the eggs into chunks. Toss the potatoes in yoghurt mayonnaise while they are still warm, sprinkle over the crisp bacon, chopped eggs, spring onions and fresh chives. Season with salt and pepper.

Serves 8

TIPS & TRICKS

- For a less creamy potato salad, just replace the mayo and yoghurt and sugar with a mustardy vinaigrette made from 1 teaspoon of mustard powder and 1 teaspoon of honey shaken up with 125 ml (½ cup) of olive oil and 60 ml (¼ cup) of good white wine vinegar. Season with salt and pepper. This is a more acidic dressing than I'd suggest for a green salad, but I think the richness of the bacon and eggs demand it.

- Want to give your potato salad a Spanish fillip? Mix 1 teaspoon of smoked Spanish paprika into your yoghurt and mayonnaise dressing. The smokiness of these dried and pounded peppers works wonderfully well with the flavour of barbecued red meat – especially if you also roast some whole red capsicums on the barbecue as well to serve as a garnish. Just scrape out the seeds and stems from the capsicums before serving and dress with a little good oil and a pinch of flake salt!

Granted, there is nothing new in cabbage salads. These two recipes are – and as always, credit where credit is due – inspired and informed by cabbage salads I've eaten at two of my favourite Sydney restaurants: Sopra and Buzo. The great thing is that they serve their purpose of adding texture and freshness to meals thoughout the year and, even better, the ingredients have a fridge-resilience which means that these salads can always be at your beck and call.

STOLEN CABBAGE SALADS

SALAD #1

¼ white cabbage, thinly sliced
1 fennel bulb, peeled and
finely sliced
1 bunch mint, shredded

100 g pecorino
juice of 1 lemon
salt flakes

When slicing the cabbage, make sure you cut out and discard the thick veins. You should have about 2 cups of thinly sliced cabbage remaining. Set these aside.

Peel off the tough outer layers of the fennel and slice the inner parts finely (cutting out and discarding the core).

Toss the shredded mint through the fennel and cabbage. Shave the pecorino over the raw vegetables and squeeze over the juice of the lemon. Sprinkle with a little flaked salt.

Serves 4

SALAD #2

¼ savoy cabbage
100 g parmesan

2 teaspoons balsamic vinegar
salt and black pepper

Strip away the outer leaves of the cabbage. Thinly slice the inner parts. Shave the parmesan and toss gently with the cabbage.

At the table, drizzle on the vinegar. Season with black pepper and salt.

Serves 4

TIPS & TRICKS

- These cabbage salads are the perfect accompaniment to an Italian pork charcuterie plate. Serve with 12 slices Italian prosciutto, 8 slices pancetta, 12 slices artisan salami, a loaf of oven-warmed ciabatta, a bowl of olives, some slices of crisp green apple tossed in a little lemon juice and a bowl of fruity olive oil.

PEA, PROSCIUTTO AND BROAD BEAN SALAD

2 tablespoons best-quality, fruity green olive oil

12 slices prosciutto

1 cup (175 g) fresh or frozen podded broad beans

8 spears asparagus

8 green beans

8 snow peas or sugar snap peas

4 baby zucchini (green, yellow or both)

1 tablespoon red wine vinegar

155 g (1 cup) frozen peas

4 eggs

4 spring onions, trimmed and thinly sliced

2 tablespoons crisp white wine (riesling is good)

small bunch mint, torn

sprig thyme

75 g (½ cup) salted ricotta, or feta, which is far easier to find

zest and juice of 1 lemon

cracked black pepper

Crack a couple of trays of ice cubes into a bowl of cold water.

Bring a saucepan of water to the boil and dig out a slotted spoon or small sieve. While the water is coming to the boil, prepare the dressing base and the veg.

To prepare the prosciutto oil, warm 1 tablespoon of olive oil in a small pan. Trim the prosciutto of any fat round its edge. Chop up the fat and drop into the warming oil. The aim is to draw some of that sweet saltiness into the oil, so keep on a gentle heat until ready to serve.

To prepare the veg, take the asparagus spears and snap off the woody ends of the stalks. They will naturally snap where the woodiness ends. Cut each spear into three pieces. Trim the stalks off the beans and the snow peas (and remove the string down the pod if necessary). Using a potato peeler, peel thin strips from the zucchini. Splash with the red wine vinegar and reserve.

Blanch all the veg (except for the zucchini) in individual batches, starting with the broad beans. To do this, pop them in boiling water for a minute or so until they are cooked but still a little snappy. Then scoop them out and immerse them in the iced water to stop them cooking. Remove and drain them on some paper towel. Slice the snow peas into halves and cut the beans in thirds.

While blanching the green beans, asparagus, snow peas and peas, do the fiddly job of slipping the broad beans out of their leathery grey jackets.

Crisp the prosciutto under the grill or in the microwave for 30 seconds between two paper towels. Break into pieces.

Softly poach the eggs in gently simmering water for 3 minutes, then remove (for perfect poached eggs see page 164).

When all the veg are cooked, cooled and drained, spread them on to a large plate starting with the larger pieces (the asparagus), then strips of zucchini (drained of the vinegar), snow peas, broad beans, peas and green beans. Add the spring onion slices. Splash over the white wine. Remove the prosciutto fat from the pan and pour the salty, warm oil over the salad.

Throw on the torn mint and thyme leaves. Top with the poached eggs, crisp prosciutto, cheese and a sprinkle of lemon zest. Drizzle with lemon juice and a little olive oil and sprinkle with pepper.

Serves 4

If you think cous cous is dull and bland then this is the dish to convert you! If you love couscous then you'll totally love all the different pops of flavor.

In fact if there is one recipe in the book that the woman I love always suggests when people are coming over – especially if it's paired with the butterflied leg of lamb on page 141 – it is this treasure trove of tastes rampaging through waves of soft couscous grains.

What makes it so wonderful is that each mouthful is an ever-changing kaleidoscope of dancing textures and flavours – the different crunches of the nuts, cucumber and celery, the sweet sticky yield of the honeyed carrots, the rich candied chew of the dried fruit, the freshness of the herbs and the citrus zests. Always make lots because it's delicious for a simple lunch the day after – and because people always seems to gorge on more of this than you expect!

JEWELLED COUSCOUS SALAD

500 ml (2 cups) water

185 g (1 cup) couscous

40 g butter

1 tablespoon honey

2 carrots, quartered lengthwise, then diced

1 celery stalk, diced

2 Lebanese cucumbers, diced

1 tablespoon cumin seeds, toasted and crushed

75 g (½ cup) currants

70 g (½ cup) pistachios

60 g (½ cup) slivered almonds, toasted

zest and juice of 1 lemon

zest of 1 orange

½ cup coriander leaves

½ cup mint leaves

sea salt and freshly ground black pepper, to taste

Dressing

250 g (1 cup) Greek yoghurt

handful of finely chopped mint leaves

First measure out all your ingredients ready to assemble the salad.

Heat the butter in a frying pan until melted, add the honey and cook the carrots over medium heat until softened. Season well with salt and pepper.

To cook the couscous, heat 2 cups of water in a medium saucepan until boiling. Remove from the heat and add the couscous. Stir and allow to stand for a few minutes until the couscous absorbs all the liquid, then fluff with a fork.

As texture is key, combine all the ingredients just before serving so the salad doesn't get soggy and maintains its riot of textures.

Combine the yoghurt and mint leaves to make the dressing and serve on the side to splash on the couscous.

Serves 4–6

TIPS & TRICKS

- If you can get barberries or pomegranate seeds, throw them in for extra crunch and colour.

Just like different people have characters so, I would suggest, do different vegetables. Iceberg lettuce is like a leggy, vacuous Californian actress – interesting as background but lacking in any real substance; butter lettuce is her more bookish sister; and bitter curly endive is her intelligent but prickly mate who you wouldn't want to see every day but who's a lot more interesting.

Tomatoes are the party vegetables most likely to misbehave saucily and cross-dress (after all they are seen as vegetables but they are actually fruit). Brussels sprouts are like snitches in the office ready to sneak to the boss and broccoli is the office airhead – no one knows what they are doing there but they always seem to turn up.

Potatoes, swedes and turnips are the tradies of the vegetable world – honest and reliable – while sweet potatoes are like those tradies with a far more adventurous and interesting past. And what of carrots? For me they are the enthusiastic geeks of the vegetable world. Sweet and friendly but all too often taken for granted. (While purple carrots, by the way, are the geeks who've discovered counter-culture, illegal downloading and tattoos.)

This dish seeks to elevate carrots to their rightful position as one of the coolest vegetables in class. Roasting them intensifies their flavour and using the bitterness of witlof makes their sweetness stand out in even starker contrast. Robing them in soft herbs, gentle milky ricotta and the crunch of almonds and sunflower seeds turns them into the sort of geek with a very nifty make-over that will win over a beauty like you!

A NOBLE ROAST CARROT SALAD

18 Dutch (baby) carrots, scrubbed
1 tablespoon olive oil
salt and pepper, to taste
1 witlof, heart discarded, sliced crosswise
¼ red onion, finely chopped

200 g fresh ricotta, crumbled
1 tablespoon sunflower seeds
1 tablespoon toasted almonds
2 tablespoons honey, warmed
chervil or dill, to garnish

Preheat the oven to 180°C.

Place the carrots in a roasting tray, drizzle with olive oil and season well with salt and pepper. Roast in the oven for 45 minutes until soft and almost caramelised. Remove from the oven and set aside to cool slightly.

To serve, transfer the carrots to a shallow dish. Scatter the witlof, onion and ricotta over the top. Layer on the sunflower seeds and toasted almonds, and drizzle with warmed honey. Sprinkle over the chervil or dill to finish.

Serves 4

Certain recipes should be filed in a lockable cabinet with the words 'Guilty Secrets' spray painted on it. This is one of these recipes. The idea of mixing parmesan, mayo and a jar of artichoke hearts seems decadent to the extreme – and it is – but when you taste how they marry up when cooked you'll forget all that. Here I've paired it with the pickled fennel so at least something on the plate is virtuous – especially as the rich fattiness of the mortadella is enhanced by warming in the microwave. This is the perfect shared dish for a night in front of the telly, so enjoy – but just occasionally!

BAKED ARTICHOKE HEARTS WITH
MORTADELLA AND FENNEL SALAD

400 g artichoke hearts in oil, drained

1 tablespoon olive oil

12 slices mortadella

250 g (1 cup) mayonnaise

100 g (1 cup) grated parmesan

juice of 1 lemon

12 slices of ciabatta, lightly toasted

Fresh pickled fennel salad

1 large or 3 small fennel bulbs

250 ml (1 cup) vinegar – a tart one such as white wine

55 g (¼ cup) caster sugar

1 tablespoon salt

Preheat the oven to 180°C.

You need to tackle the fresh pickled fennel salad first. Trim the fennel and cut the bulb(s) finely. Mix the vinegar with the sugar and salt so they dissolve. Taste and add more vinegar or sugar to balance the flavour. You want to taste acidity but mellowed by sweetness. Throw in the fennel. Leave to infuse for as long as possible – at least 30 minutes. Drain to serve.

Mash the artichoke hearts, mayo, parmesan and lemon juice together in a bowl.

Now bake in the oven for 40 minutes until hot and bubbly.

Warm the mortadella in the microwave by giving it a quick 10–20 second blast or place the mortadella on a tray and warm in the oven for 5 minutes.

Arrange the slices of mortadella on a plate, dollop the artichoke mixture in the middle, with the fennel salad on the side, and eat all together with crusty bread or toast.

Serves 4

PIES AND PIZZA

Flour, water, a little bit of fat…

It's one of the simplest combinations in the world kitchen but look at the bounty that it can provide in the hands of a smart cook – a world of pitas, pides, pizzas and all sort of different pastries for pies.

I was going to bang on now about the alchemy of the kitchen and the endless inventiveness of the peasant cook but common sense dictates that I actually try and squeeze in another recipe for you that has proved to be a huge favourites with my kids – not just to eat but also to make.

My justification – other than it's a cracker – is that this recipe for piadina uses that simplest of trinities of flour, water and a little fat that was handed down from the Etruscans 3200 years ago! It's also really good folded round fillings like melty Italian cheeses including fontina, fior de latte, taleggio, squaquerone or stracchino (which are very traditional piadina cheese; the latter like a younger, less pungent taleggio) for one of the world's best cheese toasties!

Bitter leaves such as radicchio treviso, cicoria or broccolini are also traditional in piadinas; the latter two perhaps cooked first with garlic. Other trad fillings that you can use alone or, better yet, in combinations with the cheese include rocket, silverbeet and Italian cured or cooked meats such as prosciutto, salami, pancetta or ham.

If your mouth isn't watering right now at the idea of a half-moon of warm flatbread stuffed with one of these salty and sophisticated bitter combinations then you are a more resilient than I am!

Traditional piadina is made with snowy white lard but as this is hard to come by these days, here's my recipe for a soft and velvety flatbread dough made with milk and baking powder instead. It's a cinch to make and fun to fill!

PIADINA DOUGH

250 g fine '00' four
250 g bread flour
½ tsp baking powder
salt
150 ml warm water
150 ml milk
60 ml good olive oil

Sift the flours, baking powder and salt together.

Add the liquids and knead until a smooth, pliable dough is achieved. Add a little extra water if needed to give a moist, light but not sticky dough. This will take about 15 minutes of vigorous activity.

Let the dough rest for 30 minutes to an hour. Chop, cook or prepare your fillings while this is happening.

Split dough into 70 g balls, and allow to relax, covered, on a lightly floured bench for a few minutes.

On a floured surface, roll out your dough into very thin discs about two millimetres thick (or thinner if you want).

Heat a cast-iron frying pan, tawa, clay testo, teggia or Welsh griddle. When the pan is very hot add the thin dough disc, first shake off excess flour.

The dough will bubble slightly and lift off the pan when the bottom is cooked. Using a palate knife rotate the dough clockwise, for even cooking, until it has tanned spots across the base. You can burst the bubbles that rise but I don't. They add textural adventure.

When the base side is cooked flip the piadina and turn the heat down. Add your choice of filling, fold the dough disc over and cook on each side. The dough should still be a little pliable and the filling melted/warm when you flip it out to eat. Serve immediately cut into quarters with a glass of sangiovese and a lightly dressed green salad.

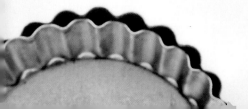

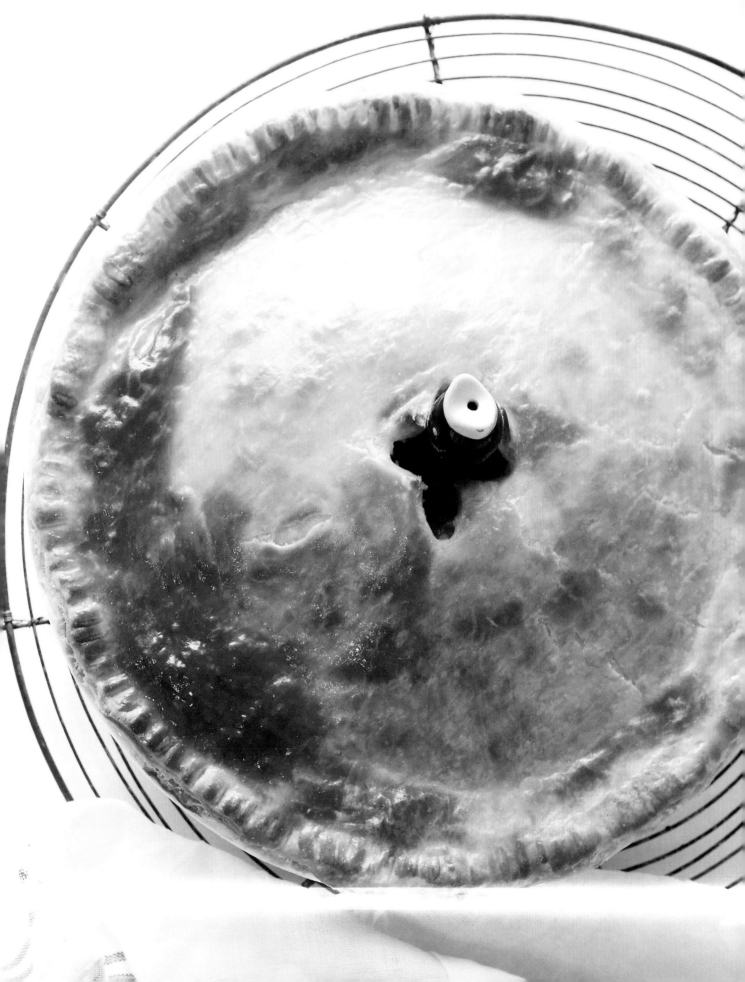

If you don't have time to make your own pastry, you can use good quality shop-bought pastry for this quiche instead. Good times!

AUSSIE QUICHE WITH BACON, CHEESE AND ONIONS

40 g butter
3 brown onions, finely sliced
2 blades star anise
6 rashers of bacon, diced
4 eggs
200 ml thickened cream
100 ml milk
50 g (½ cup) grated tasty cheese
50 g (½ cup) grated parmesan

salt and pepper
2 tablespoons chopped parsley

Pastry
150 g (1 cup) plain flour
75 g butter, chilled
pinch of salt
60 ml (¼ cup) sparkling mineral water

To make the pastry, place the flour, butter and salt in a food processor and pulse for 10 seconds until it looks like coarse crumbs. Slowly add the mineral water and pulse until it just comes together as a ball of dough. Wrap it in cling film and refrigerate for 1 hour.

To start the filling, melt the butter in a frying pan over a low heat. Add the onions and star anise, and cook for about 15–20 minutes or until caramelised. Scrape from the pan and set aside, keeping them warm. Remove the star anise blades.

Preheat the oven to 180°C.

Wipe the onion pan clean and fry your diced bacon over medium–high heat so it's a little golden. Set aside.

Roll out the pastry to a thickness of 5 mm and place evenly over the base and sides of a 20 cm x 4 cm fluted tart tin. Press in well with your fingers and allow the pastry to overhang about 1 cm around all sides. Use a fork to prick the bottom of the pastry all over. Line with foil and fill with pastry weights, dried beans or rice. Place in the oven and bake for 10 minutes, then remove the weights and foil, and bake for a further 5 minutes. Remove from the oven, but leave the oven on. Allow to cool a little then trim the pasty edges.

Spread the cooked onion over the bottom of the cooked pastry shell.

Beat the eggs, slowly adding the cream and milk until combined. Stir in the cheeses. Season with salt and pepper.

Pour half the filling into the pastry shell and sprinkle in half the bacon. Pour in the rest of the filling, sprinkle the rest of the bacon over the top and scatter with parsley.

Bake the quiche in the oven for 40–45 minutes until set and lightly browned on top. Serve while warm.

Serves 4

TIPS & TRICKS

- For a fancier quiche, replace the bacon with 6 slices of prosciutto (or Bayonne ham if you can get it). Lay this on top of the custard before baking. Oh, and replace the parmesan and the good old Aussie tasty cheese with 90 g of fancy gruyere. It doesn't matter whether it comes from Switzerland, France or Australia!

I grew up with Sunday night family dinner always being about tinned soup or fried eggy-bread. Now my family has its own Sunday night ritual and at its heart is frittata. This combo of the sharpness of parmesan and the wet bulk of zucchini hits those twin targets of getting some veg into the kids and being something that's a breeze to make when the weekend has robbed you of the will to cook again. Also any leftovers can be sliced for the boys' lunch boxes the next day. Sadie's not so keen but then she's not as obsessed with eggs as her brothers are!

ZUCCHINI AND PARMESAN FRITTATA

6 eggs
250 ml (1 cup) thickened cream
60 ml (¼ cup) vegetable oil
100 g (1 cup) grated parmesan
4 spring onions, white part only, chopped
½ cup loosely packed chopped mint

½ cup loosely packed chopped basil
zest of 1 lemon
3 zucchini, grated (use a box grater)
75 g (½ cup) plain flour
salt and freshly ground black pepper to taste

Preheat the oven to 190°C.

In a large bowl, mix together the eggs, cream, oil, parmesan, spring onions, mint, basil and lemon zest. Add the grated zucchini. Slowly add the flour to incorporate, and season with salt and pepper.

Line an ovenproof frying pan with baking paper, then pour the mixture carefully in the pan.

Place in the oven and cook for 30 minutes, or until firm and set. Remove from the oven and allow to sit for a few minutes to cool slightly. This will make it easier to handle.

Gently slide from the pan and remove the baking paper from the base. Serve while the frittata is still warm.

Serves 6–8

TIPS & TRICKS

- To make a gremolata to accompany the frittata, combine a handful of finely chopped mint leaves, the zest of 1 lemon and 1 finely chopped garlic clove. Serve slices of warm frittata with the fresh mint gremolata sprinkled over the top.

- Crumbling feta into or on this frittata is a perfect addition.

5 ways with...
A PACKET OF PUFF PASTRY

I love puff pastry. The airy crispness and the way it takes such a gorgeous colour make it a pleasure to cook with. And it's so versatile. It isn't *just* because layers of fat – usually butter – are folded into the pastry during the making to help it rise and boost its richness … although that definitely helps!

Other great things about puff pastry are that it keeps really well in the freezer and that you can buy good-quality butter puff pastry from the shops these days, rather than the endless folding and rolling of sheets that comes with making it yourself (which used to make you feel that you were working in some sort of Dickensian workhouse laundry, folding the rich folks' sheets).

Often, however, recipes call for only one or two sheets of puff pastry and that means you are left with the rest of your six-sheet pack slowly getting frostbite in the freezer. Fear not, for here are some of my favourite suggestions for how to use them all up:

POT PIES FOR LUNCH – 1½ SHEETS

Preheat the oven to 180°C. To make pot pies cut squares of the puff pastry large enough to be pushed into the greased cup of a muffin tin with the corners sticking out. Before doing this, roll the pastry out a little thinner, which will help with the problem of having a doughy bottom – a problem with which I am sadly all too familiar. Now push the squares into the holes in the muffin tins but leave enough pastry so the corners flop over the edges. Fill the resulting well with chopped ham, some herbs and a cracked raw egg, or with caramelised onions topped with crumbled feta topped with a few thyme leaves. Then bake them in the oven for 20–30 minutes or until the edges puff up and the filling cooks through.

PISSALADIERE FOR SUPPER – 1 SHEET

I also like using a puff pastry sheet to make a simple take on the Cote d'Azur/Niçoise delicacy of pissaladière. Preheat the oven to 180°C. Roll the pastry to make it a little thinner, then place on baking paper on a baking tray. Spread a cup of rich brown caramelised onions over the pastry, leaving a 3 cm edge. Top with a crisscross pattern of anchovy fillets halved lengthways and dot each resulting diamond with a ½ pitted black olive. Then bake for 30 minutes or until the pastry is golden and puffy at the edges. Serve with a green salad, or even a simple salad of sliced tomatoes in a tart vinaigrette.

PALMIERS FOR TEA – ½ SHEET

Sexy French-style biscuits called palmiers are perfect for tea. Preheat the oven to 190°C, cut a softened sheet of puff pastry in half and then take one half and sprinkle it with caster sugar and a couple of pinches of fine salt. Take a rolling pin and roll the crystals into the pastry. Now comes the fun part – rolling the pastry up so it can eventually be cut into slices to make biscuits that resemble elephant ears or palm trees (hence the name). Roll up each side towards the centre of the pastry sheet quite tightly. Place the resulting dual-roll in the fridge to firm up. When it's firm, cut into 8 mm thin slices to make those little French biscuits. Lay them on a lined baking sheet and pop in the oven for 6 minutes. It's good if they are golden but the occasional darker edge is not unwelcome for some!

APPLE SLICE FOR DESSERT – 1 SHEET

Preheat the oven to 180°C. For a simple apple slice dessert just peel and slice a couple of dessert apples like Golden Delicious or Royal Gala. Arrange these evenly across a sheet of puff, leaving a 4 cm border around the edge so the pastry can rise at the edges. Now drop a few nuggets of butter over the apples, a squeeze of lemon and a rough dusting of brown sugar. Adding a little dash of cinnamon powder with the sugar is also nice. Pop in the oven for around 30 minutes or until the pastry rises and goes golden, and the apple is cooked. If you want you can sprinkle a few sultanas over the pastry before you put on the apple. Don't sprinkle them on top as they have a tendency to burn and you want them to get plump under the apples! You know the deal – watch that the edges of the pastry don't burn and that the apple is cooked but still firm before taking it out.

TARTE TATIN FOR ANY TIME – THE LAST SHEET OR SO

This leaves us with 1 sheet, so how about going for the finest of uses by making your own take on a tarte tatin. You'll find my recipe for a lovely savoury leek tarte tatin later (see page 45), but making a classic sweet tarte tatin is just as simple.

The first thing to do is choose your fruit. The basic rule is that the softer the fruit the less time it needs to be cooked. For example, firmer fruit such as apples, quinces and pears will need more pre-cooking than pineapple pieces, while soft fruit such as strawberries, bananas, figs or (even) tomatoes will need none at all if you want them to retain some of their texture. Preheat the oven to 180°C if you're using soft fruit and 160°C if you're using hard (such as quinces or apples).

First, cut your fruit into chunks (if required). For example, you might cut figs in half, bananas into 4 cm barrels and small apples into quarters. If you want, rub any fruit that might oxidise or brown while waiting (like apples, pears or bananas) with a little lemon juice to stop this happening.

Then make a light butter caramel with a cup of sugar dampened with 2 tablespoons of water slowly heated in a large saucepan. Cook until you get a light golden caramel. If you are using chunks of apple or pear, carefully add them to the caramel to cook for a minute or so to soften slightly. Don't cook them too much as they will cook further in the oven – remember that quince will take longer, and overcooked quince is preferable to undercooked!

Generously butter a metal-handled frying pan (or any metal pan suitable for use in the oven) that is smaller than the sheet of puff. Arrange your fruit so it forms a tightly packed single layer in the pan but leave a thumb's width round the edge. Now pour your caramel over the fruit.

Here comes one of only two tricky parts. Roll out the puff a little and very carefully place it like a blanket over the fruit in the pan. Remember that the caramel will be VERY hot.

Now, using the handle end of a wooden spoon – and taking care not to touch the caramel – ease the puff sheet down and tuck it in around the edges of the fruit, like you're tucking in a snuggling sleepy child.

Cut two slots in the top for the steam to escape and pop into the oven. When the puff is golden, risen and cooked, generally around 30 minutes, remove from the oven.

Now, here comes the second tricky bit. You need to turn the tart out onto a serving plate or board. It's doubly tricky because as well as the dexterity required, there is the added difficulty of all that skin-searingly hot caramel bubbling up the sides of your tart. So here's the safest way to do it. First, place the pan on the stove. Run a blade around the very edge of the pastry to free it from the sides and then, taking care to avoid the caramel, ease and rotate the pastry top a quarter-turn to the left. This will help loosen the tart and the fruit from the pan.

Now, place a plate bigger than the pan over the top of the tart (face-side down). Next, holding the two firmly together, in one quick fluid movement turn the pan and plate over so that the tart falls out of the pan and neatly onto the plate. Hopefully the fruit will come with it! Don't worry if it all doesn't because you can always lift it out with tongs carefully and rearrange it back into the upturned puff pastry tart shell. There is no shame in this. Oh, and do make sure you scrape any of the yummy buttery caramel left in the pan onto the fruit.

Serve with cream, vanilla ice cream or crème fraîche, depending on the tartness of the fruit. My motto is 'the sweeter the fruit, the sourer the cream', but when in doubt go sourer, as the pastry is rich and the caramel sweet, so it will handle it. Oh, and warn your guests that the caramel and fruit may be hot!

And finally, don't forget to recycle the cardboard that packaged the puff, because that's all you will have left now from your once full packet.

OK, I admit that I have a bit of a thing about leeks. I love their squeaky sweetness and the way they hold together in tight juicy rings even when cooked. This tart highlights those simple virtues in the most stellar way, with the creamy goat's curd, flakes of salt and little pops of thyme essential for highlighting the sweet creaminess of the leeks and vital for building on a basic idea inspired by the lovely Anna Gare, who lit up my time filming on the first series of Junior MasterChef. *Serve it with a fresh, crunchy salad of iceberg lettuce, chunks of cucumber and batons of a sharp crisp apple such as a Granny Smith dressed with a little lemon juice for a wonderful contrast to the buttery richness of the tart.*

LEEK TARTE TATIN

6 large leeks
60 g butter
2 tablespoons water
2 tablespoons caster sugar
1 sheet butter puff pastry

100 g fresh soft goat's curd, or good feta
a few sprigs of thyme and/or tarragon, leaves picked
flake salt and cracked black pepper

Preheat the oven to 180°C.

To prepare the leeks, trim the outer layers and clean off any dirt. Cut crosswise into equal stubby lengths of about 3 cm. Make sure the leeks stay in their rounds.

Take a 22 cm metal-handled frying pan, place on the heat and melt 40 g of the butter with the water. Stand the leeks upright in the pan (cut face down) and pack them closely together so they support each other. Cook over medium heat for about 5 minutes. There's no need to turn the leeks.

Meanwhile, warm the rest of the butter with the caster sugar in another pan. When combined and hot, pour this around the outer edges of the leeks in the other pan.

Cut a large circle out of the puff pastry. This needs to be big enough so it falls like a blanket over the leeks and down their sides to the base of the pan. Ensuring you keep the leeks tightly pushed together, push the pastry down the sides of the leeks.

Pierce the pastry to let steam escape and pop the pan in the oven. Cook for 15–20 minutes until the pastry is golden and cooked (keep an eye on it so it doesn't burn). The sugar caramelises the pan-side of the leeks and the puff pastry swells up to embrace the leeks.

Take the pan out of the oven when the pastry is puffed up, golden and cooked through. Give the pan a slight shake to help loosen the tart from the pan. When you turn the tart out on to a plate it should come away neatly from the pan. Place a plate over the pan and, with one hand firmly under the plate, flip the plate and pan over in one crisp, confident motion. The toasty, golden top side of the pastry will now be on the plate and you'll be confronted by a forest of leek stumps.

If all the leeks don't come out, don't worry. Using tongs, lift the leeks out and replace on the pastry, caramel side upwards. No-one will know once herbs and goat's curd are sprinkled on.

Now dollop the goat's curd in spots over the face of the tart and sprinkle on the herbs.

Add a little flake salt and a grind of black pepper, and the tart can be taken to the table and cut into quarters to serve.

Serves 4

I love the flavours of a good old chowder but I reckon that they go together even better under this flaky pastry developed by chum and Melbourne pastry whizz Darren Purchese. Try it and be amazed that all the messing around with resting pastry, pie and filling results in such a top feed!

CHICKEN, SWEETCORN AND BACON PIE

150 g bacon, cut into 1 cm strips

1 kg skinless chicken thighs, cut into 2 cm pieces

salt and freshly ground pepper

40 g butter

2 brown onions, cut in half and then finely sliced

1 garlic clove, finely chopped

3 sprigs thyme

250 ml (1 cup) dry white wine

40 g (¼ cup) plain flour

375 ml (1 ½ cups) chicken stock

1 teaspoon Dijon or English mustard – whatever you like

500 g frozen sweetcorn kernels, thawed

4 tablespoons chopped herbs (parsley, tarragon, thyme)

1 egg, beaten, to glaze

Pastry

250 g cold unsalted butter

200 ml ice cold water

500 g (3 ⅓ cups) plain flour

1 teaspoon salt

To make the pastry, chop the butter into small 5 cm pieces and place in the fridge with the cold water until ready to use.

In a food processor, carefully pulse together the butter, flour and salt until it resembles sand and before it comes to a paste. Quickly pulse in the ice cold water and then tip the pastry out on to the bench and bring it together with your hands. Do not overwork the dough.

Cut the dough in half and wrap each piece in cling film, press it gently to flatten slightly and then place in the fridge for 2–3 hours to rest.

To make the pie filling, heat a large frying pan and add the bacon, gently frying it until golden brown. Then remove it from the pan, leaving the rendered fat behind.

Season the chicken pieces well with sea salt and freshly ground black pepper. Add the butter to the pan and melt over high heat. When the pan's hot, add half the chicken pieces and sauté until lightly golden. Remove from the pan and then cook the rest of the chicken.

After removing the last batch of chicken from the pan, add the onions and sauté over a low heat until soft. Add the garlic and thyme sprigs, turn the heat to high and cook for a couple of minutes, then deglaze the pan with the white wine and leave to simmer until it has reduced by half.

Sprinkle in the flour, stirring well to combine, then add the chicken stock and bring to a gentle simmer for 2–3 minutes. Add mustard to taste, then add all the chicken and the bacon back in the pan with the corn and simmer for 4-5 minutes or until the chicken is completely cooked. Mix through the chopped herbs and leave the pie filling to cool completely before using.

Remove the pastry from the fridge and cut into two pieces, with one slightly larger than the other. Roll out the larger piece of pastry to a thickness of around 3 mm and to fit a 26-cm pie dish. Then carefully pick up the dough by wrapping it around the rolling pin and gently lay it across the pie dish.

Fill the pie up with the chicken mixture and then roll out the second disc of pastry for the lid. Wet the edges of the pastry base with some of the egg glaze, then gently put the top on and push the edges together with a fork.

Trim off the edges and brush with egg glaze, then make a small cross on the top of the pie with a sharp knife to help steam escape. Place the pie into the fridge to chill for 30 minutes before baking then glaze it again.

While the pie rests in the fridge, preheat the oven to 220°C. Cook the pie for 40 minutes or until completely golden brown. Serve hot, warm or cold.

Serves 6

My mother used to punish me and my siblings by feeding us fish pie. Aah! Good times! It took 25 years for these emotional scars to heal and for me to start loving fish pie again. The wispy crispness of the filo and the smokiness of the trout are what helped do it! One tip – do support your local fishmonger and ask them to remove all skin, bones and bloodline from the fish when you buy it from them.

MATT'S ULTIMATE FISH PIE

60 g butter
2 garlic cloves, finely sliced
60 g plain flour
600 ml hot fish stock
100 ml pouring cream
salt and freshly ground black pepper
2 tablespoons olive oil
1 onion, sliced

500 g fresh white fish such as blue eye or snapper cut into large 3 cm chunks
½ cups chopped dill
1 whole smoked trout (approx 600 g) skin and bones removed and flesh flaked
5 sheets filo pastry
60 g melted butter

Preheat the oven to 200°C.

In a medium saucepan, melt the butter, add the garlic and cook for 2 minutes. Add the flour and stir to combine with a wooden spoon, until thickened and bubbling.

Pour in the hot fish stock slowly and use a whisk to combine. Continue to cook for 20 minutes, until thickened, stirring constantly. Add the cream, season well and set aside to cool.

In a large frying pan, add the oil and heat over high heat. Add the onion and cook for a few minutes to soften, then remove from the pan and set aside. Add the white fish to the pan and brown for a few minutes on each side.

Very gently stir the fish, onions and dill into the cooled white sauce and place in a baking dish, approximately 5–7 cm deep. Evenly arrange the smoked trout.

Top with a layer of filo pastry and brush with melted butter. Repeat with remaining layers of filo, brushing each layer with butter.

Bake for 20 minutes until golden on top.

Serves 4

TIPS & TRICKS

- If all that palaver mucking around with the filo is too much, then try this pie topped with shop-bought puff pastry or mashed potato.

- To bulk up this fish pie and give it some textural excitement, add 4 hard-boiled eggs cut into quarters when you place the fish in the baking dish. Also add 150 g of peeled raw prawns to the pie with the fish.

- To add a neat, very French, aniseedy twist to this pie, fry a diced fennel bulb and 2 diced celery stalks with the onion until they all soften – about 3 minutes – and add this mix to the sauce. Sear the fish in this pan and then deglaze it with 125 ml (½ cup) of vermouth. Cook to burn off the alcohol. Stir this reduction into the fishy white sauce. Oh, and use the fennel tops and a bunch of tarragon instead of the dill. No vermouth? No worries! Use white wine instead. You could also add 1 teaspoon of Pernod if you've got it to add a slightly different anise kick!

I once almost lost a girlfriend over shepherd's pie. She suggested that the very act of me cooking one marked me down as a peasant. She changed her mind once she'd eaten it but then she wasn't expecting the huge savoury umami hit that comes from the Worcestershire sauce and Vegemite here. Umami is the elusive fifth taste that sits alongside 'sweet', 'sour', 'bitter' and 'salty' – and it's what makes parmesan, tomatoes and dashi so delicious!

Traditionally in Australia, shepherd's pie was made with the remains of the leg of lamb, but as there never seems to be any left over in my house I've always made it with lamb mince. If you make it with beef mince, then it becomes a cottage pie. This must have carrots in it. Adding carrots to shepherd's pie is as controversial as adding pineapple to pizza!

JACKAROO PIE

3 tablespoons olive oil

500 g lamb mince

1 large onion, diced

6 spring onions, finely sliced, whites and greens separated

150 g (1 cup) frozen peas

2 tablespoons tomato ketchup

1 teaspoon Worcestershire sauce

2 teaspoons Vegemite

125 ml (½ cup) chicken stock

salt and freshly ground black pepper to taste

1½ cups cooked mashed potatoes for topping, warmed

½ cup grated parmesan

butter (as much as you're allowed)

Preheat the oven to 180°C.

Heat 2 tablespoons of oil in a heavy-based pot over a medium heat. Turn up the heat. Add the lamb mince and cook, breaking up any lumps with a wooden spoon, until browned. Stir in the Vegemite. Remove the mince and set aside.

Lower the heat a little, add the remaining oil to the same pot and add the onions and spring onion whites. Cook for 3–4 minutes until softened. Mix in the peas, tomato ketchup, Worcestershire sauce and stir thoroughly.

Return the lamb to the pan and add the stock, cooking for 5 minutes or until the liquid is reduced. Season with salt and pepper.

Mix the chopped spring onion greens through the warmed mashed potatoes.

Place the lamb mixture into individual ramekins or a large pie dish and top with the mashed potatoes and parmesan. Pattern with a fork and add little dabs of butter.

Place in the oven and cook for 20 minutes until the top is nicely browned. Remove from the oven and serve immediately.

Serves 4

TIPS & TRICKS

- If you want to make this shepherd's pie a little more adult, add a short length of fresh rosemary to the onions while they are frying. Remove before you add the lamb mince. Oh, and take out the cooked mince and deglaze the pan with 125 ml (½ cup) of red wine! Reduce this by two-thirds before returning the mince and onions.

- To make a cottage pie, use beef mince instead of lamb, use beef stock instead of chicken and fry your onions with 2 finely diced carrots and 3 rashers of bacon, diced. Otherwise, it is just the same process.

In our midst is one food that combines that life-sustaining mix of carbs, proteins and veg-loaded vitamins in one tasty, handheld package. It's the miracle that is PIZZA.

It's also one of those great meals that everyone can have a hand in. I get the kids to help knead the dough, monitor the eye-popping magic of the rise, and roll out their own bases. And there's no better way to get them to eat veg than if they've strewn mushrooms, capsicum or zucchini alongside the cheese on their own pizza.

The first rule of making pizza at home is that the dough is king. Making fresh dough yourself is both easy and delivers a far lighter, crisper result than buying a ready-made base. Secondly, the perfect pizza, once sliced into a wedge, should be crisp and not so over-laden with topping that, when held by the crust edge, the middle droops flaccidly. So be careful of having too much moisture in the chosen toppings, as we all love perky pizza! Thirdly the secret to cooking pizza is heat: massive, cheese-browning, crust-puffing heat. I'd recommend buying an electric pizza oven (you sometimes see them in the supermarket for around $50).

BASIC PIZZA DOUGH

1 teaspoon dry yeast

350 ml warm water

1½ tablespoons sugar

475 g plain flour

1 teaspoon salt

1 tablespoon olive oil

Mix the yeast, warm water and sugar together and leave for 5 minutes. In a large bowl, mix the flour and salt, and make a well in the middle of the pile. Pour in the yeasty water and the oil. Using a knife, cut the liquid into the flour. When the liquid is all mixed in, pull the dough together into a ball.

Turn out the dough onto a floured surface and knead it until it starts to feel silky and springy. You should be able to push your thumb in and have it come out clean.

Use olive oil to oil a bowl more than twice the size of your dough and put the dough in. Toss it around so it is coated with oil. Leave the dough in the bowl and cover with a damp tea towel. Place the bowl in a warm, draught-free spot for at least half an hour.

When the dough has rested and swollen to about twice its original size, flour a clean surface and tip out the dough. Punch back the rise in the dough. Cut it into four parts and roll into four balls. Pop on a floured tray and leave them to rise again (around 30 minutes).

Fire up your wood-fired oven, plug in your electric pizza oven or heat your regular oven to maximum with a pizza stone or tile in it.

On a floured surface, stretch out, or roll out, each of the balls of dough. Drop onto a very lightly floured pizza tray. Top as required, perhaps using a combination from the toppings on pages 54–55.

Place the pizza in your oven to cook. The hotter the oven, the better the pizza and the quicker it will cook. In a proper pizza oven, it will just take a couple of minutes. You are looking for a crisp base spotted with some tan marks and crisp edges.

Makes enough for 4 pizzas

10 ways with...
PIZZA TOPPINGS

MARGHERITA

The patriotic classic of tomato, mozzarella and basil is best when made with the finest cheese you can afford, whether it is buffalo mozzarella or even a more reasonably priced fior di latte or bocconcini, which will stay stringy for longer and add the required milky freshness. I use slices of the ripest tomatoes I can find, always remembering to remove the seeds to stop their moisture making the pizza topping slushy. I always add anything green and leafy as the pizza hits the table, so I don't put my basil on until the pizza is out of the oven.

PORK AND FENNEL SAUSAGE

Ripping open the skins of the snags and tossing lumps of the meat on the dough makes a great fatty and meaty hit that is perfect with a classic tomato sauce base or served *in bianco* (i.e. without red sauce), with dollops of mascarpone between the nubbly bits of snag and with a fine shaving of red onion slices over the top.

MUSHROOM

This is another pizza that works equally well with or without tomato sauce. Just remember to load the pizza with far more mushrooms than you think you'll need because they will shrink in the cooking process. To serve, sprinkle with fresh thyme leaves – or add little dollops of goat's curd or crumblings of goat's cheese if you want to go all fancy on me.

PROSCIUTTO WITH ROCKET AND RADICCHIO

This is one of those pizzas that has come to prominence in the last 10 years or so. The secret here is not to put the prosciutto on the basic tomato sauce and mozzarella pizza until after it rolls out of the oven. (If you bake the cured meat in the topping, you risk drawing the salt to the surface of the meat.) Then follow my leafy green rule and throw a handful of rocket on each slice. Add some shredded bitter radicchio leaves if you like their bitterness with the pepperiness of the rocket. I love it! The freshness of meat and lettuces is the perfect foil to the pizza's hot breadiness and the richness of tomato and melted mozz.

PANCETTA AND PEAR WITH WALNUT

For modern pizzas I like to leave out the tomato sauce, which can dominate thanks to its tang, sweetness and savoury umami notes. This pizza is a modern classic. Smear mascarpone on your base and a little mozzarella. Top with thin slices of ripe, sweet pear. Then lay over slices of pancetta – or batons of smoked bacon if that's easier to find and bake. Throw a handful of walnuts over the pizza in the last minute of cooking. You can add some nuggets of blue cheese as well but remember to balance this new saltiness against the saltiness of the pork.

LEEK AND GORGONZOLA DOLCE

A super-simple pizza – you can sweat the leeks first if you want but I just cut finger-thick rounds and layer them over the dough and then spot dollops of a soft creamy dolce latte or mild gorgonzola across the top. The combination with the sweet leeks is a modern classic oft attributed to pizzaiolo Pietro Barbagello, one of Australia's new-wave pizza pioneers.

ROAST PUMPKIN WITH FETA, RED CHILLI AND QUINCE JELLY

Next time you do a roast, throw in extra pumpkin slices and keep them in the fridge. Then partner their sweetness on a pizza with the saltiness of feta and the fruity tang of a jelly such as quince, rose, red pepper or redcurrant. A little sprinkling of fresh red chilli is the perfect contrast and looks pretty.

BACON, BANANA AND CHICKEN WITH BARBECUE SAUCE

I think the essence of great pizza is simplicity, whether it's ham and pineapple or just hot salami. I am no fan (any more!) of the tandoori chicken pizza with mango chutney, the chilli con carne pizza topped with nachos or the Greek lamb pizza. Usually I'm not a big fan of chicken on pizza, but lamb is never right – unless you replace the tomato sauce with a garlic sauce and the dough is rolled up around it souvlaki style! I do have one weakness in this territory and that is chicken on pizza with bacon, banana and a squirt of barbecue sauce. I had it in Brisbane once and, like a short passionate holiday romance, I never forgot it!

TOMATO, FIOR DI LATTE, ROCKET AND PROSCIUTTO

Place cherry tomato halves cut-side up on top of the dough. Fior di latte is similar to mozzarella cheese, but made from cow's milk. Dry five small balls of fior di latte (or bocconcini cheese) with paper towel, tear in half and place between the tomatoes. Bake the pizza, then top with a handful of baby rocket and several slices of prosciutto.

PEACH AND WHITE CHOCOLATE

A more traditional way to use banana on a pizza is with chocolate. If you haven't tried one, a sweet pizza does have a certain attraction, whether it's folded over to make a calzone stuffed with Nutella or a marbled filling of three different melted chocolates (white, milk, dark). My favourite combo is a slice of ripe peach sprinkled with loads of white chocolate and a tiny bit of flake salt. Let the white chocolate brown a little to caramelise and then the sweetness of the peach will really pop!

PASTA AND RICE

The strength of great pastas and risottos is also the strength of Italian cuisine – simple clear ideas built around a small number of complementary flavours. There is also one other abiding truth about pasta and risotto – they should always be about the pasta and the rice rather than the flavourings. The flavourings should be seen as condiments to the perfectly cooked pasta and rice, so don't overload either with too much sauce.

Also, don't get hung up on having to make fresh pasta. I make fresh pasta if I am making ravioli, want to use a light or fresh sauce, or want to romance my wife. The other times I'm quite happy with a dry pasta.

Choosing the right shape of pasta, however, is governed by the sort of set rules that are rare in Italy; basically the chunkier the sauce, the chunkier the pasta. Also, you want to look for pastas with a ridged or rough surface as these will hold on to sauce better.

When it comes to cooking pasta, there are also rules. Use lots of water that should taste as salty as the sea. Add the pasta to the water when boiling and immediately stir in a large cup of cold water. This will stop the pasta from sticking without the need to add oil. Bring the water back to the boil and then simmer the pasta until it's cooked. Cooked pasta isn't soft but has a little resistance to your teeth. It should taste a little nutty but not chalky and snappy.

When you drain your pasta, do save some of the cooking liquid. This liquid will be loaded with starch. Return the pasta and sauce to the pan along with a splash of the cooking liquid. Toss the pan to coat the pasta and to allow the starch in the water to add some extra silkiness to your sauce. This works best with oil, wine, butter or tomato based sauces. Just like the ones to follow, including one from my son, Will, age 9.

One final rule – the Italians frown on adding cheese to seafood sauces for pasta. But then, as any Italian will tell you, rules are made for breaking!

NAPOLI SAUCE

Almost all my sauces and braises start with what the French call a *mirepoix* and the Italians a *soffritto*. I'd call it a sautéed veg base, which is far less romantic but much less stuffy.

Dice 1 large carrot, 1 celery stalk and 1 onion. Then fry them together in a splash of olive oil over medium heat until soft. Add a couple of cloves of crushed garlic. Cook for a couple of minutes. Now deglaze the pan. This means add a good glug of wine and, while it bubbles away, use it to scrape any delicious burny bits on the sides and bottom of the pan. For a rich Napoli sauce that's perfect for pasta, blitzing into pizza topping or as a base for braised meats, just add 1 can of tomatoes to the well-fried veg. You can use fresh tomatoes, but tomatoes are one of the few things that are as good tinned as fresh when making a workmanlike sauce like a Napoli. Season and add a strip of lemon zest and a squeeze of juice to intensify the sauce. Remove the zest before using. Adding a little sugar is frowned upon – so if the tomatoes lack the sweetness you crave, do it when no-one is looking.

Serves 4 with pasta

TIPS & TRICKS

- For a meatier Napoli sauce, fry something porky (like a diced rasher of bacon, pancetta or speck) with your *soffritto*. This, with a good glug of olive oil, will give you a sort of basic Roman 'Amatriciana' sauce. Add some sliced red chilli or crushed dried red chilli to add some welcome 'angry' heat.

BURNT BUTTER SAUCE

Warm 100 g of butter in a clean pan over a moderate heat. The butter will melt and then foam as it heats up. When it starts to smell nice and nutty, remove from the heat and squeeze in a little lemon juice, which will accentuate the toasty flavours and cut through the fat of the butter with some freshness too. Be careful not to let the solids burn or else you'll kill that worked-for nuttiness. You can enhance your burnt butter sauce by throwing in fresh sage leaves – especially if it's destined for pumpkin ravioli – or perhaps adding plump sultanas and nuts such as hazelnuts or pine nuts.

Serves 4 with pasta

TIPS & TRICKS

- What 'burns', or more accurately 'toasts', in the butter to make it taste so deliciously nutty is not the fat but the milk solids in the butter. A cheap way to get more 'burnt butter bang' is to add 20 g (just under ¼ cup) of skimmed milk powder to every 50 g of butter. For more on using skimmed milk powder see page 3.

Will's Pesto

If you follow these steps you will have a yummy batch of pesto.

Things you will need: 1 clove of garlic, A big bunch of bazil, half a cup of pinenuts, oil, Parmesan and a mortar and pestle.

Step 1. Chop the garlic in little cubes.
Step 2. put the bazil, garlic and a splash of oil with the pinenuts in the Mortar.
Step 3. Grind the Ingredients with the pestle until it's smooth.
Step 4. If the garlic is too strong add more bazil.

Now you have made a batch of pesto

One of the great things about getting away to see friends down at the beach at New Year is cooking a succession of communal dinners using the loose roaring mob of children as a battalion of chefs. Getting them to make pasta is perfect as there are a number of tasks to share around, from feeding the pasta into the machine to cranking the handle; from making the next batch of dough to hanging the resulting silky strands. There is also the great communal wave of satisfaction they feel actually making their dinner that also eclipses the satisfaction the adults feel knowing the kids are keeping out of trouble. Once they've done it once they can usually be relied upon to do it again unsupervised, which means you can watch the Boxing Day test/Australian Open tennis/Sydney to Hobart largely unbothered!

HOMEMADE PASTA

400 g (2⅔ cups) flour
pinch of salt
4 eggs

To mix the ingredients, put the flour in a bowl with the salt and stir together. Make a well in the middle of the flour. Crack in your eggs and mix the eggs lightly with a fork. Then start pulling in the flour to mix with the egg. Work into a ball of dough that is combined to a degree that you can push your thumb into the dough and it comes out clean. (If your thumb comes out with dough sticking to it, you need to work in more flour.)

To work your dough, you should knead it with the heel of your hand until the surface feels satin-smooth and slightly elastic. Basically you need to push the heel of your hand away from you and through the dough to stretch it. Then fold the elongated dough back on itself and rotate the dough ball by a quarter-turn (90 degrees) and knead again. Keep doing this until the dough gets that silky-smooth feeling. This will take about 5 minutes of vigorous activity.

Wrap the dough in cling film and leave it in the fridge for half an hour to rest before rolling. (I have to admit I am usually too impatient to do this and the resulting pasta is still pretty good, even if it's best to let the gluten develop a little.)

Break the dough into apple-sized lumps to make it easier to handle. I usually pass each ball of dough through the pasta machine from the widest setting to the middle setting three times. When I have passed the dough through the middle setting, I fold it back over on itself, rotate the pasta 90° and start again. If at any point the dough seems sticky, dust the sheet lightly with flour. Laminating the pasta like this makes it strong and shiny.

You don't need a pasta machine and can do this all by hand but I reckon it's then easier to work with a smaller (peach-sized) ball of dough and the longest rolling pin you can find. Shape the dough into a cigar shape before you roll it out lengthways with the roller. Remember to fold the dough over on itself once or twice, rotate it and then re-roll it to help laminate it. When it gets that slightly shiny look you can cut the pasta by hand.

The rule for how wide to cut your pasta is 'the chunkier the sauce, the wider the pasta'. Pasta all'Amatriciana is, for example, quite a loose sauce, so a thin pasta is best.

Toss the pasta in a little flour after it is cut to stop it sticking. Set it aside in a dry place and in an airtight container until ready to cook it.

Cook the fresh pasta in loads of boiling water that's as salty as the sea. Pull it out after a couple of minutes while it still has some bite. Toss the cooked pasta in a pan with a little bit of the sauce and some of the cooking liquid. Tossing it in the pan like this helps emulsify the sauce.

Serves 4

Bacon, eggs, cheese – <u>there</u> is a culinary trinity to have angels singing 'Hallelujah'. They come together beautifully in this classic Roman dish. Like many classic Italian dishes however, there is much debate over what constitutes the correct way of making carbonara. Cream or no cream? Whole eggs or just egg yolks? Onions – yes or no? Guanciale, pancetta or bacon? And to make things even more convoluted, it seems that while recipes for carbonara existed before the Second World War, it was after the country was 'liberated' that the dish became popular – something blamed on the presence of thousands of US troops laden with rations of bacon and eggs!

The only other rule in my house when it comes to carbonara is that you must never overcook the sauce. The beauty of this dish is how the warmth of the pan and the warmth of the pasta gently cook the egg mix and melt the cheese to create a satiny sheen over every strand, and then the bacon adds texture and a salty explosion of smoky porkiness.

SPAGHETTI CARBONARA

250 g middle bacon
150 g parmesan
400 g spaghetti
40 g butter
splash of olive oil

5 eggs
nutmeg (optional)
freshly ground black pepper, to taste

Bring a large pot of salted water to the boil on the stove. How salty? It should taste about as salty as sea water. Your water will boil faster with the lid on. I also usually boil half the water in the kettle to make things quicker.

While the water is coming to the boil, prepare your bacon and cheese. Pull or snip any rind off the bacon before chopping it. Grate the cheese as finely as you can.

When the water is dancing madly, pour in your pasta and a glass of cold water. Stir the pasta a couple of times. This will stop it sticking.

Bring the water back to the boil and then simmer gently until the spaghetti is cooked but still a little resistant to your bite. It shouldn't crack when you bite into it but just take a little pressure to make it yield.

While the water is coming back to the boil, heat a frying pan with the butter and oil in it. When the pan is hot, add the bacon and fry until it is golden and crispy rather than overly brown and leathery like your sun-baking auntie from the Gold Coast.

While the bacon is cooking, whisk the eggs so they are broken up but not so much that they foam. Stir in the parmesan. Add a little grate of nutmeg here if you like it.

Using a slotted spoon, remove the bacon from the frying pan to a sheet of paper towel. Keep the fats in the pan.

Warm your dining plates or bowls. Call everyone to the table with some urgency as the timing is crucial.

Your pasta will be ready now. Drain it but keep some of the cooking water (about a cup). Put a good splash (about 2 tablespoons) of this cooking water back into the pot along with a smaller splash of the fat (about 1 tablespoon) from the frying pan. Fling in the pasta and toss it for a minute over the flame. This will help the starches from the pasta water and the fat to emulsify. Turn off the heat. Pour in the egg and cheese mixture and the bacon. Stir through and watch how the sauce slowly starts to thicken and the strands of cheese melt. Serve and eat immediately with a big twist of freshly ground black pepper on every plate. Overcook it and you end up with scrambled eggs pasta which is pretty horrid!

Serves 4

When I was much younger and even more foolish I found myself consorting with disreputable people. I suppose that is to be expected when my working life has been spent with nightclub owners, bands, chefs, TV people and journalists. In the culinary world too, some dishes are equally disreputable, none more so than spaghetti alla puttanesca, the so-called famous whore's spaghetti of Naples.

The story goes that this was a quick and easy dish made by the madams of Naples' bordellos in the 19th century for their hard-working girls. Sadly, the truth is that the sauce only became known in Italy in the late 1950s, decades after the Italian authorities had outlawed brothels. Thus the present culinary thinking is that the name comes from the Italian word 'puttanata', which politely translates as 'rubbish', and the sauce is the creation of a chef from the Italian island of Ischia who threw together any old rubbish he found in the pantry to make a pasta sauce. Even if this is the case, puttanesca is one of the great pasta sauces and should be listed proudly alongside bolognese, carbonara and matriciana. And with flavours as unsubtle as Sunset Strip streetwalkers' white patent thigh boots, it is certainly the most forward, no matter what the historians say.

SPAGHETTI ALLA PUTTANESCA

olive oil, for frying

1 large brown onion, diced

25 g anchovy fillets (best and pinkest you can find)

3 garlic cloves, crushed

125 ml (½ cup) red wine

400 g can tomatoes

150 g black olives, drained and pitted

60 g (⅓ cup) capers, washed and drained

1 cup chopped flat-leaf parsley leaves

zest and juice of ½ lemon

sugar (optional)

2 long red chillies, deseeded and finely chopped

400 g spaghetti or tagliatelle

1 tablespoon olive oil

vegetable oil, for frying

Heat the olive oil in a non-stick frying pan over medium-low heat and cook the onion for 6–8 minutes until translucent. Add the anchovies, pressing down with a fork to lightly mash them, then add the crushed garlic cloves and sauté for 3–4 minutes until cooked through.

Pour in the wine and cook down, scraping any caught bits on the pan back into the sauce. Add the can of tomatoes, olives and about 35 g (¼ cup) of capers. Stir and cook on a low heat for 5 minutes. Add half the parsley and squeeze in the lemon juice. Adjust the seasoning with salt and a little sugar so it is in balance (but only if needed – those capers and olives will add lots of salt). Stir in half the chopped chillies. Cook for 2–3 minutes or until the flavours are combined.

Meanwhile, cook the pasta in well-salted boiling water until al dente – or still a little firm to the bite. Drain and toss with a little oil. Keep warm.

Dry the remaining capers on a tea towel and then fry in vegetable oil until crispy. Drain on paper towel.

Serve the dish at the table garnished with the crispy capers, the lemon zest, remaining chopped parsley and chilli. Serve with crusty bread.

Serves 4

Macaroni cheese is like the cook's perfect blank canvas. Carefully pick the flavours you want to add to the classic recipe below and you'll have a hit of your own on your hands. Four rashers of diced and fried smokey bacon is always a popular choice but you can push this further by adding a cup of frozen corn, fried with the bacon. For this customisation, add four trimmed and sliced spring onions to the crumb topping. Alternatively, think of adding herbs like thyme or chives or a teaspoon of English or Dijon mustard to the cheese sauce; chopped parsley to the topping; or substituting a mix of mozzarella, gruyere and parmesan for the tasty. For something more oozily pungent try using taleggio or fontina as your cheese of choice instead. Or even add caramelised onions.

MACARONI CHEESE

500 g good-quality macaroni
2 cups roughly torn fresh bread
140 g butter
80 g (½ cup) plain flour
1 litre milk
500 g grated tasty cheese

100 g (1 cup) freshly grated parmesan
¼ of a nutmeg or ½ teaspoon ground nutmeg
sea salt and freshly ground black pepper

Preheat the oven to 200°C.

Bring a large saucepan of well-salted water to the boil. Cook the macaroni for 1 or 2 minutes short of the timing on the packet instructions, then drain in a colander. The pasta needs to be a little crunchy because it will cook more when in the oven – sludgy pasta in a mac 'n' cheese is a big no-no.

While the macaroni is cooking, make the big breadcrumbs. If the bread doesn't feel stale enough to turn into crumbs and still feels a bit moist and fresh, pop it in the toaster until it just starts to colour. Remove before it toasts. Place the slices with the crusts on into the processor. Pulse the blades to chop the bread into thumbnail-sized pieces.

Heat approximately 80 g of the butter in a large heavy-based frying pan over medium heat. Add the flour and cook for a few minutes, stirring with a wooden spoon. This will 'cook out' the floury taste and let the butter brown a little. When this roux* starts to thicken, add the milk, a little at a time, stirring to incorporate.
* fancy French word for flour and butter mixture wot thickens things.

Add 350 g (approximately 2¾ cups) of the tasty cheese, reserving a handful for the topping. Add the parmesan and stir in the pasta. Over medium heat, stir until most of the cheese has melted and you have a lovely gooey sauce.

Season with salt, pepper and as much nutmeg as you like, but beware that it is a potent spice. Finely grate in as much as your tastebuds tells you is good – which should be between an eighth and a quarter of one nut!

Pour into a large baking dish (or several individual dishes).

In a clean plastic bag or bowl, toss the torn bread with the remaining tasty cheese, then scatter this mix over the macaroni cheese. Dot with the remaining butter and bake in the oven for about 20 minutes, until golden brown and crispy on top.

Serves 4

Gnocchi has a special place in my heart because it's one of the reasons why I married the woman I love. She makes the lightest gnocchi. To match her skills I use a little trick where I cook individual trial gnocchi as I mix the flour into the potato little by little. This allows me to pick the point when the perfect gnocchi is reached. That is when the trial gnocchi has a bit of spring to it, without being all about the mash.

GNOCCHI WITH GORGONZOLA

1.25 kg clean floury potatoes
(coliban is best)

salt

300 g (2 cups) plain flour

2 bunches silverbeet, stalks
removed and leaves shredded

olive oil

50 g salted butter, melted

250 g shelled walnuts

250 g gorgonzola, roughly chopped

Heat the oven to 180°C.

Bake the whole potatoes for an hour, until they are squidgy in the middle. Scoop the flesh out of the skins. Mash until smooth while warm and season with salt. You should end up with about 500 g of cool potato. Let the flesh steam off its moisture.

Flour a work surface and dump the potato on it. Gently mix with 150 g (1 cup) of flour to make a dough. If it doesn't feel like a dough, add more flour. The gnocchi mix needs to be a little stickier than a pasta dough; if you push your thumb into the dough it should come out almost clean but not completely dry. I used about 220 g of flour for this batch, but the amount of flour depends on loads of variables such as how dry your potato is. Don't be rough when kneading the dough. You need to avoid developing the gluten in the flour too much, because that will make the gnocchi rubbery. Roll the dough into a sausage shape as thick as a bloke's index finger and cut into 3 cm lengths. Press a fork on the top to mark it slightly.

Cook the shredded silverbeet leaves in a large saucepan over medium heat with a splash of olive oil for 5 minutes.

To cook the gnocchi, bring a large saucepan of well-salted water to the boil, using water from the kettle. Drop the gnocchi into the boiling water a few at a time. When they rise to the surface they are cooked. This will take about 90 seconds, depending on how much water you are using or how many gnocchi you put in. Immediately remove the gnocchi from the water with a slotted spoon and place in a well-warmed serving dish lined with the melted butter. Try not to pile up the gnocchi; they like their personal space.

When the silverbeet starts to soften and darken, throw in the walnuts and half the gorgonzola and stir. The mixture is ready when the cheese has melted and coated the leaves, and the walnuts have warmed.

To serve, spoon the silverbeet, gorgonzola and walnut mix on top of the serving dish full of gnocchi. Top with the remaining gorgonzola.

Serves 6

TIPS & TRICKS

- Gnocchi can be made with sweet potato or pumpkin instead of potato. Again the secret is to ensure that the vegetables are as dry as possible. Officially this means you should pick a drier pumpkin such as butternut and then roast it rather than boil it. Having said that, my wife used to boil 500 g of butternut pumpkin, then drain it, mash it and let it cool, and it still worked fine enough to make me want to marry her! Work in just enough plain flour to hold the mashed pumpkin together. Roll into finger-thick ropes and cut into thumb-sized gnocchi. Cook them in simmering salted water. They are cooked when they float. Serve these drizzled with a sage burnt butter sauce (see page 57) and a grate of parmesan.

This bolognese sauce is so good it's developed its own fan club – one of whom pinned the recipe on a notice board at my publisher's. Thanks, Joybelle. The rest is history. If you want to make this bolognese even better add a parmesan crust or a couple of pieces of pig skin (ask your butcher) to the sauce when it starts cooking. Or just cook it the day before you need it. These tricks will all add further depths of flavour to your sauce.

Once you've perfected this recipe think about customizing it by adding pork, either in the form of mince or cured goodies like prosciutto, pancetta, smoked speck or even good old bacon. Alternatively step up the mince you use by choosing chicken mince, or even better, a 50/50 mix of veal and pork!

THE BOLOGNESE THAT GOT ME A BOOK DEAL

olive oil, for frying
40 g butter
2 medium carrots, finely diced
3 brown onions, finely diced
4 rashers of bacon, diced
2 celery stalks, finely diced
1 tablespoon soft brown sugar

4 garlic cloves, crushed
3 tablespoons tomato paste
1 kg beef mince
1 lemon
500 ml (2 cups) red wine
3 bay leaves
splash of Worcestershire sauce

2 x 400 g cans tomatoes
500 ml (2 cups) beef stock
salt, to taste
375 g packet of egg tagliatelle – the curly nesty ones are nicest
150 g (1½ cups) grated parmesan

Place a large pot on the stovetop over a medium–high heat. To make the *soffritto*, or base, pour the olive oil and butter into the hot pan. When the butter is melted and the oil hot, throw in the carrots, onions and bacon. Cook for 2 minutes, stirring. Add the celery and cook until the vegetables are soft and going translucent at the edges. Sprinkle over the brown sugar and stir through. Add the garlic and tomato paste, and move this around the pan to cook out for 3 minutes. Scrape the tomatoey *soffritto* into a bowl.

Splash in some more olive oil. When it's hot, throw in the mince and cook over a high heat until browned. Stir the meat the whole time so it cooks evenly.

Scrape the meat into the *soffritto* bowl. Turn up the heat and deglaze using the red wine. When the wine has reduced by half, add back in the meat, *soffritto*, bay leaves, a couple of good dashes of Worcestershire sauce, a 4 cm length of lemon peel, tomatoes and stock.

Season with salt and a good squeeze of lemon juice from one half of the lemon. Reserve the rest.

Bring the bolognese to the boil covered, then remove the lid and turn the heat right down. Cook very gently for up to 4 hours. Stir occasionally to ensure the sauce doesn't stick and burn. If the sauce gets too thick, add some more stock and stir it in. Cooking it low and slow intensifies the flavour.

The sauce is ready when it smells irresistible, and is wonderfully thick and a dark-red glossy colour. Taste and season with a little more salt and lemon juice as required. You can now either serve it straight away or cool it and refrigerate before using the next day.

Cook the tagliatelle in plenty of salted boiling water in a large pan. When the pasta is cooked but still a little firm to the bite, scoop out a cup of the starchy cooking liquid and drain the pasta.

Put a generous ladle of the bolognese sauce in the pasta pot (about 2 cups) and toss through the pasta. Moisten the combination with a little of the reserved pasta water so it isn't clumpy. Feel free to use as little or as much sauce as you like – we've got lots of plans for the sauce that's left over.

Serve it with grated parmesan over the tagliatelle, bread for mopping up the leftover sauce and a green salad.

Serves 4

15 ways with...
LEFTOVER BOLOGNESE

LASAGNE

Make a lasagne with it (see page 74). You can always add another can of tomatoes and some fried bacon to lengthen your remaining sauce.

PASTA BAKE

Heat the remaining sauce and mix with a small short pasta shape like penne, drained while still a little undercooked and fresh from the boiling water. Pile into an ovenproof and buttered dish. Top with grated tasty cheese, mozzarella and parmesan. Bang into a 180°C oven and cook for around 40 minutes or until it goes golden on the top. Serve in slabs with a fresh green salad.

FILLED CREPES

Fill crepes with the sauce and then bake in an oven dish with mature tasty cheese sprinkled over the top.

BOLOGNESE ON TOAST

Try the old penniless student treat of piling your warmed leftover sauce on toast, but top with chopped parsley and a squeeze of lemon. A gratinated grilled cheese topping is also good!

UPSIDE-DOWN COTTAGE PIE

Make a well in the middle of a pile of mashed potato and fill it with the hot sauce. Add grated cheese as an option – or mix a packed cup of grated cheese into your potato at the mashing stage so you get stringy-cheese mash. Grill.

POLENTA LAYER

Serve the sauce poured over a bowl of wet polenta. Top with a good squeeze of lemon juice, some lemon zest and loads of chopped parsley. To make this dish even sexier put a layer of thick-sliced, pan-fried field mushrooms (cooked with thyme leaves) on top of the sauce-topped polenta. Top these with a slice of melty Swiss cheese if that takes your fancy with a sprinkling of more thyme leaves and a squeeze of lemon.

BOLOGNESE PIE

Top with puff pastry and call it a pie. You can always lengthen the sauce with chunks of mushroom, whole roast shallots or any other cooked root veg.

STUFFED CAPSICUM

Take the seeds and veins out of capsicums. Fill the cavity with alternating layers of sauce and cooked rice. Then bake in the oven with grated cheese on the top until the filling is hot, the capsicum is cooked and the topping dark golden and bubbly.

BAKED POTATO

Serve on a baked potato with either grated cheese on top, or with a dollop of sour cream and some fresh chives.

BOLOGNESE COBBLER

Pour the leftover sauce into a greased baking dish small enough so the sauce is about 2.5 cm deep. Make a batch of scone dough (see page 216) and pop small scone-sized dollops of dough on top of the sauce. Bake until the scones are risen and fluffy. We'll call this a bolognese cobbler because the close-packed scones, once risen, look like cobblestones.

COTTAGE PIE

Heat the sauce and pour into a greased baking dish that's small enough so the sauce is about 2.5 cm deep. Top with piped mashed potato to make a tomatoey cottage pie. If you've got some cooked carrots left over, dice them and add them to the sauce. If you don't have enough sauce for this you can always lengthen with some more browned beef mince and some stock. Alternatively you can throw in a handful or two of peas, depending on how much sauce you have. Frozen peas are fine. Just always make sure the sauce is properly heated through before assembling.

NOT-SO CHILLI DOG

Pour it over a hot dog in a soft bun as an Aussie take on the famous US chilli dog.

PARMA

Pour over the top of a chicken or veal schnitzel for a home version of the classic Aussie counter meal.

CHEAT'S MOUSSAKA

Layer the sauce between cooked slices of eggplant and potato for a cheat's very inauthentic moussaka. Just don't tell my mate George's mum Mary or I'll get in trouble for suggesting this!

CHILLI CON CARNE

Add a 400 g can of drained kidney beans, finely chopped long red chillies, red capsicums and a good splash of Tabasco and cook through to make a Texas-roadhouse-style chilli con carne. Instead of kidney beans you can add baked beans or a cup of frozen or tinned (but drained) corn kernels. You could just add the corn and no kidney beans but then I'd also throw in a green capsicum cut into 2 cm tiles. When your fake chilli is hot, serve with warmed corn chips, on nachos, or in tacos with shredded iceberg lettuce, tomato, a little grated cheese and sour cream.

Lasagne still ranks as one of Australia's favourite dishes even though there are loads of steps to make it. To take your lasagne to another level think of infusing the milk for your cheese sauce with a sprig of thyme. Finely chopped fresh marjoram or oregano also work, especially if you've gone for a really tomatoey meat sauce. I seldom use dried herbs as they are usually too pungent. Alternatively, why not add a dollop of sour cream or crème fraîche at the end of making your sauce to add a little touch of sourness to its richness. Feel free to change-up the cheese to gruyere or be even more radical by adding a layer of thinly sliced or grated mozzarella in the middle or on top of your lasagne. Note that this will make this lasagne somewhat more expensive than the peasant dish it originally was, and I'm still not sure it would pass muster with my team of little lasagne experts back home who accept lasagne in only one form – the meaty, cheesy classic below.

LASAGNE THAT'S WELL WORTH THE WORK

1 kg bolognese sauce (see page 71)
1 small onion
4 cloves
1.5 litres full-cream milk
1 bay leaf
80 g butter
120 g plain flour

100 g (1 cup) finely grated parmesan
¼ of a nutmeg or ½ teaspoon ground nutmeg
375 g packet of fresh lasagne sheets
80 g (⅔ cup) grated tasty cheese
salt and freshly ground black pepper, to taste

Preheat the oven to 180°C.

Warm the meat sauce on the stovetop.

Stud the onion with the cloves. Pop in a saucepan over a medium heat with the milk and the bay leaf. Heat until the milk is hot but not boiling. Remove from the heat and let the spices infuse into the milk for 15 minutes.

Melt the butter and, when it starts to foam, sprinkle in the flour and stir so all the lumps are removed. Cook the flour out for a couple of minutes to make a roux (see page 66).

Remove the onion and bay leaf from the milk. Add half the milk to the roux to make a white sauce and stir it in. As the sauce thickens, add the rest of the milk steadily. Stir in the grated parmesan and taste. Add a little nutmeg – a quick grate or pinch or two should do it. When combined and thick, remove this cheese sauce from the heat until needed.

Butter an ovenproof casserole or pan. Spoon a thin layer of the meat sauce over the base of the pan. Layer sheets of pasta over the sauce. Next, slather on half of the remaining meat sauce and then half of the cheese sauce. Cover with sheets of pasta. Cover with the remaining meat sauce and then cover with pasta sheets. Pour over the remaining cheese sauce and top with the grated tasty cheese. Make sure the pasta sheets are covered.

Place in the oven and cook for 30 minutes. Check if the pasta is cooked by piercing the lasagne with a wooden skewer. There should be some resistance. Return to the oven for 10 minutes to finish and for the top to go all golden and bubbly with little burnt spots! Check the lasagne again and remove from the oven if the skewer slips in easily.

Leave the lasagne for 10 minutes to cool down from its bubbly lava-like intensity and for the lasagne to stabilise. Serve in slabs with a crisp iceberg lettuce salad and crusty bread.

Serves 6–8

A LIGHTER LASAGNE
(OOH, AND IT'S VEGETARIAN TOO)

375 g packet of fresh lasagne sheets

2 garlic cloves, finely chopped

1 bunch spring onions, trimmed and sliced into thin coins

1 celery stalk, strings removed and finely diced

2 large bunches spinach, picked, washed and shaken dry

60 g plain flour

40 g butter

400 ml vegetable stock

500 g big meaty mushrooms, sliced thickly

juice and zest of 1 lemon

¼ of a nutmeg or ½ teaspoon ground nutmeg

400 g fresh ricotta (from the deli counter)

500 ml sour cream

100 g (1 cup) grated parmesan, plus extra if you like

olive oil

Preheat the oven to 180°C.

Grease a baking pan or casserole dish with butter. Place a layer of lasagne sheets on the bottom of the pan. This will give you some nice sticky brown bits on the bottom of your lasagne as well as the top and sides.

If you want to make this dish non-vegetarian fry 6 proscuitto slices gently in a large saucepan with a little oil. When they go crispy, remove from the oil and reserve. If not using proscuitto, fry the garlic, spring onions and celery in the oil. This will take just a couple of minutes tops. Don't let the garlic brown or it will become bitter.

If the spinach has lots of thick stalks, pinch them out. Now throw the spinach into the saucepan and wilt it down. If you want to be frugal, slice the stalks finely and add to the pan as well, but you need to chop them or they will make the lasagne stringy. When that huge pan of fresh spinach has broken down to a bright green tangle about a quarter as high as it was when it went in raw, remove from the heat and let it cool slightly.

Cook the flour and butter together, stirring all the time, to create a paste. Add the stock, a little at a time, over a medium heat, until it becomes a nice thick gravy. Throw the mushrooms in the gravy and stir to coat.

When the spinach is no longer too hot to handle, use clean hands and squeeze out the excess moisture from the spinach. Layer the spinach, spring onions, garlic and celery evenly across the lasagne sheets in the baking pan, making sure it spreads all the way to the edges. Squeeze over the juice of ½ a lemon, or more if you love lemon. Sprinkle on some nutmeg. It's a potent spice, so go easy! Cover the spinach with another layer of lasagne sheets.

Layer on the mushrooms with their gravy on top of the lasagne sheets. If using the proscuitto crumble over the mushrooms. Roughly crumble over the ricotta evenly. Top with sheets of lasagne. Smear on the sour cream as thick as you like and sprinkle on a cup of grated parmesan. More if you like. Warming the sour cream in the microwave first will make it easier to spread evenly.

Pop in the oven for around 40 minutes or until the top is golden and burnished and a skewer pierces the lasagne to the bottom of the pan with just a little resistance. Sprinkle lemon zest to taste over the top of the lasagne and serve with a crispy green salad of cucumber and iceberg, and crusty warm bread.

Serves 6–8

TIPS & TRICKS

- Here are some ideas for flavourings you might like to try: prawns, zucchini and mint; blanched asparagus, green beans, sugar snaps and peas; pumpkin, chestnuts and maybe some sliced roast duck (but use red wine instead of white wine); roast beetroot, toasted hazelnuts and goat's curd; mussels and cubes of tomato and lemon zest (but cut out the parmesan). The most classic risotto is alla Milanese, which is the traditional accompaniment to that slow braise of veal shanks – osso bucco. To make it, stir in 50 g of bone marrow and add 6 saffron strands.

Risotto is perhaps the most abused dish in Australian restaurants, which is weird because making great risotto at home isn't really that hard. The secret is that old combination of the best produce and smart technique followed with patience, trust and good timing. So here is the central rule about risotto. It's all about the rice and only then about the toppings. With this in mind, I always use carnaroli or vialone nano rice as they have a higher starch count than standard arborio rice. This higher starch content means you can make your risotto without all that palaver of stirring until the end, but it may mean that you'll have to pick up your risotto rice from the deli rather than the supermarket. Yes, I know this rice is more expensive, but this is one of those few cases where I'll egg you on to spend the extra money because I believe the results are worth it.

PERFECT MUSHROOM RISOTTO

500 g mixed mushrooms, the small mushrooms halved, the larger sliced into fat strips
1 litre vegetable stock
110 g butter
olive oil

1 onion, chopped
1 garlic clove, crushed
400 g (2 cups) carnaroli or vialone nano rice
125 ml (½ cup) white wine
100 g (1 cup) grated parmesan

salt and cracked black pepper
50 g (⅓ cup) hazelnuts, skins removed and roughly chopped
zest of ½ orange
½ cup chopped parsley

Trim the mushrooms and wipe them clean if necessary. Keep any clean trimmings.

Warm the stock in a large saucepan but do not boil. Throw in any clean mushroom trimmings.

Place a large heavy-bottomed pan on the heat and melt 30 g (1½ tablespoons) of the butter with a slug of olive oil. Cook the onion gently in this pan. Soften, but do *not* let it colour.

In a separate pan, place the cut mushrooms with a little butter. Braise these mushrooms gently over a medium heat to soften slightly and go golden. Do not overcook or let the mushrooms lose too much liquid so they boil. Cook the mushrooms in batches if necessary. (If using enoki, toss these through the braised mushrooms just before serving.)

Check the other pan. When the onion softens, add the garlic and toss. Now add the rice and toss it in the pan. Keep on a low heat for a few minutes to toast the rice so it subtly changes colour.

Turn up the heat and add the white wine to the rice. Bubble this away until the rice and onion mix looks slippery rather than wet.

Add 1 litre of the stock and stir through the rice. Pop a lid on the pot and turn down the heat. Leave for 12 minutes to simmer away. Don't touch it.

After 12 minutes, check the rice. To do this, crush a grain of rice with your thumb on the back of a wooden spoon. If it squidges outwards leaving a little white star at its centre then it needs to cook longer; add 60 ml (¼ cup) of stock and stir until absorbed. Use the squidgy test again and continue adding more stock if needed. When you see three tiny white stars, then the rice is ready.

Remove from the heat. Spoon in a quarter of the remaining butter and a quarter of the grated parmesan and vigorously stir the rice with the sort of enthusiasm you might use if paddling away from the lip of a tall waterfall. This will help knock some of the starch off the rice, making the risotto creamy. Keep doing this, adding cheese and butter. This will also help to make the risotto creamy. Season with salt and black pepper to taste.

The texture you are looking for is oozy so it spreads like treacle when dolloped on the plate. When it's ready to serve, spoon on plates or in bowls and top with the mushrooms, some chopped hazelnuts, a little orange zest and some chopped parsley.

SEAFOOD

It's strange isn't it, that perhaps the easiest of all proteins to cook, seafood, is the one that gives the most people conniptions. My love affair with seafood has been more a slow-burn than a forest fire but it started on my first trip to Australia over 20 years ago when the weekends were filled with adventures out on the bay in a tinny pulling up flathead while the sun peeled my nose like a ripe satsuma. Back on the land the reward for all those handline burns was perfectly fresh fish grilled on the BBQ. Nothing is better. Well, other than…world peace, a Collingwood Grand Final win…Now the lure of perfect sashimi or a wonderful just-cooked fillet of snapper is strong, and while I'm not a massive fan of lobster I could live on plumply popping prawns, which are one of the major attractions of our biennial family holidays to Magnetic Island, for the rest of my life.

BUYING FISH

Choose the freshest fish by looking for bright eyes, firm flesh and red gills. Good fish has the fresh smell of the seas. It doesn't smell 'fishy' or have any hint of ammonia. Ideally buy whole fish and get your fishmonger to fillet it. Just like fruit and veg, fish is seasonal. Check out what fish to buy when by looking at the price, asking your fishmonger, or checking the seasonality calendar at www.sydneyfishmarket.com.au.

When it comes to buying fish I'd always rather spend my money on a small piece of wild fish than a larger piece of farmed fish. The tips to spotting wild fish are that they are generally sleeker than their farmed brethren. Also, displays of farmed fish tend to have lots of the same fish the same size. Wild fish tends to come in a jumble of sizes! One further note on wild fish: I reckon it's our responsibility to our children to make sustainable seafood choices where possible. Luckily that means whiting, the Australian sardine, calamari and blue swimmer crab are all firmly on the menu, along with favourite farmed seafood such as mussels and oysters. Avoid swordfish and orange roughy.

COOKING FISH

Cooking is all about transferring heat to ingredients. You want your fish to reach an internal temperature of between 55°C and 70°C. Over 70°C will dry the fish out, while under 55°C it will be just cooked but there will still be blood on the bone. To gauge temperature you can use a metal skewer held in the fish at the thickest part and then against your lip, but far better is a kitchen thermometer. This can cost you as little as $20. Buy one! I tend to favour the lower end of that temperature scale in the pan because when the fish hits the plate the residual heat will have cooked it. This is why fish that is perfect in the pan is so often overcooked at the table.

RICK STEIN'S TIPS FOR FISH

Every cook needs a culinary Yoda or two in their life. Rick Stein may be neither green nor pointy-eared but he does have a Jedi master–like knowledge of all things seafood. When confronting fish, his is the voice that rings in my ears: 'Use the force, Matt!' Actually the advice I hear is a whole lot more complex than that but it does result in perfect fish almost every time!

So many Australians have a fear of cooking fish; I used to be the same. Follow Rick's simple tips, however, and cooking fish perfectly is quick and easy. Here they are . . .

Pan-frying

John Dory, Mirror Dory or snapper are perfect. Flathead tastes great but isn't as pretty as a fillet. When cooking fillets Rick is no fan of the modern trend for frying the skin side down for a super-crunchy skin (as in the salmon and succotash recipe on page 86). Instead he suggests cooking fillets in a non-stick pan over a medium heat for 4 minutes on each side. It's not essential to crumb or coat fish for frying but he does – using everything from plain flour and breadcrumbs to coarse polenta or matzo crumbs. If frying whole fish, try any of the whitings – such as King George, eastern school or sand.

Roasting

One of the easiest ways to cook whole fish is to roast them. For smaller fish, give them some colour in the frying pan before you pop them in the oven. Rick's golden rule of roasting fish is to set the oven at 200°C and then give the fish 10 minutes in the oven for every inch of thickness. Check the fish has reached the right internal temperature before removing from the oven (see left). Also, buy the right sized fish for the pan you have! The fish needs to fit in the pan. This cooking method works well for large snapper, blue-eye cod and kingfish.

Poaching

When choosing a whole fish to poach, Rick suggests Atlantic salmon, snapper or ocean perch. Rather than poaching in a court bouillon (or stock), Rick prefers to use salted water (1 tablespoon of salt for every 600 ml) so as not to mask the natural flavour of the fish. He suggests choosing a whole fish over 1.5 kg in size. Pop it in a fish kettle and cover with cold salted water. Bring the water to an energetic boil and then take the kettle off the heat and leave to cool. Your fish should end up perfectly moist and cooked. Don't poach fillets as you'll lose too much flavour; braise instead.

Braising

Place your fish fillets on a reduction of sweated shallots, fish stock and white wine and cook covered on a gentle, steaming heat for 6–8 minutes – or until the required internal temperature is reached. Serve the fish with the sauce that has formed in the pan. Experiment with other bases such as a bubbling mix of tomatoes, onions and olive oil. Pop the fillets in, pop on the lid and reduce the heat to low to part-braise, part-steam the fish slowly.

Rick Stein taught me this incredibly easy dish that is a perfect light lunch or, if served with some mash, a decent healthy supper. The only thing that can go wrong with this dish is that you overcook the fish, so do use an electronic cooking thermometer. You are looking to remove the fish when its core temperature has reached 55°C and the polenta crust is lovely and golden.

POLENTA-CRUSTED SNAPPER
WITH TOMATO VINAIGRETTE

300 g (2 cups) coarse polenta

2–3 tablespoons olive oil

4 snapper fillets (about 100 g each)

32 cherry tomatoes, cut into eighths

1 garlic clove, finely chopped

8 spring onions, sliced on the diagonal (don't use the manky green ends)

1 tablespoon olive oil

1 teaspoon wine vinegar

pinch of salt

pinch of sugar

20 basil leaves, cut into thin strips

Warm four plates.

Pour the polenta onto a tray or roasting pan. Press each snapper fillet into the polenta to coat it on both sides.

Cook the fillets in a frying pan in the oil over medium heat until just cooked. This will take between 3 and 4 minutes on both sides, depending on the thickness of fillet. It's best to use two pans if you have them, so all the fillets are ready at the same time.

While the fish is cooking on its first side, move quickly and combine the chopped tomatoes, garlic and the sliced spring onions. Toss.

Roughly whisk together the oil, vinegar, salt and sugar.

After you've turned the fish fillets over to cook the other side, combine the basil and tomato mix, add the dressing and tumble everything together.

When the fish is almost cooked, remove from the pan to warm plates and serve with a mound of the tomato mixture. The fish will continue to cook after it leaves the pan through the residual heat in its flesh. Serve immediately.

Serves 4

The clinking of ice in tall glasses of Pimms. The sound of leather on willow. And the high-pitched grunts of teenage Eastern bloc tennis superstars. These are the unmistakable sounds of summer for me. Few flavours, however, conjure summer more surely than the sweet, tangy, herby flavour of this rich emulsion that's the perfect foil to the oily richness of the salmon. It's perfect with whole poached salmon as well.

SUMMER DAZE SALMON WITH HONEY MUSTARD

8 x 200 g salmon steaks
2 tablespoons olive oil

Honey mustard sauce
1 bunch dill
1 tablespoon clear honey

3 tablespoons Dijon mustard
1 egg yolk
200 ml grapeseed oil (plus a little extra if needed)
salt and lemon juice, to taste

Start the fish in a cold heavy frying pan large enough to fit 4 steaks in easily. Pour in half the oil. Cook the salmon for 5 minutes on one side over a medium–high heat then gently turn the fish over to finish for 2–3 minutes. Remove the steaks from the pan and set aside to keep warm while you repeat for the other 4 steaks.

To make the sauce, first finely chop up the dill and set aside. Now warm the honey in a small saucepan over a slow flame. Place the Dijon mustard in a cold bowl, pour on the honey and mix together. Leave to cool. The exact proportion of mustard to honey depends on two things: the acidity of the vinegar and the sweetness of the honey. Your palate is your best guide here. The honey mustard base must be balanced so neither the mustard nor the sweetness dominates!

Now drop the egg yolk into the mixture and whisk. When well combined start very slowly drizzling in the grapeseed oil as you whisk to create an emulsion. Continue adding until you have a thick mayonnaise. You may not need to use all the oil. Add salt and a little lemon juice to taste. If this mayonnaise-like sauce is too thick, then add a little hot water. Gently stir in the dill and place in the fridge to let the flavours infuse.

Serve the steaks with a generous dollop of the dill/honey/mustard concoction.

Serves 8

TIPS & TRICKS

- Potatoes and cucumber salad make delicious accompaniments to the honey mustard salmon:
- To make the cucumber salad, peel 2 long English cucumbers and cut them in half lengthways. Using a teaspoon, scrape out the seeds from the centres. Turn the cucumber halves over and cut into half-moon slices about 5 mm thick. Sprinkle with 2 teaspoons of caster sugar and toss. Leave in the fridge until ready to serve. Prior to serving, add 2 tablespoons of white wine vinegar.
- To prepare the potatoes, chop 1 kg of small waxy potatoes into two-bite sized portions. Place them in cold water in a large saucepan and bring to the boil, then simmer until just cooked. Pierce them with a knife to check if they're ready – they should slowly slip off the blade. Drain the potatoes, then dab with butter and serve sprinkled with thinly sliced mint leaves.

The crispy salmon here partners really well with the corn-based succotash that is a classic from the US Southern States. Good times!

CRISPY SALMON AND SUCCOTASH

4 x 160 g salmon fillets, skin on
flake salt
60 ml (¼ cup) vegetable oil

Succotash
400 g can lima beans, drained and rinsed

2 medium smoked ham hocks (or 6 rashers of bacon, see tip)
40 g butter
450 g (3 cups) frozen sweetcorn or fresh, cooked and cut from the cob
60 g (½ cup) sliced spring onions

200 g (1 cup) diced yellow squash
black pepper
80 g (½ cup) diced green capsicum or green chilli
60 g (½ cup) sunflower seeds, toasted
1 bunch coriander, torn

Simmer the ham hocks covered with water for 2 hours, or until the flesh comes away easily. Making sure to keep the cooking liquid, remove the hocks and strip off the meat. Discard the bones and skin.

Take 2 cups of the pork poaching liquid, strain it and reduce it by half over a low heat. You can do this all in advance if you want.

Bring a pan of water to the boil and add the lima beans; simmer for 10 minutes or until soft.

While this is going on, you have another task to attend to. Take a large frying pan and whack it on a high heat so it gets very hot. Toss in about 10 g butter, the sweetcorn kernels and the spring onions, frying them until they start to get a little brown and caramelised at the edges. Now add the yellow squash and a loose-packed cup of the ham hock meat.

Taste the porky-reduced cooking water. Assuming it's not aggressively salty, pour in a cup to moisten the dish. If it's very salty, only use half a cup. Cook the succotash for about 5 minutes or until the liquid is absorbed and the succotash is dry rather than soupy. Season if you have to – but note the hock will add saltiness so, as always, taste.

Serve garnished with the green chilli or capsicum, sunflower seeds and coriander. The succotash is great by itself but for a dinner, top it with a fillet of crispy salmon.

To make the crispy salmon, first rub salt into the salmon skin and pop in the fridge for 1 hour. Remove and scrape off the salt with the back of a knife. Pat dry with paper towel. This will help draw out moisture from the skin, helping it to crisp up.

Start the fish in a cold heavy frying pan large enough to fit the 4 steaks in easily. Pour in the oil. Cook the salmon for 5 minutes skin-side down over a medium–high heat then gently turn the fish over to finish for 2–3 minutes. The skin should be really crispy and the fish should hold its shape.

Remember to take the fish off a little before it's cooked. It's good if the fish is still pink in the middle, as the fillet will continue to cook with its residual heat once it's out of the pan. You'll know it's ready because the internal temperature will be about 57°C and the fish will flake apart easily.

Serves 4

TIPS & TRICKS

- If you're using bacon rashers rather than ham hocks, just dismiss the first three steps and put diced fried smoked bacon into your succotash instead. It won't be quite as delicious but it'll still be yummy. Where the recipe suggests adding the pork liquid, just splash in a little of the pork fat (½ tablespoon) rendered from cooking the bacon.

7 ways with...
PRAWNS

GARLIC PRAWNS

I love how the Spanish load prawns with an obscene amount of garlic. To make this classic tapas dish, pour a good glug of olive oil into a large pan. Finely dice 5 garlic cloves and finely chop up a bunch of washed and dried parsley. The easiest way to do this is to strip the parsley leaves from the stalks. Then put them into a large cup and snip at them madly with scissors until they're in teeny pieces. When the oil is hot and sizzly, throw in 32 peeled raw prawns and jiggle the pan. Wait a minute and then throw in the chopped garlic. Fry for a minute or so until the prawns curl up and are cooked. The garlic should just be going golden and slightly chewy. Throw in the parsley and toss. Serve the prawns from the pan with crusty bread and a lemon cut into wedges. Feel free to toss the prawns in a little paprika (about1 teaspoon) before frying.

PRAWNS IN SWEET CHILLI SAUCE

First put on some rice! Now halve 10 long red chillies, deseed them and de-stem them. Blitz half with 3 garlic cloves, a 3 cm peeled piece of ginger, 1 tablespoon of fish sauce and 60 ml (¼ cup) of malt vinegar. Slice the remaining 10 chilli halves (5 chillies) crossways into 3 mm wide slices. Pour the garlic and chilli paste into a frying pan. Fry for a minute. Then add 150 g (1 cup) grated palm sugar and the rest of the sliced chilli. Stir and cook for about 5 minutes to thicken and reduce. Throw in 500 g of peeled raw prawns. When the prawns are almost cooked (in a couple of minutes), stir in the juice of a lime or two to balance the sweetness and heat as well as give the caramel its pep. Pour the prawns and sauce over hot rice. Serve with some soy sauce on the side.

BARBECUED HEAVY PRAWN TACO

Cook 20 peeled raw prawns on the barbecue until they firm and curl. In the minutes while this is happening, warm your tortillas or soft taco shells on the flames too. Lay 1 cm thick slices of creamy ripe avocado on the bottom half of the warmed taco. Lay the cooked prawns on top. Sprinkle on thin rings of green chilli, lime juice and coriander leaf. Fold over and serve. You can add a squirt of mayo or a dollop of sour cream if you are a bit of a piglet. I quite often do but I'm trying to set a good example here!

ELEGANT PRAWN SANDWICHES

Mix cooked prawns cut into 1 cm chunks with mayonnaise and a few drops of Worcestershire sauce or with finely chopped dill and lemon juice. Chop iceberg lettuce into 3 cm long ribbons. Butter soft inelegant white bread and slather the prawn mayo on one side. Evenly top with lettuce and pop the other buttered slice on. Press down to combine. Eat with a slack-jawed smile on your face.

PRAWN COCKTAIL REVISITED

Halve an avocado and remove the pit. To make the Rose Marie dressing, mix 125 g (½ cup) of mayo with 120 g (½ cup) of crème fraîche. Add a few drops of Tabasco and about 140 g (½ cup) of tomato sauce to taste and colour. Season with lemon juice and a drop of Worcestershire sauce if required. Hook the fat end of 7 cooked peeled prawns into the well of the avocado; then fill it with dressing.

PRAWN TEMPURA

Chill some fizzy water and a metal or glass bowl until very cold. Take 20 peeled raw prawns. Make a small slit near the base of the tail and, using a skewer, hook out the poo chute if present. Make two more slits across the back and then stick a soaked wooden skewer into the length of each prawn so it sits straight on the stick. Make a dipping sauce by heating 60 ml (¼ cup) of mirin with 125 ml (½ cup) of water and 2 tablespoons of soy sauce. Add a small sachet of powdered dashi stock if you can find it. Heat in a small saucepan on the stovetop over a low heat until combined. Then cool. Dust the prawns lightly with flour. Pour vegetable oil into a large saucepan to a depth of 10–15 cm and heat to 170°C–180°C, or when little bubbles immediately appear around a wooden chopstick or wooden spoon handle dipped in the oil. While the oil is coming to temperature, use chopsticks to whisk 175 g (1 cup) of rice flour through 250 ml (1 cup) of icy chilled fizzy water in the chilled bowl. It can be the consistency of a slightly lumpy crepe batter. Immediately dunk the prawns three times in the batter. Fry in batches of four for about 2–3 minutes or until the batter is golden and crispy. Keep warm on a rack, then serve immediately with the dipping sauce. Cut this sauce with a squeeze of lemon if you want.

TIPS & TRICKS

- Try oysters or asparagus fried in this tempura batter. Experiment by replacing the icy fizzy water with chilled lager or by replacing the rice flour with a 3:1 ratio of plain and cornflour and a pinch of bicarb. Try marbling 125 g (½ cup) of mayo with a little soy sauce and a squirt of sushi takeaway wasabi as a dipping alternative.

- The main thing about tempura batter is that it should be really cold as the difference between the hot oil and cold batter makes it crispier. Also avoid developing any gluten (if you are using a wheat flour) by over-beating or by not using the batter immediately!

FRESH PRAWN, MINT & ZUCCHINI SALAD

Take 4 firm small zucchinis and use a potato peeler to make long thin strips. Tumble these with 1 tablespoon of lemon juice and 2 tablespoons of olive oil. Split 20 cooked prawns in half lengthways and toss with the zucchini and a handful of carefully picked mint leaves (about 20 leaves). Sprinkle on a little flake salt and a few specks of zest from the lemon. Pre-cooked, steamed greens or barbecued prawn tails will all do for this dish – each giving this fresh and rather healthy salad a slightly different edge.

TIPS & TRICKS

- Feeling decadent? Try adding 10 or so small teaspoon-sized dollops of taramasalata across the top of the salad and serve with hot pocket or pita bread.

Spain's national dish is a party in a pan. It's also easier to make than most risottos – just have faith in the recipe and don't stir the rice until all the liquid has been absorbed and a suitably crunch crust has formed on the base of the pan. Serve your paella with a salad of iceberg lettuce and orange segments dressed with sherry vinaigrette.

GOOD TIMES PAELLA

3 chicken thighs, skin off

olive oil, for frying

1 brown onion, diced

1 chorizo sausage, cut into 1 cm slices

2 garlic cloves, chopped and crushed

300 g Spanish short-grain rice (calasparra or bomba); if you can't find either in your local Spanish store or foodie shop, then arborio will do

1 red capsicum, cut into 2 cm cubes

½ green capsicum, cut into 2 cm cubes

1 teaspoon paprika

700 ml (just under 3 cups) chicken stock

12 saffron strands

80 g (½ cup) fresh or frozen peas

6 large or 12 small prawns

1 lemon, cut into 6 wedges

To cook the chicken, first cut each thigh into 3 equal-sized pieces. Turn a hob on to high and pop your paella pan – or the widest frying pan you have – on the heat. Pour in a generous amount of olive oil to coat the pan with a thin layer. When the oil is hot, fry the thighs until their main two sides are turning golden in places, then remove the chicken pieces to a separate bowl. Note that some pieces will take longer than others. Scrape up any strands of chook that may have stuck to the base of the pan. You can leave these tasty bits in the pan as they'll add flavour.

Toast the saffron on a little sheet of foil over an open flame then add to the stock.

To create the paella, splash in more olive oil so once again the pan has a thin coating all over it. Fry the onion and the chorizo over a medium heat until the onion starts to soften, then add the garlic and the rice. Stir and toast the rice for 2 minutes. Add the chopped capsicums and paprika, and pour in the stock. Bring the paella to the boil and then turn it down to a simmer.

Do not stir it again – ever! You want a nice toasty crust to form on the bottom of the pan. Cook for 20 minutes.

The rice will swell and absorb the stock but while there is still a little stock covering your rice it is time to arrange your prawns over the top of the paella like the spokes of a wheel. First, sprinkle on your peas over the top of the paella. Now push the prawns down into the rice and stock so that they come halfway up their flanks, and arrange the pieces of cooked chicken between your prawns. Leave to cook for another 10 minutes until the liquid stops bubbling out on the surface of the paella. Check the rice is cooked at this point.

Now turn the heat down to low. Leave so the paella can dry out slightly for about 5 minutes or until the edges become slightly crusty and the *socarrat* (the layer of toasted rice) has fully developed. If you can be bothered now rest the paella, partially covered, for 5 minutes which should help the crust develop as the hot pan further toasts the paella's ricey bottom.

Serve at the table with lemon.

Serves 4

I have a long-running love affair with the street food of the world – whether it's the chips and mayo of a smoky late night in Amsterdam, a plate of pani puri at dusk on Juhu Beach in Mumbai, or a really crunchy-edged, post-club lamb souva dripping in garlic sauce from any number of fine Australian establishments. Madrid's contribution to this front line ranged against late-night hunger are rolls filled with crunchy rings of calamari that are served in a number of less-than-salubrious establishments around the C17th Plaza Mayor. Oddly, these always seem vaguely reminiscent of the fish finger sandwiches I used to make as a teenager.

MADRID BATTERED CALAMARI ROLLS

125 g (2½ cups) panko breadcrumbs (available from Asian food shops or the Asian section of most supermarkets)

75 g (½ cup) plain flour, seasoned

3 eggs, lightly beaten

sunflower oil, to deep-fry

750 g baby squid tubes, cleaned and cut into 1 cm rings

½ cup flat-leaf parsley leaves

good-quality aioli, to serve

6 long white bread rolls, split

lemon wedges, to serve

Place the breadcrumbs in a shallow bowl.

Place the flour and eggs in separate bowls.

Half-fill a saucepan or deep-fryer with oil and heat to 190°C (a cube of bread will turn golden in 30 seconds when the oil is hot enough).

Dip the squid in flour, shaking off the excess, then coat in egg and breadcrumbs. In batches, fry the squid for 1 minute or until golden. Remove with a slotted spoon and drain on paper towel. Keep warm.

Press the parsley between paper towels to dry. Deep-fry for 10 seconds, remove with a slotted spoon and drain on paper towel.

Spread aioli on rolls, top with calamari and parsley, and serve with lemon wedges.

Serves 6

It was only a month or so ago that my eldest son tried his first mussel. Looking on dispassionately at those rather strange, fleshy, salmon-pink bivalves I could understand why he hesitated before he tried his first one. After all, mussels do look more anatomical than edible. His eventual bravery was rewarded by the biggest smile and the exclamation – 'Why did no one tell me mussels were this good?' This recipe is a classic version of that same dish but it also has another, more poignant edge. It was one of the last things my maternal grandmother ate before she died, on holiday with her best friend in Brittany. Well, mussels and also lobster. It's become rather the benchmark for the perfect way to go in our family!

GRANDMERE'S MUSSELS MARINIERE

120 g unsalted butter

6 shallots – those fancy, small, sweet brown-skinned onions celebrity chefs lurve more than a pan endorsement deal, minced

6 garlic cloves, finely chopped

2 thyme sprigs

1 bunch parsley, stalks trimmed (reserve the chopped leaves for garnish)

white pepper

500 ml (2 cups) dry white wine (don't be too fussy or worried about this choice – riesling, sauvignon blanc, chardonnay, pretty much anything that isn't sweet will do!)

2 kg mussels

125 ml (½ cup) cream

sea salt and freshly ground black pepper, to taste

Melt the butter in a large pot. Add the shallots and cook for a few minutes to soften. Then add the garlic, thyme, parsley stalks and pepper.

Add the white wine. Stir, remove from the heat, place the lid on and set aside to allow the flavours to develop.

Clean the mussel shells thoroughly. Discard any that are broken or gaping open. Only remove beards once they have cooked or you risk killing the mussels before you cook them (no-one likes having their beard pulled while they are still alive).

Place the mussels in the pot and cover with a lid. Bring to the boil and continue to cook until the mussel shells start opening. This will take about 5 minutes. Remove the mussels from the pot as they open. Remove any beards and then pop the mussels in a warm pot to keep warm.

When all the mussels are open, remove the thyme and parsley stalks from the cooking liquid. Discard any unopened mussels. Add the cream to the pot juices, bring to the boil and reduce to thicken slightly. Adjust the seasoning but be aware that the mussels will have made the sauce salty already! Return the cleaned mussels to the pot, add the reserved parsley leaves, jiggle the pot to coat, and heat through.

Serve in deep bowls with all the cooking liquid and crusty bread to mop up the juices.

Serves 4

Salty foods like seafood help the brain release oxytocins, while eating also tends to make us produce serotonin. This perhaps explains why eating this dish of clams and jamon makes me so very, very happy!

BARBECUED CLAMS WITH BREADCRUMBS

60 ml (¼ cup) olive oil

3 garlic cloves, very finely chopped

3 spring onions (green and white parts), trimmed, peeled and sliced into coins

6 slices of any cured ham, such as prosciutto or Serrano, cut into batons (or 4 rashers of bacon, diced)

160 g (2 cups) fresh breadcrumbs

3 fresh bay leaves (crumpled), or 1 dried (de-stemmed and very finely chopped)

1 kg clams, cleaned and purged of sand (if necessary)

1 bunch fresh parsley or dill (or better yet, a ½ bunch of both!), chopped

1 lemon, cut into wedges

Add the olive oil to a frying pan and place over a medium heat. Fry the garlic and spring onions until they soften but don't brown. Add the prosciutto and stir. Whack up the heat and get the oil hot. As soon as it's hot, add the breadcrumbs and bay leaves, and stir. Fry so they go golden, then remove from the heat.

Place the clams carefully on their sides on the barbecue grill until they open. Make sure they are sitting level so when they pop open most of the clam juice stays in the shell! If you have a barbecue lid, put it down and they will open more quickly. Beware of opening clams spitting! When they do open, carefully remove them, keeping as much of their juice as possible, to a large warmed serving pot, leaving those unopened on the barbecue to finish cooking. Do remember that the barbecue, the clam shells and the juice will all be HOT, so take care!

At this stage, stir the chopped parsley or dill into the breadcrumb mix. When all the clams have opened – and you've discarded any that don't open – pour the parsley and porky breadcrumb mix over the clams and stir. Serve immediately with a squeeze of lemon over the crumb-stuffed clam shells. Eat with your fingers, sucking the clams and the juice-soaked crumbs out of the shells. This is not an elegant dish but a beach-shack feast. It is perfect with a bottle of beer or a crisp white.

Serves 4

TIPS & TRICKS

- Place a double thick layer of foil over the barbecue to control any spilt clam juice if you are neat like that or hate cleaning the barbecue. I don't, but . . .

- Clams can be gritty, so check any you buy have been purged of sand. If not, just put them in a large bowl or a sink full of cool water (salted, so it tastes like seawater) for a few hours or overnight. Discard any that have broken or cracked shells or those that aren't tightly closed when touched. Even if the clams have been purged, wash them thoroughly anyway. Try to eat clams as close to the moment that their shells pop open during cooking – this is when they will be at their most tender. Try to save as much of the liquor in the clams as possible, as it's delicious. In New England, they add the clam juice to their Bloody Marys! Eat clams as soon after purchasing as possible. If you need to store them, do so wrapped in a damp tea towel in the crisp drawer of the fridge. Take them out 30 minutes before cooking.

CHICKEN

(and a cheeky Turkey recipe)

I always loved my mum's roast chicken. For my first decade of food writing, that was my benchmark against which I judged all restaurants I reviewed. The question was always simple: 'Was this meal as good as my mum's roast chook?' And if it wasn't, then why would you pay for it?

My benchmark could have been set higher. I could have been measuring against Maggie Beer's roast chicken, which eclipsed even my mum's in terms of flavour and juiciness – sorry, Mum – when I ate at her kitchen table in the Barossa. It was a pilgrimage of sorts. Maggie is an inspiration for her honest, delicious and achievable cooking, her infectious smile, and her unbridled and obvious appreciation of great food. Also, I've never met anyone – home cook or chef – that could roast a bird as well as our Maggie.

For the record, yes, she is as fun as she appears. She laughs easily and deeply, her head thrown back, and while she makes much of her slightly shambolic approach in the kitchen she has a steel-trap mind for business. She's also been incredibly generous teaching me how to make the perfect roast bird, whether it's a chook or a turkey. This is what I learnt – and what she was happy to share!

MAGGIE'S MAGNIFICENT BIRD-ROASTING TIPS

- Make sure you bring the turkey or chicken up to room temperature before cooking.

- Preheat the oven and make sure that the oven racks are at the right level to fit the bird in and keep it high enough in the oven.

- Use proper breadcrumbs for your stuffing; ideally homemade with 'proper' bread such as unsliced sourdough.

- To keep your stuffing light, don't use egg to bind it and always ensure that the yummy bits – nuts, herbs, dried fruit, bacon – outnumber the breadcrumbs.

- Make the stuffing the night before. Don't refrigerate it, but keep it in a cool place.

- Make a stuffing that tastes good before it goes in the bird. It will taste even better when it comes out.

- Always turn your wings so the tips are under the bird. This will help the breast cook more evenly.

This recipe makes for wonderfully silky chicken that's especially succulent. It feeds 8. Good times!

PERFECT ROAST CHICKEN

The best 2 kg chook you can find
olive oil and flake salt for rubbing
100 ml verjuice (or lemon juice)

Stuffing
½ head of garlic (optional), chopped
250 g onions, finely chopped
60 ml (¼ cup) extra-virgin olive oil

35 g (¼ cup) hazelnuts
40 g (2 slices) streaky belly bacon, cut in to 2 cm squares
4 chicken livers, cleaned
80 g (1 cup) fresh breadcrumbs
½ cup picked herbs, such as rosemary and thyme
30 g (¼ cup) dried cranberries (craisins)

To make the stuffing, cook off the garlic and onions in lots of olive oil in a frying pan over a medium heat, until caramelised.

Roast the hazelnuts on a roasting tray in a hot oven. Then remove the skins by putting the nuts in a tea towel and rubbing.

Sear the bacon in a hot frying pan, then set aside. Quickly sear the whole livers and take out the connective tissue. Rest the bacon and the livers out of the pan. Then cut the livers into 2 cm chunks.

Mix the caramelised golden onions and garlic in a pan with the breadcrumbs, hazelnuts, bacon, rosemary and thyme, and cook over a moderate heat for 2 minutes to soften the herbs. Make the stuffing by mixing this cooked herb, onion and crumb mix with the dried cherries and the liver pieces. Add extra oil if necessary to loosely bind it all together. Leave the stuffing to cool.

Preheat the oven to 200°C.

Clean the chook and dry out the cavity. Fold the wing tips under the bird. Stuff the chook. Rub the bird with olive oil and salt. Put it on a trivet or grill rack and place in a low-sided baking tray – this will help the bird cook evenly. Cover the breast with a strip of foil to protect it from drying out. (The experienced cook needn't do this step as they can tell how the chook is cooking by feel and therefore can minimise the risk of over-cooking it.) Place the chook in the oven.

Check the bird after 40 minutes. Remove the foil and oil the breast with 2 tablespoons of oil. Drizzle with 85 ml (⅓ cup) of verjuice or lemon juice. Return to the oven for a further 30 minutes.

Test the bird with the thermometer and remove if the legs are at 68°C, or are cooked. Turn it over to breast-side down. Leave to rest for 20 minutes minimum – but 30 minutes is even better.

Remove the fat from the roasting pan and then heat the juices to reduce. Add a little more verjuice or lemon juice if the sauce needs more acidity.

Carve and serve with the reduced pan juices and the stuffing.

Serves 8

This approach to turkey results in a very juicy bird with a stuffing that's a million miles from the very stodgy old-fashioned bready stuffings of yesteryear. The downside is that since using this technique two years back with spectacular results, I'm now the one getting up at 6 am to prep the turkey on Christmas morning, not my mum. I should have never told her Maggie's chook was better.

PERFECT ROAST TURKEY AND STUFFING

1 x 5.6 kg turkey
(You'll also need a turkey-sized oven bag from the supermarket and a meat thermometer if you don't have them.)
½ lemon
olive oil and flake salt for rubbing
flour, for dusting

Stuffing
250 g onions
olive oil
1 blade of star anise
4 rashers of bacon, cut into 2 cm squares
zest and juice of 1 orange
130 g (1 cup) dried cranberries

1½ cups mixed fresh herbs, such as parsley, sage, marjoram, rosemary and thyme
320 g (4 cups) fresh breadcrumbs
155 g (1 cup) roasted salted cashews

Glaze
2 tablespoons orange marmalade (fancy Seville orange is best)
extra-virgin olive oil

Gravy
125 ml (½ cup) white wine
salt
juice of ½ lemon
1 tablespoon orange marmalade (optional)
60 g butter (optional)

To make the stuffing, caramelise the onions with lots of olive oil and the star anise blade. Fry the bacon over a high heat.

In a small saucepan, warm the orange juice with the cranberries – when almost boiling, remove from the heat and let it stand.

Now, remove the star anise blade from the onions and discard. Drain the cranberries. Mix the herbs, cranberries and orange zest into the onions and bacon and then add the breadcrumbs. Mix until combined so it is feeling juicy but not sludgy. If the mix is too dry, splash in a little extra olive oil. Let the stuffing cool.

To prep the turkey, first take the bird out of the fridge 2 hours before you want to cook.

Clean out the internal cavity of the turkey. Wipe it dry and with 2 quarters of lemon, rub some lemon in there.

Preheat the oven to 170°C.

Mix the cashews into the stuffing. Do this last so they stay crunchy. Fill the bird with the stuffing. Really push the stuffing into the bird. Pull the flaps of skin over to close the cavity. Secure with a skewer if you need the security. Massage the bird with olive oil and salt. Dust the inside of the oven bag with flour. Now pop the bird into the oven bag breast-side up and tie it off. Place it in a deep oven dish in case the bag splits. This is a safety measure so you can save the vital juices if this happens!

Pop the turkey in the oven. Maggie notes it's really dangerous to give a total cooking time as all ovens and birds cook differently. She suggests it's better to look for the meat pulling away from the bone, which shows that the bird is cooked.

After 1 hour carefully turn the bird over to breast-side down. After 15 minutes turn the oven down to 150°C.

After a further 1½ hours take the bird from the oven. Cut the bag and pour the juices into the pan. Now scrape the turkey pan and pour the juices and any pan scrapings into a tall jug. You should get about 250–275 ml of juices.

Chill the juices in the fridge. This will help later when you need to take the fat off the top easily.

Glaze the bird with the marmalade and a drizzle of extra-virgin olive oil. Return to the oven and turn up the temperature to 200°C for 10–15 minutes. (But check if it needs more.)

Check the bird with a meat thermometer. You can get these for $20. When the probe in the leg reaches 68°C, the bird is almost cooked.

Now take the bird out of the oven and rest it upside down (on its breast) for 40 minutes covered with foil. Serve when the bird's breast gets to 68°C. Resting the bird on its breast makes this lean part extra succulent and juicy.

While the turkey is resting, make the gravy. Deglaze the turkey pan with the wine and reduce by half. Get the jug of juices from the fridge and remove the fat from the top. Pour the juices into the pan, stir and reduce over the heat until it thickens to a saucy consistency. Season with salt and a squeeze of lemon juice.

If you want to, you can add some extra marmalade to the gravy and then some cold butter cut into squares and whisked into the hot gravy to make it velvety.

Now carve the bird and serve with the stuffing, the gravy and all the usual seasonal trimmings such as loads of roast potatoes, cranberry sauce and bread sauce. Eat the turkey warm or at room temperature rather than hot.

Serves 12–16

TIPS & TRICKS

- If your turkey is too big for an oven bag, use the fat off your Christmas ham to lay over it and protect it as it roasts. Or slather the bird in heavily buttered baking paper. This is especially important with turkeys as you must do whatever you can to keep them moist – they're a lean bird and therefore at risk of drying out. The marmalade glaze is important for this for it gives the turkey a burnished look without drying it out through prolonged cooking.

It was the Dutch who gave the world coleslaw – or 'koolsla' as they called this dish of cold (kool), cabbage (sla) when the name passed into the English language in the 1600s. The main thing here is to cut the veg rather than grate them so they retain their juicy, wet crunch under the dressing.

Coleslaw is one of the great reasons to buy a mandolin, which makes cutting things finely about 100-times quicker. In fact after a good knife, a stick blender, a microplane or fine grater, and a kitchen thermometer, the mandolin is the most-used tool in my kitchen. Also, do whiz up your own breadcrumbs to use up the ends of the bread. Store them in the freezer until you need them.

CHICKEN SCHNITZEL AND COLESLAW

2 large chicken fillets, cut in half lengthways
160 g (2 cups) fresh breadcrumbs
40 g (⅓ cup) finely grated parmesan
zest of 1 lemon
¼ cup finely chopped parsley

freshly ground black pepper
1 egg, beaten
125 ml (½ cup) milk
plain flour, for dusting
olive oil, for frying
2 lemons, cut into wedges to serve

Coleslaw
¼ savoy cabbage, finely shredded
1 carrot, shredded
½ red onion, thinly sliced
235 g (1 cup) good-quality mayonnaise
½ bunch parsley leaves, washed and dried
40 g (¼ cup) currants

To prepare the schnitzels, beat the chicken until flat between two pieces of plastic wrap. Mix the breadcrumbs with the parmesan, lemon zest, parsley and pepper. In another bowl, whisk together the egg and milk. Dust the chicken with flour, dip it in the egg wash and coat in the breadcrumb mix. Place in the fridge for 30 minutes to allow the crumbs to set.

Meanwhile, to make the coleslaw, mix the cabbage, carrot and red onion in a medium bowl with enough mayonnaise to bind. Set aside for 20–30 minutes to soften.

Heat the oil in a shallow pan and cook the schnitzels for 4–5 minutes on each side until golden. Drain well on paper towel. Keep your schnitzel warm while you cook all the fillets.

Toss the coleslaw with the parsley and currants, pile onto plates with the schnitzels and serve.

Serves 4

TIPS & TRICKS

- Use red cabbage instead and add 2 heaped teaspoons of seeded Dijon mustard to your mayonnaise. Feel free to add an apple cut into batons and a few sultanas.

- Feeling in need of crunch without creaminess? Simply dress the cabbage with a vinegar dressing. Mix a couple of tablespoons of cider vinegar with a little sugar (approximately 1 teaspoon) to take the edge off it, and toss through the salad. Alternatively, use Japanese rice vinegar and add some daikon radish cut into fine strips. Season the dressing with a splash of soy. You can tweak the schnitzels by using Japanese panko breadcrumbs with a tablespoon of sesame seeds added to them instead of the plain breadcrumbs.

- If you want more creaminess, replace half the mayonnaise with sour cream and add a squeeze of lemon to make a sort of herb-free ranch dressing. Some celery seed, black pepper and ½ teaspoon of horseradish will give this dressing some pep.

14 ways with...
A SUPERMARKET ROAST CHOOK

I am proud of pretty much every column that I write for my column in the 'Taste' section of your favourite metro newspaper. In fact they form the very foundations for this book and the great things about those ideas first explored there is that now I get to take them further in this book. Like these ideas for how to soup up a supermarket roast chook.

As far as I see there are three ways you can pimp up your supermarket roast chook: with a glaze, with a sauce or with an accompaniment or two.

GLAZES

Your supermarket chook has already been cooked, so really all you want to do is anchor on any glaze you apply to the skin by giving it a blast at 240°C for about 5 minutes.

Middle Eastern

Try giving your supermarket chook a Middle Eastern twist by blitzing 2 teaspoons of coriander seed, 1 teaspoon of cumin seed and ½ cup of slivered almonds or pistachios. Don't overwork it or you'll get a sort of almond butter – so use the pulse button on your processor or blender if you have one. Add 1 teaspoon of flake salt. Spray the chook with olive oil and then sprinkle on the spiced almond powder. Bang in the 240°C oven for 5 minutes until the powder starts to colour. Juice and zest 2 oranges. Place the juice on the heat in a small saucepan and reduce with 2 cups of chicken stock to create a simple sauce. If you have some dates– fresh or dried – chop them into small pieces and add to the sauce. When they are soft, mash them into the sauce. Take the chook out of the oven. Sprinkle with the orange zest and serve with the orange gravy on the side. This is perfect with buttered couscous. Feel free to splash the chook with 2 tablespoons of marmalade (melted on the stove with a little splash of sherry) instead of spraying with oil. Then sprinkle this sweet sticky coating with the spiced almond powder.

Anglo–Indian

For an Anglo–Indian twist, toast 1 teaspoon of good-quality curry powder in a small hot saucepan. When it starts smelling aromatic, dollop in 1 tablespoon of apricot jam (or sweet mango chutney) and the juice of ½ a lemon. When it's runny and warm, paint this glaze onto the chook and bang in the 240°C oven for 5 minutes until the glaze starts to go sticky and burn or catch in places. Serve with steamed rice, 1 cup of thick Greek yoghurt mixed with finely chopped mint and finely diced red onion (about ¼), as well as a salad made from a long cucumber cut into ribbons with a potato peeler and dressed with salt and lemon juice.

North American

The US loves its buffalo wings, so why not take that as your inspiration for a glaze. Melt 100 g of butter with 1 tablespoon of Tabasco sauce. Paint one-third of this on the chook and pop in a 240°C oven for 6 minutes. Baste the chook with the second third of the hot butter after 3 minutes. Remove from the oven when the chilli glaze looks set. Carve. Drizzle the cut chook with the last of the hot butter sauce and serve with a simple salad of sliced celery, chunks of blue cheese and butter lettuce dressed with some dollops of sour cream. If your sour cream is a little thick, loosen it with a slash of milk. Adding some short snipped chives is a good addition.

Chinese

How about a Chinese taste for your chook? First peel wide strips of zest (no white pith) from a lemon and set aside. Then in a small pan, heat 1 cup of hoisin sauce with 1 tablespoon of soy sauce and the juice of ½ a lemon. Cook until it thickens. Paint half this glaze on the chook and pop in the 240°C oven for 4 minutes until the glaze is sticky on the bird. Reapply some more glaze and return to the oven for another 3 minutes. Gently toast a cup of white sesame seeds and, in a separate pan, bring 175 g (½ cup) of honey to a bubbling boil with the strips of lemon zest. Cut the chook up into portions. Squeeze over the juice from the remaining ½ lemon, drizzle with the hot honey (remove the zest), and then sprinkle over the toasted sesame seeds. If you have some sesame oil you can flick a few drops across the plate as well, but no more that 1 teaspoon in total as it's so strongly flavoured. And make sure it's well distributed – hence the flicking! Serve with steamed bok choy and rice. For a side dressing, blitz a bunch of trimmed and peeled spring onions with a small drizzle of neutral vegetable oil and a pinch or two of salt.

SAUCES

Let's start with classic combinations.

Sage and onion

Roast chicken loves sage and onions, so combine them to make a thick sauce. Thinly slice 4 large brown onions and gently fry in a knob of butter with 4 sage leaves. When golden, add a heaped tablespoon of plain flour and stir over the heat until it looks tanned like the onions; now raise the heat and slowly add 2 cups of good chicken stock, stirring as it thickens. Remove the sage leaves, blitz the gravy and pass through a sieve. Serve as gravy with the chook broken down into segments.

Mandarin

Given that our chickens are all descended from a jungle fowl that roamed through South East Asia and China 10,000 years ago, it's apt that it goes so well with Chinese flavours and with the mandarin, which shares common geographical roots. So how about glamming up your supermarket roast chook with a mandarin sauce. First, put a little fat or oil into a pan. Gently fry 2 chopped garlic cloves and a bunch of finely sliced spring onions until soft, then add a grated thumb-sized knob of ginger. Deglaze the pan with 60 ml (¼ cup) of Shaoxing wine (or sherry). Add 250 ml (1 cup) of chicken stock and reduce by half. Take 6 mandarins, zest one and juice them all. Add juice and zest to the sauce and cook for 5 minutes. Strain out the bits and put the sauce back in a clean pan (wipe clean if using the same pan). Reduce and season with a little sugar and soy sauce – about 2 teaspoons of each should do it, but let your palate decide. If you want a richer, more velvety sauce use 40 g (2 tablespoons) of cold butter cut into 2 cm cubes. One at a time, whisk these cubes into the sauce. Serve it immediately in a jug with the chook.

Coriander seed, cranberry and tamarind

While the classic partnerships for roast chook are pretty well known, there are some other, less traditional ingredients that share flavour compounds with the humble roast chook – and each other. These can make surprisingly good combinations, as in a coriander seed, cranberry and tamarind gravy. Along with roast chook and pine mushrooms, these three ingredients share loads of flavours that make them wonderfully compatible. To make this, slice 300 g of pine mushrooms (or chestnut mushrooms if you can't get pines) and fry them in a little butter with 1 teaspoon of freshly ground coriander seeds. Once the mushrooms are slippery, take them out of the pan and keep them warm. Now fry 2 teaspoons of bottled tamarind in that pan with a good handful of craisins (dried cranberries). Deglaze this with 250 ml (1 cup) of chicken stock. Leaving it on a low heat, reduce it by half to make a rich but sour gravy. Season and serve with the mushrooms and the chook. It's odd – but also oddly delicious.

ACCOMPANIMENTS

Hazelnuts, Thyme and Mushrooms

Roast chicken loves the warm, brown flavours of hazelnuts, thyme and mushrooms with an almost unmatched ardour, so pan-fry 500 g of different sliced mushrooms – oyster, chestnut, horse, pine, shiitake, button, etc – in some foaming butter with a leafy stick of thyme taken from a bunch. Toast 140 g (1 cup) of hazelnuts on an oven tray in a 180°C oven for 8–10 minutes, then remove their bitter skins by rubbing them in a clean tea towel between your palms. Test one first: if the skin doesn't slip off easily they'll need a couple more minutes in the oven. Remove the cooked mushrooms with a slotted spoon. Reserve any mushroom liquid from the pan. Deglaze the pan with a little (60 ml/¼ cup) sherry vinegar. Bubble it away, then add 250 ml (1 cup) of chicken stock and any of the cooking liquid. Reduce by half. Slice the chook breast onto hot plates. Arrange with the mushrooms, toasted hazelnuts and the sauce. Sprinkle on a few more fresh thyme leaves taken from the bunch to complete the dish.

Sweet Potato, Smoked Bacon and Maple Syrup

While supermarket roast chook might love those woodland flavours, it's also great friends with the sweet fairground flavours of the USA. Bake 8 clean orange-fleshed sweet potatoes in a preheated 200°C oven. These will take 45 minutes to cook and are ready when the skins are sort of papery and the flesh squidgy. Make a slit two-thirds of the way along the top of each sweet potato and tease apart. Do this carefully as steam will billow out. Put a little knob of butter in each potato and return to the bottom of the oven while you prep the other sides. We want the inside flesh of the sweet potato to dry out and get a little toasty and crusty. Rub 4 rashers of smoked bacon with a little maple syrup or brown sugar and microwave between two sheets of kitchen paper for 60 seconds until crispy. Alternatively, grill them. Now carve the roast chook and serve with loads of cooked peas (frozen is fine), boiled and buttered corn cobs and a baked sweet potato garnished with strips of maple bacon and a dollop of sour cream on the side. Use the remains of the chook to make stock (see pages 2–3) and live on simple chicken broth for a week to atone for the sugary, junk food excesses of this meal!

Roast Carrots, Peaches and Potatoes

A slightly out-there combination comes from the research into odd complementary pairings done by my chums, the scientists at the always intriguing www.foodpairing.com. It's the combo of large chunks of carrots, peaches and roast potatoes! Just roast the lot in a 180°C oven, remembering that the peaches will take a third of the time of the carrots and potatoes (which will take around 1–1½ hours). Serve with a simple velouté gravy. To make this, create a brown roux by cooking and stirring a large knob of butter with a tablespoon of plain flour until the resulting paste goes a golden brown. Then stir in chicken stock until the gravy reaches the required thickness. For me that's about 500 ml (2 cups) of stock. Feel free to grate in some fresh mandarin zest to finish if you want. This gravy will help pull all those elements together. Serve with the chicken, carrots, peaches and potatoes.

Bananas, Mango, Popcorn and Peanuts

Another interesting, odd but delicious flavour combo identified for roast chicken by the research scientists is a very Caribbean one of bananas, mango, popcorn and roasted salted peanuts. Slice 4 ripe bananas in half lengthways, sprinkle with ½ teaspoon of allspice and slowly pan-fry them in 40 g (2 tablespoons) of butter. Deseed and dice a long red chilli. Pop 90 g (½ cup) of corn and blitz with a little salt to make a coarse powder – ooh so trendy! Cut 2 cm cubes of mango from 2 mango cheeks. Cut up the chook and serve with the bananas from the pan, drizzled with buttery sweet pan juices, sprinkled with the diced red chilli and a good handful of roasted salted peanuts. Toss the mango in the popcorn crumbs and add to the plate. Dig in!

Apples, Grapefruit and Cashews

Supermarket roast chicken also works wonderfully well with a warm salad – and without quite the same negative health connotations as roast potatoes! Try serving the meat with a salad made of a head of butter lettuce, batons of 2 golden delicious apples, segments of flesh cut from 3 yellow grapefruits and 155 g (1 cup) of roasted cashews for crunch. Dress with a little olive oil, some salt and drizzle with a couple of teaspoons of honey, warmed so it is runny!

Grapes, Lemon and Tarragon

A sweeter option is to warm a couple of cups of seedless grapes in a large frying pan with a little olive oil. Toss with 125 ml (½ cup) of lemon juice and immediately remove from the heat. In a salad bowl, tumble these plumped grapes with a bunch of French tarragon leaves and the choicest juicy roast chicken flesh sliced from the carcass. Pick the rest of the chook meat off to make chicken mayo sandwiches for tomorrow's lunch. Trick these sangers up by mixing a handful of toasted pine nuts and soft herbs such as dill, finely chopped chives or parsley into the mayo.

Celery, Almond, Leek and Cannellini Beans

In the colder months, partner the chicken with a warmed salad of celery, almond, leek and cannellini beans. The poet in me likes this salad because the green of the leeks and the celery looks like spring shoots breaking through the snowy paleness of the beans and the almonds. The hungry man just likes the contrast of flavours – salty cheese, sharp acidity from the dressing, sweetness from the leeks – and the craggy range of textures, from the creamy beans, the firm bite of the almonds, the crumbly cheese and the crunch of raw celery against the soft slipperiness of the leeks and the juiciness of the sweated celery. Peel and slice 2 leeks into 1 cm rounds and slice 2 celery stalks in half lengthwise and then across into 5 mm crescents. Reserve the celery's pale leaves. Fry half the celery and all the leeks with olive oil in a frying pan. Cook until the leeks soften and become more intensely green. It's good if they have a few burnt edges. Now add a 400 g can of cannellini beans (that you've drained and rinsed) and 100 g (⅔ cup) of whole blanched almonds. As soon as the chill is off the beans, remove from the heat and splash with good olive oil and a good squeeze of lemon juice. Serve topped with the reserved raw celery crescents, the palest celery leaves (if you have them) and curls of pecorino or parmesan.

For other great accompaniments to supermarket roast chook, try the potato salad on page 24, the coleslaw on page 102 or drizzle with the chimichurri sauce from page 120.

It has to be said that when I cook it's often a bit of a maelstrom in the kitchen, which is fine in that I do get a lot done in a short period of time, but the aftermath can be a little terrifying in terms of washing up. This has led to the suspension in my house of the Geneva Convention that whoever cooks doesn't wash up. Now that I get to do my own washing up I seem to have become far keener on simple, one-pot dishes like this one – and the others the follow. Sure, the flavours that come from long, slow braising are delicious and as warming as a snuggly doona with puppies in it, but the lure of one pot to wash is almost as sweet.

COQ AU VIN

1.6–1.8 kg chicken, cut into 8–10 pieces; or 4 Marylands

salt and freshly ground black pepper

40 g butter

2 tablespoons olive oil

3 thick slices streaky bacon, cut into matchsticks

16 small pickling onions, peeled (or shallots if you want to splash out!)

150 g small button mushrooms, trimmed

4 garlic cloves, peeled and chopped

2 tablespoons plain flour

2 tablespoons tomato paste

750 ml (3 cups) red wine

a few sprigs of fresh herbs (thyme, parsley, rosemary, bay leaf)

6 allspice berries

500 ml (2 cups) chicken stock (or water)

Preheat the oven to 180°C.

Season the chicken with salt and pepper.

Melt the butter in a large heavy-based ovenproof pot and add the oil. Cook the bacon, onions, mushrooms and garlic over a medium heat for about 5 minutes or until softened, then remove and set aside.

To start cooking the chook, add the pieces to the same pan and brown on all sides for about 10 minutes over a medium heat. Add the flour to the pan, coating the chicken, and allow to brown for a couple of minutes. Add the tomato paste and wine to the pan and stir. Add the fried bacon, mushrooms, onions and garlic, the fresh herbs, allspice berries and stock. Bring to the boil on the stovetop, cover and place in the oven. Cook for about 1 hour, or until the chicken is tender and falling off the bone.

Remove from the oven and serve immediately with crusty bread or boiled potatoes and a green salad.

Serves 4–6

TIPS & TRICKS

• For a really speedy way to peel those pesky onions, blanch them for 30 seconds in boiling water to loosen their skins – they should just slip out of the outer skin – easy!

7 ways with...
CHICKEN WINGS

Chicken wings are that wonderful combination of being very versatile and cheap. Handled right they can also be darned delicious. The first thing you need to do is divide the wings into their three segments. First, chop off the wing tips. These are too fatty to be much fun to eat but are great for adding to stock to boost its flavour. Then divide the rest of the wing into the two obvious portions of drumette and wingette at the joint.

- It's then really just a matter of working out which part of the world you want to take your culinary inspiration from, whether you want to bake Indian wings that have been marinated overnight in tandoori paste, or give them a French twist by mixing olive oil, lemon juice, smooth Dijon mustard and 2 crushed garlic cloves for the marinade. After a couple of hours, shake off the excess marinade and grill or barbecue slowly.

- My kids love their chicken wings with a Chinese twist. The easiest way to achieve this is to marinate 1 kg of the wing pieces for an hour or more in a sauce made from combining 90 g (¼ cup) of honey, 125 ml (½ cup) of soy sauce and the juice of 1 lemon. Then lay the wings in an oven tray and bake in a 190°C oven for about an hour until the wings are cooked and the marinade has turned into a sticky glaze on the wings. Toss them a couple of times during cooking. For a more adult version, very finely grate a thumb-sized piece of ginger and 2 garlic cloves into the marinade.

- Alternatively, make a dry rub of 1 tablespoon of sugar, 2 teaspoons of salt and 1 tablespoon of five-spice powder mix and rub into the chicken pieces. Arrange the wings in one layer in a baking dish and leave them (covered) in the fridge for at least 30 minutes for the rub to flavour the skin. Bake these wings in a 220°C oven for 45 minutes on an oven rack. If you want, serve these wings drizzled with threads of a salty caramel sauce spiked with deseeded slices of red chilli and sprinkled with toasted white sesame seeds.

- The wings can also be braised with Chinese flavours. In a large frying pan, heat some oil and brown 1 kg of divided wing pieces. Then add about a cup of sliced mushrooms of your choice – shiitake are great but ordinary button mushrooms are fine. Trim and peel a bunch of spring onions. Cut off the white parts and stir into the pot. Reserve the green parts of the spring onions. Now pour in 250 ml (1 cup) of chicken stock plus 125 ml (½ cup) of sweet soy and 125 ml (½ cup) dark soy. You can find these in the Asian section of your local supermarket or at Asian delis. Cook the wings at a gentle simmer for 30 minutes, or until the wings are cooked but still juicy. To finish the dish, drizzle 1 teaspoon of sesame oil over the wings, snip the green part of the spring onions as garnish and serve with rice. For more pizzazz in the braise, add 1 cinnamon stick and 3 blades of star anise to the chicken stock.

- Braising works equally well with other flavours. For Italian-accented wings, brown 1 kg of them in a large high-sided frying pan or heavy saucepan with a little olive oil until they are all toasty and golden. Finely grate (or chop) 2 garlic cloves into the pan and jumble the wings so the garlic is well distributed among them. Deglaze the pan with 125 ml (½ cup) of balsamic vinegar when the wings are golden. Then add a 400 g can of tomatoes, 250 ml (1 cup) of chicken stock, 35 g (¼ cup) of capers and 70 g (½ cup) of pitted and halved black olives. Cook on a medium heat, just quietly bubbling away, for 30 minutes. Finish by stirring in a handful of chopped parsley and 1 teaspoon of balsamic vinegar just before serving.

FRIED WINGS

1 kg chicken wings
250 ml (1 cup) milk
2 teaspoons salt
1 teaspoon dry mustard
¼ teaspoon ground allspice
1 teaspoon garlic salt or 2 minced garlic cloves
150 g (1 cup) flour
1 teaspoon salt
freshly ground black pepper
125 ml (½ cup) tomato sauce, barbecue sauce, sweet chilli sauce or groovy sriracha chilli sauce
250 g (1 cup) good-quality egg mayonnaise

To prep the wings, cut into three sections – but discard the wing tip section to use in making stock. Mix the milk with the salt, mustard, allspice and garlic salt, and add the wings to soak. After at least 1 hour but ideally longer, drain the wings and dry on paper towel.

Season the flour with a teaspoon of salt and a good grind of black pepper, and flour the wings.

Cook the wings in three batches. Fry the wings using a deep-fat fryer or a medium-sized pan with vegetable oil, at 180°C for 10 minutes until nice and golden. Test the chicken is cooked by piercing the fattest part of the wing with a sharp knife and checking the juices run clear. Leave to rest on paper towel until all the chook is cooked.

To make the marble mayo, pour the tomato sauce, barbecue or chilli sauce in a small serving bowl; dollop the mayonnaise on top to cover it. Draw the back of a knife through the mayo so the red sauce marbles the snowy white expanses.

Serves 2

KFC – KOLA FRIED CHOOK

1 litre Coca-Cola
230 g (1 cup) packed brown sugar
3 garlic cloves, crushed
1 large onion, grated
2 tablespoons soy sauce
juice of 2 lemons
1 kg chicken wings, segmented and tips removed

Preheat the oven to 140°C.

Mix 750 ml (3 cups) of Coke with the sugar, garlic, onion, soy sauce and lemon juice in a shallow casserole. Add the drumette and wingette pieces. Top up with Coke to ensure the wings are almost covered.

Bake in the oven for 3 hours or until the liquid has evaporated and the wings become sticky. This can take up to 4 hours, but watch them after 3 hours as they can get too dark too quickly at the end, given the amount of sugar in the cooking liquid!

Serves 2

TIPS & TRICKS

- You can make these with Diet Coke and no sugar, but only use one lemon – and don't expect them to be quite so evilly sticky.

YOGHURT CHICKEN SKEWERS
WITH IRANIAN BUTTER CRUST RICE

Yes, I know that these days some of my chums in the US like to hold up Iran as a rogue state or pariah nation but we've actually got rather a lot to thank that country for. Bricks, the windmill, polo, the lute and gold coins for starters; and you know those jars with blue designs that the Chinese favour – they're Persian too.

There's also increasing evidence that they were the first to make wine as well. Neolithic pottery found in the Zagros mountains in Iran contains strong traces of tartric acid (usually a sign that they had held wine), suggesting Persians made wine 7000 years ago. This is 4500 years before the first French evidence of wine making. Other claimants to the title of the first wine makers are Georgia, where grapes are supposed to have originated, and Armenia, who can point to the earliest winery discovered last year complete with a 6000 year old wine press, fermentation vats, jars, and cups.

Either way, the Persians have the best myth about how wine was first discovered – a story that has no little resonance and relevance today. A girl jilted by the Persian king was so unhappy that she tried to poison herself with a jar of rotting table grapes. She rather liked the boozy effect and shared the discovery with the King who liked it so much he reinstated her as his girlfriend, gave her riches and insisted that all grape production in the land be turned over to vinous purposes.

Wine isn't the only contribution that Persia made to our gustatory pleasure. The good people of Shiraz were strewing their salads with edible flowers centuries before France's Michel Bras pioneered this practice that now grips almost every fancy modern restaurant. Saffron use, pistachios, the pomegranate, the quince, mulberries and ice cream are all claimed to have originated here too. Look further east and it isn't just in buildings like the Taj Mahal that you see the influence of Persia but also in the food of the Parsees of Mumbai and in Moghlai cuisine.

Several of my keenest tricks in the kitchen I have learnt from Persian cooks: sparking up carbs like rice or couscous with the sour snap of little red barberries; pounding walnuts to make fesenjoon; or marinating lamb in the juice of grated onions to make it especially succulent, as you'll see if you make the chops with toum on page 136.

The Iranians also have a special way with chicken and run some of the best chicken shops in the world. It's that part of the Iranian kitchen that these too recipes celebrate. The chicken skewers show the clear link between the Persian and Indian worlds but the buttered rice is another thing altogether – like some smart Shah decided to get the delicious crusty rice on the bottom of a paella without all the kerfuffle.

In a Persian chicken shop they might just give you a foil wrapped pat of butter on your rice but for this very sumptuous buttered rice, the grains are par-boiled ('chelo' as it's called in Iran) then steamed for really fluffy rice with a wonderful crunchy golden crust on the bottom of the pan. This much prized crust is called 'tah-deeg'. Even though I've reduced the amount of butter used from the huge traditional quantities, it's still rich so serve it with roast meat like these skewers rather than oily stews.

To buy Persian/Iranian ingredients such as dried rose buds or barberries see www.pariya.com – or look in Arab or some Indian delicatessens.

2 onions, chopped
1 teaspoon saffron threads
1 tablespoon boiling water
500 g (2 cups) Greek yoghurt

salt and freshly ground black pepper, to taste
800 g chicken thigh fillets, cut into neat 5 cm cubes
80 g melted butter

CONTINUED

To make the kebabs, blitz the chopped onion in the food processor so it is almost a paste. Mix the saffron with a tablespoon of boiling water and leave to infuse for 5 minutes.

Mix together the yoghurt, saffron water, minced onion and a grind of black pepper, and season with salt. Take out and reserve one-third of this marinade.

Toss the chook in the remaining yoghurt mix, then pop in the fridge for at least 1 hour.

Push the meat onto skewers, then place your chicken skewers under a grill over a high heat. At first, baste while cooking with the reserved yoghurt marinade that didn't have the chook in it. This will build up a nice crust on the chook. Then finish by basting with the melted butter.

Serve the kebabs with this delicious rice below.

IRANIAN BUTTER-CRUST RICE

2 litres water

2 teaspoons salt

400 g (2 cups) long-grain rice
(basmati is the closest to the rice
you'd find in Iran)

70 g melted butter

250 ml (1 cup) boiling water, plus
an extra 125 ml (½ cup)
if necessary

chopped dill, to garnish (optional)

Find a big pot with a lid. Non-stick would be good. In this pot bring the water to the boil.

Wash the rice in a sieve until the lost starch is washed away and the water runs clear. You needn't be too fastidious about this.

Add the rice to the boiling water, return to the boil and cook for about 7 minutes until the rice is parboiled (or partially cooked).

Drain the rice in a sieve, then return to the pot and pour boiling water from the kettle over it. Give it a gentle swirl and drain it again. This will help give you fluffier rice.

Pour half the melted butter into the pot and swirl it round to coat the base and a little way up the sides. Bang it on a low heat.

Mound the rice in the pot so it covers the base but is pushed away from the sides into a mound.

Using the handle of a clean wooden spoon, make five holes in the mound. Pour the remaining butter into these holes, followed by 50 ml (⅕ of a cup) of boiling water in each hole.

Put a dish cloth or paper towel over the top of the pan to stop the steam condensing on the lid of the pan and dripping back on the rice, making it soggy. Pop the lid on. Keeping the heat low, steam the rice until it's all fluffy on top and dark golden and crunchy-crusted on the bottom. You'll see this at the sides of the rice. (That's why you mounded it away from the sides, after all!)

This should take about 30 minutes but check after 15 minutes to see if the crust is getting too dark. If it is and the rice needs longer to cook, just drizzle in another 125 ml (½ cup) of water into those holes, but avoid peeking too often as you'll let the steam out of the pot.

Spoon some fluffy rice from the top of the mound onto each plate. Pop the base of the pan into a sink of cold water for 30 seconds. This will help the crusty rice contract and come away from the pan easily. Using a fish slice, top each pile of fluffy rice with tanned, golden rice crust.

Serve with chicken kebabs and dust with some chopped dill if you like.

Serves 4

You'll find that my mother-in-law pops up a fair bit in this book, but then I've learnt so much from her in terms of some of those tasty flavour-bomb dishes that have been forgotten about in our headlong rush of the twin goals of 'crispy' and 'fresh'. These are old country dishes that were destined to sit in a wood-burning stove or over a slow-smouldering hearth while everyone is out in the paddocks. These are also invariably simple, one-pot dishes that might occasionally take sneaky 70s shortcuts like using canned tomato soup. Purists might sneer and prefer to knock up an authentic 'chicken cacciatore' – albeit that the only thing they've ever 'hunted' or 'cacciatored' for is cheap antiques in quaint rural bric-a-brac stores. Forget the snobbery! I'm all about results and this is one of our regular favourites for a mid-week supper. That daggy canned tomato soup is a vital element – not just for flavour but also for the connection to a period of Australian cuisine that it represents. Good times!

JUDE'S CHICKEN ITALIENNE

2 tablespoons plain flour
1.5 kg chicken drumsticks
3 tablespoon olive oil
2 onions, chopped
2 garlic cloves, crushed

1 large can tomato soup
125 ml (½ cup) dry sherry
½ cup flat-leaf parsley, plus extra to garnish

Preheat the oven to 180°C.

Flour the chicken drumsticks and fry them in a large frying pan in 2 tablespoons of the oil over a high heat until golden brown, usually around 10 minutes. Place in a casserole dish and keep warm.

In the same pan, cook the onions and garlic until translucent. Add the tomato soup, oil, sherry and parsley, and simmer for 5 minutes. Transfer to the casserole dish, add the chicken and then cook in the oven for about 1 hour.

Serve the drumsticks with some buttered risoni or orzo pasta.

Serves 4

MEAT

So what is the Holy Grail in the kitchen? There are many, but the most vexing must be the perfect cooking of meat. Perfect cooking ensures taste, texture and safety but it's made difficult by all the variables involved, such as the thickness of the meat, the heat of your oven (or heat source), the temperature of your meat when you start cooking it and what cut or beast you are cooking.

Experienced chefs and cooks learn to tell how far a piece of meat is cooked by the touch and feel (basically how firm the protein has become); by the sight; by the smell; or even by the sound that the cooking meat or fish makes in the pan. Another way of checking *cuisson* – to use the cheffy French word for achieving the correct point of cooking – is to pierce the thigh of a turkey or chook and look at the juices that come out. If they are clear then the bird is cooked; if there is any redness in the juices then it needs longer in the oven.

Far, far simpler, and more fail-safe, is a food or meat thermometer. This is a simple piece of kit with a metal needle that you can insert into your cooking meat to see the internal temperature. Food thermometers cost between $12 and $40, which is a comparatively small price to pay to ensure that your expensive meat is cooked the way you want it. No wonder I think every kitchen should have one! So there it is, the secret to perfect meat and fish cookery is as simple as buying a thermometer! Oh, and then using it!

To use a food thermometer, stick it into the thickest part of the meat, ensuring it doesn't touch bone or gristle. If you are cooking a whole piece of meat you can follow these simple guidelines for internal temperature that I use to cook meat rare, medium-rare or medium.

	Rare	Medium–rare	Medium
Meat	50°C (125°F)	55°C (130°F)	60°C (140°F)

Remember, these are only guidelines. You need to work out which is the ideal internal temperature for you. Basically I like my steak rare, my lamb pink, my pork with a little blush on it and my chicken juicy. Maggie Beer recommends removing roast chook or turkey from the oven when the thermometer reads 68°C in the leg. I have found that beef can be cooked a little less to be rare (around 45°C), while 70°C or above will give you a well-done steak. Lamb and chook need a little more heat to achieve the desired cooking point and you'll find that lamb cooked with the bone will read a lower temperature to be rare than lamb with the bone out.

The Food Safety Information Council advises that poultry, sausages, hamburgers and rolled roast meats should reach an internal temperature of 75°C to ensure all food poisoning bacteria are killed. This is because most bugs live on the surface of meat and are killed by the far higher external temperature of the meat while cooking. Mincing and rolling puts that potentially bug-carrying exposed meat into the interior of what you are cooking, where it is not exposed to direct heat, hence the need for that higher internal temperature!

Once perfectly cooked all meat should be rested, as it allows the meat to relax and the juice to redistribute back into the meat. How long you rest the meat is a matter of some debate. I think the 'rest for as long as it cooked' brigade must just love cool food, but certainly at least 5 minutes for chops or steaks and 15 minutes for large roasts are the bare-minimum times. Rest your meat on a warm serving plate loosely covered with foil. Drape over a newspaper for insulation if resting in a cold place.

Resting results in more tender and juicy meat. But remember, while this is happening, the heat from the outside of the meat will also be working its way into the meat's centre, increasing its internal temperature! Basically your meat is still cooking while it's resting, so allow for this. The amount that the internal temperature rises ranges from minimal to 6°C. This depends on the size of the piece of meat, where you rest it, how long you rest it, and the difference between the surface temperature and the internal temperature when it comes out of the oven.

4 ways with...
SAUCES

BARBECUE SAUCE

Once you have tried the barbecue sauce recipe here, experiment to create your own signature sauce. Honey, molasses, smoked paprika, soy sauces and different vinegars will each give your sauce a unique character. If you want to serve barbecue sauce with pork, try a strong shot of espresso as a nod to the red-eye gravies of the American south.

250 ml (1 cup) tomato sauce

2 teaspoons onion powder

1 teaspoon garlic powder

1 teaspoon English mustard powder

120 g (4 tablespoons) treacle

1 teaspoon ground allspice

1 teaspoon paprika

2 tablespoons Worcestershire sauce

3 tablespoons maple syrup

3 tablespoons apple cider vinegar

½ teaspoon liquid smoke (optional)

2 tablespoons brown sugar

3 tablespoons good-quality bourbon

Mix together the tomato sauce, onion powder, garlic powder, mustard powder, treacle, allspice, paprika, Worcestershire sauce and maple syrup in a large pan.

Place over a medium heat and cook for 20 minutes so it thickens. Stir in 2 tablespoons of the cider vinegar and the liquid smoke, if using.

Taste and adjust the flavours. If the sauce is too tangy, add some of the brown sugar. If it's still too sweet, add more cider. Cook a little longer, then remove from the heat and gradually add the bourbon to taste. I reckon you'll need most of it but it's up to you!

Makes 500 ml

CHIMICHURRI SAUCE

On and off I spent a year or so trying to perfect a chimichurri but was never perfectly happy with the results. Too often the sauce was too sharp or too green. This recipe uses honey for sweetness, and red wine vinegar rather than ordinary cheap white vinegar, which I think helps mellow it out a little. Try it yourself and then, using this recipe as a template, tweak it until it matches your palate.

3 garlic cloves

¼ cup roughly chopped flat-leaf parsley

2 tablespoons chopped coriander

2 tablespoons thyme leaves

1 tablespoon oregano leaves

2 small red chillies, deseeded and chopped

zest of 2 lemons

2 spring onions, green part only

60 ml (¼ cup) red wine vinegar

pink sea salt and freshly ground black pepper

80 ml (⅓ cup) extra-virgin olive oil

1 teaspoon honey

Gently blend the herbs, chillies, lemon zest, spring onions, vinegar and salt and pepper together. Next, add the oil a little bit at a time. The oil should bind the chimichurri, not dominate it.

Taste and add the honey a little at a time until a good balance is achieved. Taste again and add more salt, oregano and oil to suit your taste.

Serve the sauce with Easter lamb, steak, beef ribs or any meat that is begging for some zesty, herby tang!

Makes 250 ml

TIPS & TRICKS

- You can also include bay leaves, ground cumin or sweet paprika in your chimichurri.

PINEAPPLE KETCHUP

One of my favourite sauces to squeeze on chicken and especially pork is pineapple ketchup. This is one of those really cool thrown-together sauces that grew from experimenting with US-style barbecue sauce. The pineapple brings sweetness, acidity and brightness, while adding strong coffee balances with bitterness.

50 g sultanas
1 onion, roughly chopped
2 garlic cloves
90 g (⅓ cup) tomato purée
160 ml (¾ cup) vinegar
360 ml (1½ cups) water
70 g (⅓ cup) brown sugar
2 teaspoons salt
pinch of cayenne pepper
8 canned pineapple rings
1 teaspoon ground allspice
½ teaspoon ground cinnamon
2 cloves
grate of nutmeg or ⅛ teaspoon ground nutmeg
2 teaspoons coffee powder (or a double shot of espresso)
120 g (4 tablespoons) light honey

Combine the sultanas, onion, garlic, tomato purée and vinegar in a food processor until smooth. Scrape the purée into a large heavy saucepan and stir in the water, brown sugar, salt and a big pinch of cayenne pepper. Don't wash the processor – we'll use it again. Bring to the boil, then simmer uncovered gently for 60 minutes. Stir regularly.

Purée the pineapple rings and add to the ketchup along with the allspice, cinnamon, cloves, nutmeg, coffee and honey. Simmer to thicken for another 10 minutes. Stir regularly as a thick mixture always risks getting burnt.

When the ketchup is thick, pass it through your finest sieve and return it to a clean pan. Heat and balance the seasoning by adding splashes of cider vinegar if it's too sweet or salt if it's too bitter. Drizzle in a little honey if it's too tart or some more of the coffee if it needs some added complexity.

Use immediately or bottle in clean sterilised glass bottles or jars. Use within the month.

Makes 750 ml

TOMATO SAUCE

As you may not have a wonderful mother-in-law like mine who makes this delicious sauce, here's a recipe for tomato sauce that should give some warm spicy zing to your footy pies. This is not an overly sweet sauce.

2.5 kg ripe tomatoes, roughly chopped (make sure you use the seeds and juice in the sauce)
400 g onions, peeled and roughly chopped
10 g (1½ tablespoons) whole cloves
10 g allspice berries
10 g (1 tablespoon) sweet paprika
1 garlic clove, peeled and bruised
½ cinnamon stick
50 g salt
330 g (1½ cups) sugar
500 ml (2 cups) clear white malt vinegar

Put the tomatoes and onions in a jam-making copper (or a wide-mouthed, heavy-bottomed saucepan) with the cloves, allspice berries, paprika, garlic, cinnamon and salt. Simmer gently for 1 hour until the tomatoes are nice and soft.

Add the sugar and vinegar and cook until it tastes suitably saucy and thickens up. To test this, you can always put a dollop on a plate and see how much liquid seeps out of the cooked tomato mush. If it's only a little, then the sauce is done. Taste and adjust the seasoning if required.

Pass through a coarse sieve so that you remove the bigger bits of skin and whole spices. Collect the sauce in a clean, sterilised bowl or jug. To help work the sauce through the sieve, roll the round bottom of a ladle over the sauce in the sieve.

Bottle in old whisky or gin bottles in the true country fashion (labels removed and fully sterilised obviously.) I don't know why but homemade tomato sauce always seems better poured from an old Teacher's or Gordon's bottle.

Serve with 4 Four 'n' Twenty pies or similar.

Makes a bit more than 2 litres

BEEF

There's been a revolution in beef in Australia in the last decade. For so long Aussies have been obsessed with the fillet and the steak, but we've now re-embraced the whole cow in all its delicious glory, from meltingly tender slow-cooked cheeks to rich, meaty oxtail. Furthermore, the quality of our top grass-fed, dry-aged beef now matches the best in the world, making it our king of meats.

As a beef lover, the main revelation I have had over that time is that I'd rather spend my money on a small piece of great beef rather than a large piece of cheap beef that's been stored in a plastic bag and has picked up the liverish, wet cardboard flavour too often associated with 'wet ageing'. Your butcher will be your biggest support in your search for great beef, so look for a butchery that maintains the traditional skills where the meat is properly stored and butchered each day on-site.

The good thing about this strategy of eating 'a little of the best' is that it then justifies you going crazy on the accompaniments to your steak, whether it is a technicolour blizzard of salads, condiments or delicious and slightly decadent hot sides.

If beef is the king of meats then there is no doubt that the potato is its queen. The trouble is that too often the noble potato has been associated with peasant food. This can be avoided by following the five faithful rules for respecting potatoes.

RULE #1 MASHED

Mash has to be made with lovely fluffy potatoes such as spunta or coliban, which are gently mashed while warm with warm milk. Then a little butter can be added to loosen and enrich the whole mass. I don't mind the sticky mash that comes with using loads of olive oil, or those Paris mashes that seem to be more butter than potato, but ideally my favourite mash is still all about the potatoes. The only way this mash can be improved is by pouring over cubes of fried speck (and the fat that renders when cooking them) along with some finely snipped chives to make you think you are eating your greens! Otherwise, add sliced spring onions, another lump of butter and call it 'champ' like my Irish forebears did. The one cardinal rule with mash is always to use a proper masher or ricer to ease the starch-filled cells of the potato apart. Never be tempted to blitz with a stick blender or a food processor as this will split the cells and usually make for a disgustingly gluey mash.

RULE #2 ROAST

For the perfect roast potatoes, parboil a nice floury potato cut into quarters or thumb-length chunks until their edges have softened. Drain well – letting some of the steam blow off them will help this – and return to the pan. Hold the lid on firmly and give the pan a good shake to bash up the potatoes' soft edges a little. Now place these potatoes in a hot oiled roasting tin and cook in the oven with the roast until golden and crunchy all over. Only turn the potatoes when their bases are properly crunchy. I like to turn up the oven to give the potatoes a blast while the meat is resting and I am making the gravy.

RULE #3 FRIED

I never make chips, potato croquettes, wedges or gems at home. They never seem worth all the hassle to do them perfectly, and as for the amount of oil needed for the deep-fat fryer … It's far easier to order them when eating out or at a decent takeaway shop! Instead I might slice thin wedges of potato and bake in the hot oven at 180°C as a healthier alternative but with a similar crunch. These are also far quicker than normal baked potatoes as they take only about 20 minutes.

RULE # 4 BOILED

There is an admittedly small place in my world for boiled potatoes, but they need to be waxy potatoes like kipflers or, even better, young ones like Jersey royals. A little butter, some fresh mint and a sprinkling of salt is all they need to be perfect. It also helps that none of these potatoes need to be peeled, as I hate peeling spuds – and that was even before I peeled 15 kg of them for a big lunch. Cook them until they're at the stage when they slowly slide off a blade that they've been stabbed with. Rather they are under-cooked than over! I always boil extra because the dehydrating effect of spending the night in the fridge makes a wonderful change in the cooked potatoes. This makes them perfect for adding to curries or sautéing. A waxy potato, such as pink eye or pink fir apple from Tassie, is perfect for making potato salad as they resist soaking up the mayo and going all soggy on you. One of those cold day-old potatoes from the fridge will be even less thirsty for the dressing and will work well with a vinaigrette as well as a creamy-based dressing.

RULE #5 GRATIN

Potatoes are wonderful boiled, mashed or roasted but they reach a level of divinity when baked with lots of leeks and something creamy in a classic gratin. Serve your gratin with any roast meat, chops or steaks. Or even just on its own with a little green salad and a very guilty grin. There is no side more decadent, more delicious, more jaw-droppingly gorgeous than an old-fashioned gratin – that simple combo of potatoes and something oniony baked into oozy submission with the help of a few good glugs of cream.

CLASSIC LEEK AND POTATO GRATIN

50 g butter

3 large leeks (about 500 g), trimmed, halved lengthwise, rinsed and sliced into 1 cm pieces

1 garlic clove, finely chopped

400 g potatoes, sliced very thinly (use a mandolin if you have one)

salt and freshly ground black pepper

300 ml cream

2 bay leaves

¼ teaspoon grated nutmeg or ⅛ teaspoon ground nutmeg

100–125 g (1 cup) grated cheese (gruyere mixed with parmesan if you are going all fancy; good grated tasty if not)

40 g (½ cup) fresh breadcrumbs

Preheat the oven to 180°C.

Warm the butter in a big pan and, when hot, cook the leeks and garlic over a medium heat for 5 minutes until they soften.

Butter a baking dish.

Assemble the gratin with alternate layers of potato slices, then leeks, then potato, then leeks and finally potato. Season each layer.

Heat the cream to almost boiling with the bay leaves and the nutmeg.

Pour the cream over the leek and potato layers. Season with salt and pepper. Top with the grated cheese and then the breadcrumbs.

Put the dish in the oven covered in foil for 45 minutes. Check the potato is cooked with a skewer. If the skewer goes through the potato slices easily then it's cooked. If not, pop it back in the oven with the foil still on.

When cooked, remove the foil and pop back in the oven for 15 minutes to brown the top.

Serve with perfectly cooked meat.

Serves 2

Remember that a great burger has a balance of crunch, creaminess, freshness, saltiness and tang to contrast against the soft sweet bun and the properly crusty-edged meat. It also has a structural integrity that means the middle doesn't drop out the back onto your shoes when you take the first bite. Serve with fries or salted potato chips warmed in the oven, and loads of pickles, sauces and mustard on the side.

CLASSIC AUSSIE HAMBURGER

20 g butter

1 kg onions, sliced

2 teaspoons brown sugar

600 g beef mince

150 g sausage meat (optional) – I think the ideal fat content for a burger is about 20%, so add the sausage meat if the beef mince is very lean

2 spring onions, finely sliced

1 teaspoon Tabasco sauce or 1 tablespoon Dijon mustard

salt and freshly ground black pepper

1 teaspoon white sesame seeds

1 cup shredded iceberg lettuce

½ cup shredded white cabbage

juice of 1 lemon

4 large bread rolls, round and soft butter, for rolls

4 rashers of middle or streaky bacon, ideally smoked

4 slices cheese

4 pineapple rings (or 4 sweet and sour pickled cucumbers, or 1 x 225 g can of sliced beetroot)

tomato sauce

mayonnaise

2 large ripe tomatoes, thickly sliced

fresh, salted hot chips, to serve

Warm the butter in a frying pan and slowly cook the onions and sugar, stirring occasionally, until the onions caramelise (about 40 minutes).

In a large bowl, mix the mince, sausage meat and spring onions. Add Tabasco or mustard, a generous pinch of salt and pepper. Use your hands to just combine the meat – don't overwork it.

Mix in the sesame seeds. Using wet hands, form into small cricket balls and place on a baking tray lined with baking paper.

Press flat so they are the same diameter as your rolls. With a spoon, press down to form a little well in the centre of the top of each burger patty to deal with the slight swelling in the middle that tends to come with the cooking of the meat. Place the burgers in the fridge until you need them.

Combine the lettuce and cabbage. Dress the salad with a squeeze of lemon juice.

Grill the rolls (outsides first) and lightly butter.

Heat the grill to a high heat and cook 4 burgers and the bacon. The burgers will take about 4 minutes each side, depending on the thickness – they do not need to be cooked through.

Lay a cheese slice on each burger. Cut the bacon rashers into 4 and push these into the cheese. Keep the burgers warm so the cheese melts.

In a dry frying pan, fry the pineapple over a medium heat so it gets a little tanned.

Now, to assemble the burger, put a layer of the caramelised onions on the bottom bun. Place the burger patty on next. Squidge some tomato sauce on the cheese and bacon-topped patty. Now, put on the pineapple ring. Scatter with a handful of the lettuce and cabbage mix. Spread mayo on the bun top, anchor 2–3 ripe tomato slices in the mayo and then place on top of the rest.

Serves 4

My memories of being a small child are punctuated by warm, fuzzy images of my mother cutting slices of steaming and bronzed meatloaf, paired with the sound of thick tomato sauce splattering on to the hot meatloaf, and satin-smooth mounds of mashed potato. It would return the next day sliced and sandwiched between white bread for school lunch. I don't know why this memory resurfaced recently but it sent me off on a quest to rediscover a meatloaf that would match this rose-tinted recollection. This is it. The kids love it; the woman I love doesn't but then she still labours under grim memories of meatloaf being bland slabs of grey, and while this isn't that sort of meatloaf sometimes these synaptic connections to the past are hard to break. If you want to play with this recipe, try pushing about twenty 2 cm cubes of tasty cheese into the meatloaf after you've hand-shaped the mince. This will give you a succession of gooey cheese kransky-like surprises when you eat the meatloaf hot from the oven.

This title will <u>really</u> embarrass my mother which is why I wrote it!

THE BEST MEATLOAF – THANKS MUM, I LOVE YOU

1 kg beef mince
½ red onion, finely chopped
3 garlic cloves, finely chopped
125 g (1 cup) rolled oats
1 large egg
250 ml (1 cup) milk
salt and freshly ground
black pepper

Glaze
125 ml (½ cup) tomato sauce
1 tablespoon Worcestershire sauce
2 tablespoons brown sugar
(the darker the better)
1 tablespoon mustard (Dijon is best)
½ teaspoon cayenne pepper
(optional)

Preheat the oven to 180°C.

Mix the mince, onion and garlic together. Stir in the oats, then add the egg and mix. Stir in the milk. Pull the mixture together but do not overwork it. Season with salt and pepper.

Line a baking tray with foil and then baking paper. Hand-shape the mince mix into a long loaf of equal thickness on the baking tray and pop in the oven.

When the meatloaf starts cooking, heat the tomato sauce, Worcestershire sauce, sugar, mustard and cayenne (if using) in a saucepan over a medium heat until it looks thick and syrupy. Taste and adjust seasoning. Add a little extra Worcestershire sauce if it's too thick. The sauce will be used as a glaze, which means when you eat it, it will be greatly reduced with flavours intensified, so don't be too tempted to add loads more cayenne.

After 30 minutes, pull out the meatloaf and pour two-thirds of the sauce over the top of the meatloaf. Use a pastry brush or knife to spread the sauce over all sides of the loaf.

Return to the oven for 40 minutes but check the meatloaf after half an hour as the cooking time will be affected by the thickness of your meatloaf, the starting temperature of your ingredients and your oven. Reglaze any bits of the meatloaf that need it. When cooked (if you have a meat thermometer, its internal temperature should have reached 65°C), take it from the oven.

You want the meatloaf to be cooked through and the glaze to have gone all sticky, tangy and caramelly. Rest for at least 5 minutes.

Serve sliced with mashed potatoes, roast tomatoes (which you can do in the oven on the shelf under the meatloaf) and a dark-leaf green such as silverbeet.

Serves 4

Stop, yes, I know that this recipe has the most boring name in the book and that, yes, I am a wee bit obsessed by bay leaves, but let me let you this is one of the must-try recipes! It looks so simple and unassuming, but what happens is that while you barbecue both the fresh aromas of the bay leaves and the smoke from its charring give a wonderful complex flavour to the beef. It's also one of the recipes that I can leave up to Jono, Will and Sadie to knock up with minimal supervision – other than to try and ensure that they don't try to brand each other with the BBQ. Oh, one further thing, this idea comes from Portugal. I don't know why this is important, but I feel it is.

BEEF AND BAYLEAF SKEWERS

3 garlic cloves
1 teaspoon coarse salt
3 black peppercorns
2 tablespoons red wine vinegar
3 tablespoons oil

800 g porterhouse, cut into 3 cm cubes
bamboo skewers, soaked for 30 minutes
About 35 fresh bay leaves

Mash the garlic with the salt and black peppercorns, or blitz in a processor. Loosen the mix with the vinegar and 2 tablespoons of oil. Slather on the meat and leave in the fridge for 3 hours.

Thread the steak cubes on the soaked wooden skewers with a bay leaf wrapped around each one.

Brush with the remaining oil.

Cook the skewers on a hot flat grill for a few minutes each side, turning only once. Then rest on a plate covered with a clean tea towel or loosely with foil for 5 minutes.

Serves 4

TIPS & TRICKS
- These skewers are delicious served on warm pita bread (see page 141) and a simple sauce of 125 g (½ cup) Greek yoghurt stirred with lots of black pepper, a squeeze of lemon juice and some soft cheese like feta. Or be all conciliatory and serve 'em with the Greek Salad on page 20 or 'the Jewelled Couscous Salad' on page 30.

Growing up in England, I have a well-developed love of wet, cold winters. That's because those sorts of days were always an excuse to build a large open fire, crack a bottle of red and enjoy a dish like this – the taste, the aromas of it cooking that wafted through the house, and the inevitable snooze that would follow. The basic idea is built on a southern French 'carbonade', which is one of the few examples of beer replacing wine in that country's cookery. The secret to the flavour here, however, is the very English balance between the sophisticated bitterness of the dark beer, the sweetness of the prunes and the saltiness of the anchovies which add a complexity without any hints of fishiness! There might also be something in the fact that I associate this dish strongly with winters in the woody warmth of English country pubs with their low ceilings, roaring inglenook fireplaces and frothy pints of bitter seared with plunging a hot poker from that fire into its malty, hoppy depths to make a sort of traditional mulled ale.

SLOW-COOKED BEEF IN STOUT

4 rashers of bacon, chopped

1 celery stalk, diced

2 onions, diced

olive oil, for frying

1.2 kg beef chunks (beef shin or stewing steak), cut into 3 cm pieces

plain flour, for dusting

3 anchovy fillets

330 ml beef stock

4 carrots, cut into big chunks

1 bay leaf

110 g (½ cup) prunes

330 ml stout (Guinness)

salt and freshly ground black pepper

Preheat the oven to 150°C.

In a large heavy metal casserole dish (with a lid), fry the bacon, celery and onions in a little oil until translucent. Remove and reserve.

Dust the meat with flour. Pop the pieces in a sieve and give them a jiggle to remove any excess flour. Fry the beef quickly in oil, and in 3 batches, in the same pot until browned on all sides. Remove and reserve each batch until the final batch is browned.

Mash up the anchovies in the base of the pot and then deglaze the pan with the stock. Throw in the carrots, bay leaf, prunes, beef, bacon, celery, onions and stout. Put the lid on the pan and place in the oven for 3 hours. At the end of cooking, check the braise and add salt and pepper if required. The prunes and the saltiness of the anchovies should temper any excessive bitterness from the stout but a little extra salt at the end can help highlight the stew's flavour and counter bitterness.

This delicious beef stew goes wonderfully well with mashed potatoes and carrots (see Tip below).

Serves 4

TIPS & TRICKS

- Serve with roast purple carrots and a parsley potato mash, which is basically your normal mash but with very finely chopped parsley stirred through it when you add your butter and milk but before you add the extra dollop or two of butter you suspect the mash secretly needs before serving!

OK, so there is nothing actually wrong with a nice steak – well, apart from the fact that it's expensive, but ask yourself … is it really ever quite as sexy as the rich, succulent, falling-apart-at-the-barest-whisper-of-its-name romance of beef cheeks; a beef cheek that has been coddled in a thick red-wine gravy, loaded with the warm medieval intrigue of cinnamon and orange, that speaks of a dark history of centuries of European misadventure across the Holy Land on crusades. Hungry?

BRAISED SPICED BEEF CHEEKS

2 tablespoons olive oil
40 g butter
2 large carrots, diced
2 celery stalks, diced
2 brown onions, diced
4 cloves garlic, finely chopped
75 g (½ cup) plain flour
4 beef cheeks
750 ml (3 cups) red wine
zest and juice of 1 orange

2 tablespoons coriander seeds
3 bay leaves
½ bunch thyme
2 cinnamon sticks
1 tablespoon black peppercorns
750 ml (3 cups) beef stock

Garnish
zest of 1 orange
½ cup thyme leaves
½ cup parsley leaves

Preheat the oven to 140°C.

Heat 1 tablespoon of oil and the butter in a large ovenproof pot. Add the carrots, celery, onions and garlic, and cook over medium-low heat for 10 minutes until softened. Remove the vegetables from the pot and set aside.

Lightly flour the beef cheeks – yes, I did blush when I wrote this, but let's focus here – increase the heat, add 1 tablespoon of oil and brown the cheeks in a pot.

Return the vegetables to the pot. Add the wine and the remaining ingredients. Add enough beef stock to cover the beef cheeks and bring to the boil. Cover with a lid (or a layer of baking paper, then foil).

Transfer to the oven and cook for 4 hours, until the beef cheeks are meltingly tender. When ready, remove the cheeks from the cooking liquid.

Finish the cheeks with a sprinkling of freshly grated zest of extra orange, thyme leaves and parsley leaves. This is vital to wake up the warm slumbering flavours of the beef gravy. Drizzle with some of the cooking liquid and serve with potato mash.

Serves 4

LAMB

Once lamb was oh so humble. It was the centrepiece of the classic Aussie meal – chops and two veg. Yet just as lamb was the logical flagbearer for a young country whose wealth was built on the sheep's back, so it was also the hero protein of many migrants who moved here over the years. There's the lamb rogan josh and saag gosht of the Indians, the lamb tagines of the North Africans, the celebratory whole roast lamb of the Greeks, the kebabs of Turkish arrivals, and even the barbecued lamb cubes rubbed with Sichuan pepper that are a signature of the plains food from China's most Western province.

Now, of course, rising prices have moved better cuts of lamb out of the realm of cheap food for cash-strapped newly arrived Australians. This means that if you are going to spend your hard-earned on Larry Lamb, then you better make it a bit flasher than just grilling it and serving with potatoes, boiled peas and carrots.

There are all manner of delicious lamb recipes to follow, from slow-roasted lamb shoulder that pulls apart as easily as a Greek unity government, to Persian Chops and Toum (page 136) or Lamb and Barley Braise (page 142). First up, however, let's turn our attention to the original Aussie icon – the lamb chop.

Sure, there's always the attraction of herb-crumbed lamb chops served with a dark, richly spiced plum sauce made with sugar and vinegar to accent the natural flavours of the plum – something that's an Australian CWA classic of sorts. Then, if you're looking for another easy yet perfect partnership, try serving your chops with a dollop of black or green olive tapenade. I prefer the black one, which is as simple as making a coarse paste by blitzing 1 cup of pitted black olives with 6 capers and an anchovy with a drizzle of olive oil. Feel free to tweak those proportions to match your palate.

If you can find those fancy, strangely sweet but rather expensive Cantabrian anchovies like Ortiz, then make an anchovy butter instead. Roughly chop 50 g of those anchovies and scrape them into 80 g of room-temperature butter. Mash together with a tablespoon of finely snipped chives and shape into a rough log. Dump into plastic wrap, roll up and twist both ends tightly to compress the butter and make a neater, more even shape. Refrigerate until needed (and it has hardened). Serve your chops with a cut, cold round of the butter on them. Do remember to remove the plastic film!

The classic English way to serve lamb chops is with a sweet vinegary mint sauce. To make this, dissolve 1 tablespoon of caster sugar with a good splash of hot water. Stir until the sugar has dissolved and then add ½ cup of very finely chopped mint leaves and 125 ml (½ cup) of malt vinegar. Taste. If it's too intense, then mix in water little by little. If the vinegar dominates, stir in a sprinkling of more sugar to balance it out.

The other classic English accompaniment, other than delicious quince, redcurrant or medlar jelly, is an onion sauce. Fry 3 finely sliced brown onions in 40 g of butter until they start to look brown and caramelly. Stir in 60 g of flour and keep cooking for a couple of minutes to toast the flour and cook out any floury taste. When everything is looking suitably tanned, stir in 100 ml of milk. When this is combined, stir in another 300 ml and bring to the boil. The sauce will bubble and thicken. Add more milk if the sauce is getting too thick. Serve this sauce poured over the chops. It can be very nice if you drop a strand of thyme into the onions while they are cooking.

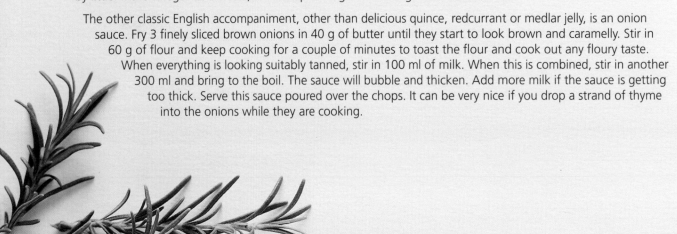

For a classic French onion sauce (aka soubise sauce), slice the onions very thinly and then fry them in butter for about 20 minutes very slowly. This is so they soften but stay pale and don't colour; next, purée the onions before adding to a béchamel or white sauce made from 60 g flour, 40 g butter and 500 ml (2 cups) milk. Once combined, the sauce should be passed through a fine sieve to ensure it's as smooth as a penniless French playboy in Cap d'Antibes. Rewarm in a clean pot before using.

Cheaper lamb chops like forequarter chops can also make the basis of a lovely stew but I prefer something sunny and tomato based rather than the greyness of a classic potatoey Irish stew. It is perhaps no surprise, given what we said about tapenades and anchovy butters, that the rich flavours of the puttanesca sauce on page 65 go really well with lamb. So brown the chops with some diced onions, then deglaze the pan with red wine and add tinned tomatoes, capers, olives, chilli, anchovies, a strip of lemon zest, crushed garlic and the lamb chops. Cook for 40 minutes until everything has cooked down to a lovely rich dark mess. Let the paste recipe proportions guide you!

Other great partnerships with lamb chops include feta, mint and cucumber – either as a salad or chopped and added to yoghurt as a sauce. Similar things can be said for beetroot, hazelnuts and goat's cheese!

My current favourite sauce for chops, however, is something that I stumbled across while playing around with batches of balsamic syrup (see page 15). When you throw in the balsamic, sugar and cider vinegar, also add 1 cup of kalamata olives, which you have pitted yourself. Cook to reduce the sauce and combine. The salty, slight bitterness and juiciness of the olives are the perfect contrast to the sweet–sour syrup. If it takes your fancy, add a handful of black-skinned blueberries to the sauce for the last minute of cooking for the occasional fresh fruity surprise. Spoon this black-on-black-on-blue syrup over barbecued or grilled chops.

PERSIAN CHOPS AND TOUM

2 large onions
juice of 2 lemons
salt and freshly ground black pepper
12 lamb chops

Toum (Lebanese garlic sauce)
1 head of garlic, cloves peeled and trimmed
juice of 1 lemon
salt
200 ml sunflower oil
1 tablespoon iced water

To make the marinade, grate or blitz the onion. Mix with lemon juice, a pinch of salt and black pepper. Slather the lamb chops with marinade.

Place in a covered bowl with the remaining marinade for at least 4 hours. Overnight is better.

If you like your toum with that raw garlic heat, then use the cloves simply trimmed. You can cut some of the heat by cutting out the root from each clove. If you want to mellow the garlic further, cut the cloves in half, remove the root from the centre and blanch in boiling water for 1 minute. Refresh in iced water.

Now blitz the cloves with the juice of ½ lemon and ½ teaspoon of salt. I've found that a stick blender with its plastic blending cup works best, as it has some space around the blender head for the toum to grow. But a mortar and pestle is traditional.

When you have a smooth garlic paste, keep the blender going (but at a slower pace if it can). Now drizzle in half the sunflower oil very slowly and a very little at a time. The emulsion will start to form and the toum will start to look fluffy like a mayo. Now slowly drizzle in the remaining lemon juice and then the remaining oil. The garlic and oil will emulsify magically together.

Keep blending and sprinkle in the iced water. This makes the toum go more white and billowy. Then it's ready.

When ready to cook the chops, scrape the marinade off and grill them on a hot grill until the fat is crispy and the meat is still pink (usually around 2–3 minutes on each side depending on the thickness of the chop).

Serve the chops with the toum and grilled tomatoes.

Serves 4

TIPS & TRICKS

- If the garlic and oil fail to emulsify, don't panic. Just drop in an egg white and whisk. This should pull the recalcitrant toum together and you'll get a lovely cloudy toum.

BAHARAT CHOPS WITH CARROTS AND HAZELNUTS

12 lamb chops
1 tablespoon ground cumin
½ tablespoon ground coriander
1 teaspoon ground cinnamon
½ teaspoon ground cloves
½ teaspoon grated nutmeg or ¼ teaspoon ground nutmeg

Carrot and hazelnut salad
500 g carrots, cut in half
1 head of garlic
70 g (½ cup) hazelnuts, toasted
1 teaspoon coriander seeds
zest of 1 orange

To make the baharat, mix together the spices. Rub the lamb chops with 2 tablespoons of the spice mix. Pop in a bowl. Cover and leave in the fridge for the rest of the day to infuse.

Preheat the oven to 190°C.

Toss the carrots and garlic in olive oil and roast for 45 minutes or until soft. Set aside and keep warm.

Cook the lamb chops on the barbecue over a high heat for 2–3 minutes each side. Rest the chops after cooking under foil.

Serve the chops with roast carrots, roast garlic tossed with hazelnuts, coriander seeds and orange zest.

Serves 6

PERFECT GRAVY

For me the perfect gravy is made by just removing the fat from the roasting pan and then reducing the juices, but this seldom makes enough for the gravy-holics who surround me. Hence, here are three easy versions.

The Old-school Version

- Heat 40 g of butter with 60 g plain flour in a small saucepan until it starts to change colour from pale buttercup yellow to a sort of camel-coat brown. This is now a roux. Little by little, stir into this roux 300 ml of stock to match the meat you need the gravy for. The butter adds flavour and the flour will swell with the stock to create a velvety gravy called a velouté.

Mum's Gravy

- My mum's no traditionalist but she takes a sort of velouté approach. Put the roasting tray on the stovetop while the meat is resting and drain off a couple of tablespoons of the fat. Into this, quickly stir a tablespoon or two of cornflour (or plain flour) so that it makes an oily paste. It will start to bubble and cook out the flour flavour. Then throw in a cup of booze of some form – wine, sherry, brandy – and scrub it round the pan, trying to dissolve all the stuck-on pan juices. The booze reduces and sizzles, which helps to burn off the alcohol. Incorporate any juices that are in the pan or that have seeped from the roast. Pour in the cooking water from your veg or some stock and stir. This will thicken and you now have a gravy. Add more stock or veg water if needed so your gravy is at the required consistency.

Glossy Gravy

- Drain the juice and fat from the pan, and put the juices in the fridge. Once cold, remove the fat. Deglaze the roasting pan on the stovetop with a cup of booze (as above: red wine, white wine, verjuice, sherry, muscat, brandy, etc), remembering that sweeter or heavier booze is best with the darker, heavier meats. Ensure that all the browny bits in the pan are incorporated. Reduce this liquid by half and add a cup of stock to match your meat. Strain this base gravy and return to the pan (which you have wiped clean). Pour in the pan juices through the sieve without the fat. Taste and season if required with salt or a little acid (lemon juice or even vinegar) if the gravy seems dull and lifeless. Now reduce this combination a little until it is at the required consistency. For a glossier, richer sauce, cut up 50 g (2½ tablespoons) of cold butter into cubes and whisk into the HOT (but not boiling) sauce, piece by piece to emulsify the sauce. This will mute the flavours but improve its velvety texture.

Slow roast lamb. Thick, sweet onion gravy. 'Nuff said. Good times!

SLOW-ROASTED LAMB SHOULDER WITH ONION GRAVY

1 tablespoon olive oil
30 g butter
1.4 kg shoulder of lamb
1 kg brown onions, sliced
10 garlic cloves

125 ml (½ cup) white wine
salt and freshly ground pepper
1 teaspoon instant coffee granules
20 marjoram leaves

Preheat the oven to 180°C.

Pour the olive oil and butter into a heavy roasting pan. Heat on the stovetop over a high heat until sizzling. Brown the shoulder on all sides. Remove the pan from the heat and the meat from the pan.

Place the onions in the pan, and stir them through the pan juices and fat. Place the lamb on top of the onions and place in the oven. After 30 minutes, add the garlic to the roasting pan and turn the heat down to 120°C. If the onions start to char before the lamb is cooked, remove them and set aside.

Depending on your oven, the shoulder will be cooked in about 90 minutes. It's ready when the meat easily pulls apart. Remove the meat from the pan and wrap it in foil. Cover with a newspaper and rest.

Scrape the onions and garlic to the side of the pan and place the pan over medium heat. Pour in the wine so it sizzles and deglaze by scrubbing the crusty meat bits off the bottom of the pan while the wine evaporates slightly and the alcohol burns off. Mix in the browned onions, garlic and coffee (if you want).

Pour the onion, garlic and wine mixture into a tall narrow vessel and blitz with a stick blender, making a smooth paste. Add any other meat juices, salt, pepper and the coffee, to taste. Coffee and garlic share some of the same flavour compounds so they work very well together.

To serve, tear lamb pieces from the shoulder. Put a generous splash of the onion purée across 4 plates. Dot each with 5 marjoram leaves and pile the meat on top. Serve with bowls of roast potatoes, sweetcorn kernels and baby peas.

Serves 4

TIPS & TRICKS

Love onion flavours? To amp up the allium appeal, try these accompaniments.

- To make leeks à la grecque, cook 2 washed, sliced leeks gently in olive oil until translucent. When softened let them cool. Mix in a splash of sherry vinegar.

- To make caramelised shallots, melt 50 g of butter in a pan big enough for 500 g of peeled shallots to lie in one layer. When melted, add the shallots and cook slowly for 15 minutes. Add another 50 g of butter and stir until it melts. Pour the shallots into a baking tray and pop into the oven with lamb. They will go dark and sticky. Remove just before serving.

- To make pickled red onions, slice 500 g of red onions as thinly as possible. A mandolin is great for this. Put half in a heatproof bowl. Pour over boiling water. Count to 20, drain and refresh them in cold water, then pat dry. Mix with the unblanched onions. Toss them in 60 ml (¼ cup) of red wine vinegar with 35 g (¼ cup) of currants.

BARBECUED BUTTERFLIED LAMB

juice of 2 lemons
250 ml (1 cup) olive oil
6 large sprigs thyme, roughly chopped
6 large sprigs rosemary, roughly chopped
5 garlic cloves, crushed
1 tablespoon cumin seeds, toasted and roughly crushed

1 x 1.5 kg boned leg of lamb (get your butcher to do this)
sea salt and freshly ground black pepper
lime zest, finely grated, to serve
natural yoghurt with finely chopped mint leaves, to serve

To make the marinade, mix together the lemon juice, olive oil, thyme, rosemary, garlic and cumin seeds in a large bowl. Add the lamb, cover it all over with the marinade and refrigerate for a minimum of 12 hours.

Preheat a large grill pan or barbecue to high.

Remove the lamb from the marinade, season well with sea salt and freshly ground black pepper and place on the hot grill pan or barbecue. Cook for 5 minutes on each side.

Now, either continue to barbecue for around 20 minutes, turning once or twice more, or place the lamb on a tray and cook in a 180°C oven for 15–18 minutes, or until cooked to your liking.

When the meat is cooked, leave it to rest for 20 minutes, loosely covered with foil, before carving.

Serve with pita bread and garnish with lime zest and yoghurt mixed with finely chopped mint leaves on the side.

Serves 4–6

PITA BREAD

310 ml (1¼ cups) tepid water
1½ teaspoons dry yeast
1½ teaspoons caster sugar

450 g (3 cups) plain flour
½ teaspoon sea salt
125 ml (½ cup) olive oil

Mix together the water, yeast and sugar in a small bowl and leave in a warm spot until the mixture foams (around 20 minutes).

In a large bowl mix the flour and salt and make a well. Add the olive oil and the yeast mix and combine. Work the mix until it comes together and then turn out onto a lightly floured bench and knead for a few minutes until the dough becomes silky and smooth.

Put it back into the bowl, cover with a tea towel and leave to prove for around 15–20 minutes.

Preheat the barbecue to a medium heat.

Divide the dough into 12 and roll out into flat, thin, even discs approximately 16 cm in diameter.

Brush the flat bread with some olive oil and place it oil side down on the barbecue. Gently brush a little oil on top as well.

In a matter of seconds the bread will start to puff. After 20–25 seconds, flip them over and cook for 20 seconds more. Do not cook for too long or they will dry out too much and become crisp.

When they are cooked, stack them one on top of the other and wrap them tightly in a clean tea towel to keep them warm and help them sweat a little and stay soft until ready to use.

Makes 12 pita breads

LAMB AND BARLEY BRAISE

330 g (1½ cups) pearl barley
1 litre (4 cups) water
1 kg lamb shanks (4 shanks)
4 garlic cloves, sliced
2 teaspoons instant coffee
olive oil
butter
8 shallots, finely diced

4 carrots, finely diced
6 celery stalks, finely diced
4 anchovy fillets, drained
750 ml wine (big red shiraz)
750 ml beef stock
salt and freshly ground
black pepper

100 g speck or smoky bacon,
cut into ½ cm cubes
½ bunch flat-leaf parsley, chopped
¼ head savoy cabbage,
finely sliced

Heat the oven to 180°C.

Put 1 cup of the pearl barley in a saucepan and cover it with 4 cups of water. Bring to the boil and simmer for 30 minutes or until the barley is cooked but still a little nutty. Drain and reserve.

Make incisions in each shank and slip the garlic in these holes. Rub each hole with a few grains of instant coffee. Lamb loves garlic and coffee.

In a heavy ovenproof pot (with a lid), pour enough olive oil to coat the bottom of the pan and a walnut-sized knob of butter. Fry the shallots until translucent, then add the carrot and celery. Cook them along with the anchovy fillets for 5 minutes or until the carrots soften a little and the anchovies break down into the vegetable *soffritto*. Remove this *soffritto* with a slotted spoon and reserve, but leave the oil and fat behind.

Reheat the oil and fat. When hot, brown the shanks in batches, then set aside.

Deglaze the pot by pouring 2 cups of the wine into the hot pot – it will hiss wonderfully – and scrub all the brown bits into the wine. This will add more lovely rich flavours.

In a small ovenproof bowl or ramekin (deeper than it is wide), pour in the remaining ½ cup of uncooked barley and cover with 1 cup of wine. Cover with foil and place in the oven for an hour.

Return the vegetable *soffritto* to the pan and nestle the shanks on top. Gently pour over all the remaining wine and the stock. Season with a good pinch of salt and a couple of good grinds of black pepper. Put a lid on and place the pot into the oven. Cook for about 1½ hours. Check the shanks and barley after 30 minutes and then again after an hour to make sure there is enough liquid. If not, top up with a little water.

Remove the red wine barley pot from the oven after an hour, and check if it's cooked and all the wine absorbed. Only return it to the oven if it is not! Stir 2 tablespoons of butter through the mixture, which will be a beautiful red colour. Don't eat it all even though barley cooked this way is shockingly addictive.

Remove the main pot from the oven after 90 minutes. The lamb meat should be juicy and falling off the shank bone. The vegetables will be red, reduced and soaked with wine and meat juices. Season with salt and pepper.

Turn off the oven but keep the oven door closed.

Fry the cubes of speck or bacon over a high heat for 5 minutes, so they are brown.

Lift out the shanks so you can gently stir in both the plain-cooked barley and the red barley. Add the browned speck. Moisten it all with a little water (about 1 cup) if dry.

Pop the shanks back on top. Top with the chopped parsley and then a layer of the cabbage. Bang the lid on and return to the hot oven for 15 minutes or until the cabbage has softened but still has crunch.

Serves 4

Meaning 'head of the shop', ras el hanout is a Moroccan spice mix that differs from kitchen to kitchen, but might include any or all of the following: black pepper, cumin, coriander, cardamom, mace, licorice, ginger, allspice, cinnamon or other aromatics. If you can't find ras el hanout, toast and then grind together a powder of ¼ teaspoon cumin seeds, ½ a blade of mace, a cardamom pod, ¼ teaspoon of black pepper, ½ teaspoon of coriander seeds and ¼ teaspoon of cinnamon. Why all this ramble? Well, you'll need it for this dish.

MOROCCAN LAMB WITH PARSNIPS AND DATE PURÉE

2 x 6-cutlet racks of lamb
(each about 225 g)
1½ teaspoons ras el hanout
spice mix (see introduction)
1 kg parsnips
125 ml (½ cup) cream
125 ml (½ cup) milk

180 g (1 cup) dried pitted dates
150 ml water
90 ml muscat
2 tablespoons olive oil
4 celery stalks, plus a few
young celery leaves

1 tablespoon red wine vinegar
½ bunch flat-leaf parsley
½ bunch mint
8 soft fresh dates, pitted
juice of 1 orange
50 g butter

Rub the lamb racks with the spice mix. Cover and leave by the stove.

Add the parsnips to a large saucepan, cover with cold water, bring to the boil and simmer for 20 minutes until cooked.

To make the parsnip mash, blitz them in a processor, adding the cream and milk bit by bit until the right consistency is achieved. You should end up with a smooth purée with a texture of creamy mashed potato.

To make the date purée, cook the dried dates slowly in half the water and the muscat for 10 minutes, stirring to ensure that they don't boil dry. Mash the dates and add the remaining water. You should have a thick stringy paste. Pass the mixture through a fine sieve to remove those fibres. You will be left with a fine date purée.

Fry the meat in a pan with the oil over medium heat, making sure you brown all sides. Remove the meat after cooking and rest under foil for 10 minutes.

To make the celery salad, finely slice the celery into thin crescents. Pour in the vinegar and swish the celery around in it. Pour off any excess after doing this. Toss with one-third of the amount of chopped parsley. Garnish with picked celery leaves.

To make the mint and date salad, tear the mint leaves (you should have about ⅓ cup) and place in a bowl with the fresh dates, orange juice and chopped quince paste. Toss to combine.

Gently warm the date and parsnip purées. Whisk small hunks of butter into the warming date purée to make it extra velvety – this will also make the purée less fruity.

Slice the cooked racks and plate with a dollop of parsnip mash, date purée, mint and date salad and a pile of celery salad for crunch and freshness.

Serves 4

TIPS & TRICKS

• To doll up the date salad, add 50 g of quince paste chopped into 1 cm pieces.
  Quince loves lamb like politicians love a photo opp.

Don't tell the other recipes, but this might well be the best dish in this book. Why? Well, it's not just that everyone who tastes it falls in love with it. It's not just because the use of curry powder and Chinese flavours like soy and ginger show a strong historical influence from the waves of European migrants who reached our shores from Calcutta, and the Chinese migrants who first came to chase a living on the diggings. It's not just because pineapple is a supremely daggy but also supremely Australian ingredient that here becomes the secret agent, adding savour and tang to the rich gravy of the lamb without ever really announcing its presence. It's not just that the walnuts add crunch but they also have a direct link to the hills of north-east Victoria where this recipe comes from. No, it is because this is what I remember my future mother-in-law cooking me after I asked the woman I love to marry me. No dish ever tasted sweeter.

LAMB, WALNUT AND PINEAPPLE BRAISE

1.2 kg lamb forequarter (ask the butcher to chop it), fat trimmed and lamb diced

2 tablespoons plain flour

2 tablespoons oil

3 garlic cloves

500 ml (2 cups) pineapple juice

2 teaspoons curry powder

140 g can tomato paste

80 ml (⅓ cup) soy sauce

2 tablespoons vinegar

2 tablespoons brown sugar

1 cm knob of ginger, grated

75 g (¾ cup) walnuts

salt and pepper, to taste

Preheat the oven to 180°C.

Toss the meat in the flour and fry in oil over a high heat to brown. Transfer to a casserole dish.

Fry the garlic, then add the pineapple juice, curry powder, tomato paste, soy sauce, vinegar, brown sugar and ginger, and bring to the boil. Pour over the meat, cover and cook in the oven for about 2 hours.

When cooked, add the walnuts and season to taste.

Serve with buttered egg noodles or some nutty brown rice.

Serves 4

PORK

Sizzly, crackly, juicy, fatty, crispy, sticky, crunchy – some of my favourite words used to describe food sit most comfortably with the most versatile of all meats – pork.

Roast it, cure it, fry it, braise it, grill it, mince it, stuff it, BBQ it, bake it, brine it, smoke it or salt it – pork isn't just a meat but also something far more essential, a true building block of flavour and the cornerstone of so many great dishes. In fact much of our happiness and the success of our civilisations can be traced back to that happy moment when man and pig realised they could live together harmoniously. The pigs lived off our scraps and then repaid that hospitality with their meat. Yes, we did get the best from that deal, didn't we?

The best pork leaves your eyes glazed with pleasure and your lips glazed and smacky from its sweet fat but you'll also find it popping up all over the place in this book whether in a stuffing, a carbonara or as the base of a soup. Here, however, the pork is out, proud and here for use to celebrate in all its porky glory!

I  NEW PORK and HAM and COTECHINO and LARDONS and PANCETTA and BACON and CHIPOLATAS and ZAMPONE and SPECK and BACON BITS and JAMON and BRAWN and CAPOCOLLO and PROSCUITTO and SPAM and LARD and CHITTERLINGS and SPARE RIBS and RILLETTES and LARDO and DEVON and CULATELLO and LIVERWURST and KNUCKLE and SCRATCHINGS and BELLY and CRACKLING and GUANCIALE and NJUDA and BLACK PUDDING and HOT DOGS and KULEN and PEPPERONI and LOMO and SMOKED HAM HOCK and SCOTCH EGGS and GAMMON and PORK CHOPS and CHORIZO and APPLE

I've tried a few methods for slow-cooking pork shoulder for the best results and crackling, but the extremely slow (ie eight hour!) process used by the River Café seems to produce the best results. The really slow cooking allows the fat to render and keeps the meat moist. The meat is ready when it falls apart. OK, admit it, I had you at 'crackling'!

ROAST PORK WITH CRACKLING AND APPLE SAUCE

1 x 2 kg boned pork shoulder, (get your butcher to slash the pork fat)

12 garlic cloves, peeled

30 g (5 tablespoons) coriander seeds

2 tablespoons ground allspice

1 teaspoon dried chilli flakes

1 teaspoon salt

juice of 5 lemons (around 250 ml)

125 ml (½ cup) oil

Apple sauce

50 g butter

2 sage leaves

5 green apples, peeled, cored and diced

1 tablespoon brown sugar

1 teaspoon Dijon mustard (or 2 teaspoons hot English if you're into that sort of punishment)

salt and freshly ground black pepper

1 extra green apple

Heat the oven to 230°C.

Smash your garlic, coriander seeds, allspice, chilli and salt together. Rub it in to the slashes on the pork skin. Leave to stand for at least 10 minutes.

Mix the lemon juice with the oil.

Put a wire rack into a roasting tray. Pop the shoulder on top, skin side up, and bang it in the oven. Watch it. When the skin begins to bubble up and brown all over (after about 30 minutes), turn the heat down to 120°C. Drizzle about half the lemon oil mixture over the shoulder.

Cook for 8 hours, turning it over when you remember. When you do flip, you should baste it with the lemon and oil mixture again.

While the pork is cooking, make your apple sauce. Melt the butter in a pan. Fry your sage leaves in the pan until crispy but still green. Remove. Now fry the apple dice in the butter with a splash of the rendered pork fat from the roast.

When the apple starts to soften, stir in the brown sugar and the Dijon mustard. Cook down for 10 minutes or until collapsed and saucy. Remove from the heat, season and keep warm.

Grate the extra apple into a sieve over a bowl. Squeeze out the juice. Just before serving the pork, warm the sauce and stir in the fresh apple juice. This gives your sauce a great green freshness. Serve.

Serves 6–8

TIPS & TRICKS

- If the crackle doesn't finish in the oven, just cheat! Remove the sheet of it while the pork is resting and pop it under the grill. Watch it, don't let it burn and take it out as soon as it goes golden!

I should pay tribute to Victoria's Roy Rigoni, who shared the secret to his miraculous pork chop at his Mount Beauty restaurant (the secret was pineapple juice) in a manner that I still remembered the next day after one of the funniest and most disreputable nights. This inspired my experimentation with the golden nectar and pork, and hence this dish. Sounds weird, maybe, but once tried you'll be a convert!

PINEAPPLE BRINED PORK STEAKS

2 tablespoons salt

1 tablespoon soy sauce

2 tablespoons soft brown sugar, packed

1 litre pineapple juice

2 tablespoons olive oil

4 x 125 g pork loin steaks

½ cup white wine

Make the brine by mixing the salt, soy, sugar and pineapple juice together. Place the pork steaks in a large ziplock bag (or baking dish/mixing bowl). Pour in the brining solution. Bang in the fridge for 3 hours or longer to marinate. Make sure you massage the marinade all over the meat. Turn it over a couple of times while it is marinating in the fridge so all the meat receives a good coating.

When you are 15 minutes out from serving, pull out the chops, drain, rinse and dry them. Throw the brine away. Before cooking the chops, make sure your vegetables are cooking (see Tips & Tricks) and the table is laid.

Now oil the chops and, in a hot, dry frying pan, fry (or grill) them for 3 minutes on each side, taking care to turn at least once. The sugar will caramelise quickly and may easily burn.

You'll need to cook them for longer if the steaks are thick or you want your pork well done. The pork should reach an internal temperature of 65°C. Rest covered for at least 5 minutes. Drain the veg and keep the boiling or steaming water.

While the pork steaks are resting, keep the pan with all its juices on the heat and pour in half a cup of the green veggie's cooking liquid and the wine.

Use the liquid to scrape away any of the delicious burny bits so that they incorporate into the sauce. The sauce will bubble, the wine flavour will burn off and it will reduce. Pour in any of the juices that have leached out of the resting meat.

Reduce the heat and simmer for 5 minutes or until the sauce thickens to coat the back of a spoon. Sieve the sauce into a small warmed jug to serve.

Serves 4

TIPS & TRICKS

- Serve these delicious pork steaks with mashed potatoes, broccoli or beans. Make sure your veggies are well underway before whacking the pork steaks in the pan.

It seems that a couple of years back we had all forgotten ribs in our rush to praise and cook secondary cuts like neck, belly and cheek. Cooked right, all of these are meltingly delicious, but ribs also give you the added primal pleasure of tearing the meat away from bones with your teeth and then licking your fingers of the remnants of the all-important sticky BBQ sauce. Cooking ribs is one of those simple things that can be done 100 ways. In my book (and for once I can mean this literally – tee hee hee) there are only two rules. Firstly – no matter what experts tell you – never boil ribs before cooking. I usually use the oven then the barbecue, but the grill in your oven can be used for the final stage instead. Secondly, always remove the fine silver skin on the underside of the ribs before cooking, as it is both horrid to eat and stops the marinade or dry rub working its way into the meat. To remove this, bump the nose of a teaspoon inwards along the edge of the rib underside (concave side) until a little tag of skin is visible. Using paper towel or a clean cloth, grab the tag and pull back the silverskin until it is
all removed from this side of the ribs.

When it comes to flavourings, ribs love a vinegary mop sauce or something sweet applied during cooking that will become a sticky glaze (like the barbecue sauce or pineapple ketchup on pages 120–121) but for me there is a certain elegance about a dry spice rub like this one. And it's this approach that won the most votes in the latest family 'rib-off'. The ribs can be glazed at the end of the cooking time, but I reckon they are just dandy as they are, because the fat from the meat combines with the rub residue with glorious results.

PORK RIBS

2 kg pork ribs
3 teaspoons cumin seeds
1½ tablespoons coriander seeds
1 teaspoon allspice
3 teaspoons fennel seeds

12 fresh bay leaves (or 7 dry)
3 teaspoons onion powder
3 teaspoons garlic powder
1 tablespoon flake salt (or
2 teaspoons table salt)

Prepare the ribs by peeling off the silver skin on the underside of the ribs. Then blitz all the dry rub ingredients together (or pound them into a powder in the mortar and pestle). Generously massage the rub into the ribs.

You may well have some dry rub left over that will keep until the next ribs session. Place the ribs on a rack or in a plastic container, cover them, and put in the fridge for a few hours or overnight.

To cook the ribs, preheat the oven to 140°C. Knock the ribs together to remove any excess rub and place on a baking tray. Bake for 60 minutes. Check if they are ready by cutting one of the racks in half. Depending on the thinness of the ribs and the speed of your oven, the ribs may need up to 30 minutes more.

When they are cooked, cut the ribs into portions and serve them with a crisp green salad or rice, and your choice of sauce or dressing.

Serves 1, but I suppose you could share with 3 others!

TIPS & TRICKS

- This rub is versatile and can be used for chicken, lamb or beef – just omit the fennel seeds.

- The onion and garlic powders are very traditional in US barbecue rubs and sauces. They add a certain savour, but aren't essential.

4 ways with...
SAUSAGES

Sausages have a special place in my life, whether it's those cheap snags spitting on the fundraising sausage sizzle barbecue or eaten at kids' footy in squidgy white bread with even cheaper red sauce. Then there are those old-school snag dishes like bangers and mash with onion gravy, or even curry sausages. I once shared a flat with a woman whose go-to meal was curry sausages and that wasn't a bad thing. For her, Jane was her name, here are four simple ways that she could quintuple her culinary repertoire with minimal skill or effort!

BAKED SNAGS

It's distinctly daggy but there is something rather reassuring about baked snags. Basically toss 500 g of the best fat pork snags into an oiled metal baking pan and pop in a preheated 200°C oven. While they are cooking (this will take about 30 minutes or longer if they are big fatties), make a Cumberland sauce for the sausages. This is a delicious combination of a jar of redcurrant jelly with port and orange. To make the sauce, heat 250 ml (1 cup) of port to burn off the alcohol. Then add the zest and juice of 1 orange, ½ cup of redcurrant jelly and a generous teaspoon of English mustard. Cook gently to reduce to a syrupy consistency. Adding a little lemon juice or vinegar will give some balancing acidity. When the snags are cooked pour over the Cumberland sauce and turn the oven up to 220°C. Cook for 5 minutes. Serve with roast potatoes, roast onions, roast pumpkin and roast carrots. Pop these veg in the oven 20 minutes before you start the snags.

SAUSAGE PASTA

Good chunky butchers' snags can be pulled apart and used as the meat on your pizza or in a simple pasta sauce. I'd pick a nice pork and fennel snag for this role. Gently heat a little oil in a pan. Pull the skin off the snags and, using your fingers, pull apart the sausage meat and drop chunks into the pan. Toss with ½ cup of 3 cm long spring onion pieces. Wash your hands. Fry until the snag meat is firm and almost cooked. Remove the snags and spring onions. Deglaze the pan with 250 ml (1 cup) of white wine and cook merrily until reduced by half. Throw in a 400 g can of tomatoes, a pinch of salt and a crushed garlic clove. Stir madly to combine and to break up the tomatoes as well as to incorporate the fat rendered from the snags. Cook on a good heat for 5 minutes, then throw the snag bits back into the pan. Serve spooned over a chunky dried pasta like big penne with a good grating of your favourite cheese.

SAUCY SNAGS AND APPLES

Pork loves apple like Romeo loved Juliet. The sweetness and tartness of the apple are the perfect partners for the salty, porky sausage. Barbecue (or grill) the snags. While you – or your duly appointed sous chef – are cooking them, fry 2 apples that you've peeled and cut into 8 wedges in 50 g of butter with a cinnamon stick or a teaspoon of mustard seeds. When they start to brown, throw in 45 g (¼ cup) of brown sugar and toss to coat. Slice the cooked snags at an angle to maximise the meaty face of each slice. Toss with the apples. Throw in some finely sliced sage leaves if you like but these aren't essential. A dash of cider vinegar will add some pep but again it isn't essential. Serve the saucy snags and apples with a buttery potato mash and some finely sliced cabbage cooked in a little butter and just a little water so it's still crunchy.

PORK SAUSAGE, GREEN LENTIL AND RED WINE BRAISE

600 g coarse fat pork snags
2 large brown onions, finely diced
2 rashers of streaky or the fatty end of middle bacon,
cut into 1 cm pieces (If you can find a chunk of smoked
bacon in your supermarket deli counter, even better!)
20 g butter
1 tablespoon olive oil
1 large carrot, finely diced
2 celery stalks, finely diced
3 garlic cloves, crushed
500 ml (2 cups) red wine
2 sprigs thyme
2 x 400 g cans green lentils

Grill the pork snags.

In a heavy-based saucepan, fry the onions and the
fatty bacon in a little butter and olive oil. Add the
carrot and celery, and cook until they all get little
browny edges then add the garlic and toss for
1 minute. Deglaze the pan with the wine and cook
to reduce by half.

Throw in a couple of sprigs of thyme and add the
lentils. Cut the pork sausages into chunks and lay
them on top. Pop a lid on and place on a low heat
at the back of the stove for 30 minutes.

Serves 4

4 ways with...
CHORIZO

Once a delicatessen rarity, now Spanish-style chorizo sausages, ruddy with dried capsicum, are stocked at most supermarket deli counters. I reckon these plump, slightly yielding sausages are one of the most versatile and exotic things you can have in your fridge at home. Using it is limited only by your imagination.

In Spain, tapas bars will serve little bowls of fried chorizo slices with the 'tortilla' (potato omelette), or on little toasts topped with a quail's egg, both an Iberian take on pork and eggs. Chorizo adds meatiness to paella and to many regional bean stews. In the north they cook it slowly submerged in cider; wine or sherry is used elsewhere.

I love chunks of chorizo tossed through pasta with clams, and while it's probably culinary heresy it also works really well sparking up a classic ballsy Italian 'puttanesca' pasta sauce of olives, tomatoes and anchovies. I'll slice it through spicy Spanish potatoes ('patatas bravas') or pop it on top of pizza with slices of red capsicum echoing the sausage's sweetness.

Of course if you are lazy and just after a snack, dispense with all this laborious cooking and just grill chorizo topped with slices of salty Spanish manchego. You can always amp up this combo by making little manchego and chorizo tarts or sprinkling the two on roasting figs or deseeded, roasting peppers. Add some toasted almonds for crunch and serve with a chilled glass of nutty sherry.

The three recipes here play on some of those classic combinations whether it is eggs stained with the rusty fat rendered from the cooked sausage or something that cuts against the fatty salty richness of the sausage like the juiciness of grapes with the sherry-braised chorizo. It is however the combination of mint with the chorizo in a tomato sauce that is the most surprisingly delicious. Sure, the mint adds some peppy freshness but there is also something rather wonderful about the accompanying tomato sauce that is dense and pale from the emulsification of some of the sausage's fat into the sauce.

CHORIZO IN SHERRY WITH GRAPES

4 fat, fresh chorizo sausages, sliced into thick (1 cm) rounds
125 ml (½ cup) of sherry
20 small round black grapes, halved and seeded if necessary

Prepare the chorizo just before serving.

Fry in a hot, heavy, dry pan over a high heat. Don't add oil – the chorizo will give off loads of its own. Turn the chorizo after 4–5 minutes once the first side is nice and charry. When the second side starts to go golden, pour in the sherry.

Cook for 2 minutes, tossing the chorizo through the reducing sherry. Throw in the grapes to warm through.

Serve with crusty bread or over potato mash.

Serves 4

TIPS & TRICKS

• You could use tiles of capsicum or even chunks of stone fruit if you have no grapes.

CHORIZO IN TOMATO SAUCE WITH MINT

1 punnet cherry tomatoes
olive oil
4 fat chorizo sausage, chopped into
finger-fat slices
½ lemon
1 teaspoon brown sugar
bunch of mint, chopped

Slice the cherry tomatoes in half and keep the juice that oozes out.

Fry the chorizo in a litttle cheap, hot olive oil on both sides so the slices are crispy on the surface but still juicy in the middle. The chorizo will give off a lot of fat.

Remove the slices but keep the pan with the ruddy chorizo-kissed oil on the heat. Place the tomatoes, cut side down, into the fat and fry the little darlings until they start to break down. Shake the pan gently to stop them sticking but don't stir them and break up the tomatoes' form too much.

Just before serving, stir in a squeeze of lemon and some brown sugar. Throw the chorizo back in. Toss and serve dressed with chopped fresh mint.

Serves 4

TIPS & TRICKS

- You could save dollars and just use a can of chopped tomatoes.

CHORIZO WITH SCRAMBLED EGGS

8 eggs
salt and freshly ground black pepper
2 chorizo
1 red capsicum, deseeded and diced
4 soft tortillas
paprika
1 jalapeño, deseeded and sliced
1 serrano chilli, deseeded and sliced
2 spring onions, sliced
bunch coriander, chopped

Make the scrambled eggs by cracking the eggs into a warm pan and stirring together. Season with salt and pepper.

Keep the pan on a low heat and stir regularly. While the eggs are cooking, cut the chorizo into chunks about 2 cm wide.

Check the eggs and stir in the red capsicum dice.

Place the chorizo in a dry pan to fry. They will give off their own oil. (Check and again stir the eggs.) When the chorizo corners go crispy, remove to paper towel to drain. Check and stir the eggs.

As soon as the eggs are scrambled to your liking, remove the pan from the heat and warm the tortillas in the microwave for 20 seconds. Place the tortilla on one side of the plate. Fill half the tortilla with scrambled eggs.

Top with a sprinkling of chorizo chunks and a pinch of paprika. Garnish with the sliced chillies, spring onions and chopped coriander leaves.

Serves 4

At the religious prison school that I went to they would feed us a plate of white rice for lunch each Friday so we could remember the poor of Peru. Not allowed off campus, this meant that every Friday lunchtime the school's fire alarms would go off and the elderly electrics would short out as five levels of kids plugged in power-hungry heating elements to make soup, or lit illegal camp stoves to fry bread in butter pilfered from the canteen. Little, and thus easily hidden, cans of baked beans were the luxury we all craved for these impromptu feasts. We would have killed for these far fancier beans that are so darned tasty. I suggest you make them in the huge quantity below so you can boastfully share them with all your friends. The secret is the usually left–right flavour combination of maple syrup and smoky bacon paired with the cheeky smack of the anchovy and tamarind complexity of a good Worcestershire sauce.

HOMESTYLE BEANS WITH
SMOKY BACON AND MAPLE SYRUP

2 tablespoons oil

4 slices thick-cut smoky bacon, thinly sliced

1 onion, finely diced

400 g can diced tomatoes

1 tablespoon dark brown sugar

80 ml (⅓ cup) maple syrup

2 tablespoons Worcestershire sauce

4 x 400 g cans cannellini, drained and rinsed

1 bay leaf

500 ml (2 cups) water

salt and freshly ground black pepper

2 tablespoons raw sugar

Heat the oven to 160°C.

In a large ovenproof cast-iron dish, heat the oil and sauté the bacon and onion for 5 minutes. Add the tinned tomatoes, brown sugar, maple syrup and Worcestershire sauce. Stir well.

Add the drained beans and bay leaf. Add the water and season with salt and pepper. It will all taste a little weird but don't worry, like a good party, time and heat will bring these disparate ingredients together to a riotous conclusion. Cover tightly with foil, place in the oven and bake for 1½ hours.

Remove the foil and sprinkle over the raw sugar. Continue to bake, uncovered, for 30 minutes.

Serves 6

TIPS & TRICKS

- To make that darker, more mysterious, Boston strangler style of baked beans, add 3 cloves, 1 teaspoon of ground allspice, 2 tablespoons of black treacle or molasses and a couple of teaspoons of dry English mustard. Reduce the maple syrup to 2 tablespoons. Otherwise, the process is the same.

- Crack eggs on the beans about 10 minutes before you want to eat. Return to the oven and bake until cooked.

4 ways with...
BACON

There is something about the smell and sound of sizzling bacon – whether green or smoked, dancing in the pan or twisting on the grill – that sings to me. It is a song loaded with umami and rebellion as our love of bacon seems to flip the bird at the rising army of health-conscious wowsers. Yeah, OK, I'll do 30 minutes on the treadmill after eating bacon. Deal?

I sometimes think I could live without meat – perhaps – but it is bacon that is the unscaleable rampart between me and vegetarianism.

Bacon is indispensable in my kitchen. It is the foundation of so many great dishes, whether it's adding savour and saltiness to a bolognese, or complexity to classic French dishes like coq au vin or beef bourguignon. And it's an integral part of many a Tuesday plate of fried rice. When you can't be bothered to find char siu pork or lap cheong sausage, there's always that other great porky contribution to a good suburban Chinese fried rice, cubes of Spam! Bacon is essential whether it's binding a terrine, wrapped around a beef fillet, adding protection and juiciness by covering the lean breast of a chicken or adding a savoury punch to its stuffing. In my kitchen, bacon is a building block of much of what I cook and it's a condiment to add salty crispy smokiness, but it can also have a starring role in many simple dishes.

WITH BREAD AND PASTA

Bacon loves bread. Add it to your burgers, join it between the sheets with lettuce and tomato for a BLT, or partner it with slices of turkey breast, lettuce, tomato, mustard, mayo and three pieces of toast in a classic triple-decker Club sandwich.

If that's too much faffing, then there are few things easier or more consoling than a 'bacon butty'. Try this buttered white bread sandwich with both back and streaky bacon cooked not too crispy with a good dollop of sweeter tomato ketchup rather than tangier Aussie tomato sauce. If you want to step up your butty, add grilled tomato pressed into the bread instead of the ketchup and omit the butter – or just try mayonnaise spiked with a teaspoon of horseradish. More radical is using crispy bacon between slices of plump golden toast with marmalade – a very English tradition.

Bacon enjoys an ongoing love affair with flour. It's paired with French toast or with pancakes as a salty counterpoint to the sweetness of maple syrup to make a classic Canadian breakfast. It can also add a whole other dimension to your muffins, dumplings or scones when partnering any of the veg that go so well with it, such as corn or zucchini. It's also fantastic added to the sweetness of corn fritters for breakfast or a light lunch. Flour – or at least a rich tasty browned roux – is at the heart of a good chowder and one of my favourites is a corn and bacon chowder with the pig replacing the usual seafood.

Now, if we take the flour thing one step further, then bacon is perfect with pasta. Fry 200 g of it with a couple of crushed garlic cloves, added when the bacon is almost cooked. Now mix a can of tomatoes and some chilli (fresh or dried) into the pan to make an arrabiata sauce for penne pasta. The fat rendered from the bacon will make the sauce velvety and extra delicious against the heat of the chilli. Or mix instead pieces of grilled bacon with egg yolks and parmesan to make a carbonara (see page 62). Pair bacon with mushrooms and cream, however, and you make boscaiola (or woodsman) sauce, which is ideal with orecchiette pasta.

WITH SEAFOOD

The saltiness and smokiness of bacon both go very well with seafood. Bake oysters with matchsticks of bacon and a splash of Worcestershire sauce for oysters Kilpatrick, or top clams with bacon, breadcrumbs and garlic to make the US dish of clams casino. Grilled oysters wrapped in bacon are angels on horseback, but the technique works equally well with prawns or even prunes. A bacon and scallop pie or chunks of bacon and prawn tossed through penne pasta moistened with a little stock are more substantial versions of the same flavours.

WITH EGGS

Abbott and Costello, Gary and George, Eggs and Bacon – all great classic combinations but I'd advise only cooking with the latter two. Think about using bacon along with your custardy eggs in your quiche Lorraine (see the quiche recipe on page 38), with mushrooms at the heart of your omelettes or with zucchini in a frittata. Or just serve it grilled with poached eggs and a couple of crunchy-edged rounds of fried black pudding for breakfast.

WITH MEAT

It isn't just for beef bourguignon or coq au vin (see page 108) that lardons (fat matchsticks) of bacon can be used to add some complexity to the sauce. Use it as the base for other stews or braises. It's especially good with rabbit – particularly if you spike the stock and white wine braising sauce with a good dollop of Dijon mustard, garlic and celery. Oh, and then finish it by stirring in a big spoonful of cream and some fresh thyme just before serving. Rabbit meat can be very lean so cook it slowly at a gentle low heat to keep it from drying out. And if you need to thicken the sauce further after the rabbit is perfect, hook out the meat and then reduce the sauce by itself. Also think about mixing lardons of bacon with cooked chicken as the filling for a deliciously savoury chicken and bacon pie.

The venerable dish of liver and bacon (with loads of onions of course!) has become rather unfashionable these days. If that still brings back too many memories of bad lunches at Nan's house, try skewering cleaned chicken livers wrapped in bacon on wooden skewers and grilling them. The bacon should be cooked and the livers should still have the faintest pink colour at their centre. Serve with a drizzle of red wine, sweet sherry or port boiled up with a little sugar to make a sticky sweet-sour dressing. And yes, a splash of

cream in this sauce adds extra decadence too, and it gives you something to mop up with crusty bread.

The Italians love to wrap birds in thin-cut bacon or prosciutto, especially in their classic dish of saltimbocca. Try this with boned quail or chicken thighs that you roast in the oven. Rest the meat before serving. While this is happening, deglaze the pan with a couple of cups of marsala or fruity white wine or half the amount of verjuice. When the tasty brown bits from the pan have been incorporated into the wine, take the heat down and reduce the sauce for a few minutes. Finally, add a couple of handfuls of seedless grapes (ideally sweet red ones) and toss the bacon-wrapped birds through the sauce to coat. Serve immediately with a crisp green salad and some soft polenta. You can add sliced green chillies to this too.

If that all sounds too French and fancy, then wrap your favourite pork snags in strips of streaky bacon and bake them in the oven slathered in a rib sauce. To make the sauce, cook up some tomato ketchup, brown sugar, cider vinegar, Worcestershire sauce, English mustard and some cayenne pepper until you get a coatable sauce that's sweet, tangy and a little bit fiery. If it gets too thick while you're making it, add some black coffee, which will add some liquid and a little edge of bitterness! These bacon snags are perfect in a roll with loads of crunchy iceberg or just served with mash and roast pumpkin. Oh, and maybe something green too!

8 ways with...
EGGS

Egg cookery is a kitchen skill all of its own, but for all that is written about the humble egg, the essential truths of egg cookery can sometimes lie buried among myth and misinformation. Here's my essential guide to getting the best out of cooking eggs.

The first rule of egg cookery is to always use the freshest eggs you can get. Checking the dates on the packaging can help, but the best way to gauge the freshness of the egg is how it looks when cracked. In a fresh egg, the raw white will be thick enough to stand proud from the plate like a small mound on which the yolk perches.

To spot a fresh egg without cracking it, fill a bowl with water. Slip in the egg. If it sinks immediately it is fresh; if one end floats and the other end sinks, then the egg is about a week old, as an air sac has formed at the floating end. Don't use it if it totally floats!

The second rule is to use eggs that are at room temperature, rather than straight from the fridge. This is especially important when boiling, as the shock of going from the cold of the fridge to a hot pan of water can cause the shells to crack.

The third rule is that there are no rules. For example, how long your boiled egg will take to cook depends on a number of variables such as the size of the egg, the size of the pan, how much water there is in the pan, the core temperature of the egg that you put into the water, and how many eggs you are cooking (as having more eggs in a pan of water affects the heat of the water). The altitude of where you are cooking your egg will also affect how long it takes to boil!

SOFT-BOILED EGGS

Place the eggs in a pan just big enough to hold them and cover them with cold water. Place on a high heat and bring to the boil. When the water boils, remove from the heat and leave covered for 3½ minutes. Serve with 'soldiers' of toast buttered and spread with the yeast spread of your choice. The old-school way is just to put the eggs into boiling water for 4 minutes.

HARD-BOILED EGGS

As above, but leave for 10 minutes. Cooking them slowly like this will stop that unsightly dark ring forming around the yolk, which is caused by cooking your eggs too long and at too high a temperature. Remember that cooling the eggs down like this stops them continuing to cook through the presence of residual heat. If you want to put boiled eggs with softer, juicier yolks on your salads, cook them for 7 minutes. Having said all that, I have also dropped eggs into boiling water for 8, 9 and 10 minutes and got lovely hard-boiled eggs with moist, vibrant yolks and not a trace of 'ring', so don't sweat about it!

TO CHECK HOW HARD-BOILED OR SOFT-BOILED YOUR EGGS ARE

- If you spin the egg on a benchtop, this will tell you how well the egg is cooked. If the egg is hard boiled it will spin evenly. If it is very soft boiled or uncooked, the liquid (that is, the unset yolk) inside will make the egg wobble unevenly and fall over. Soft-boiled eggs tend to wobble just slightly.

- The best way to get perfect eggs, if you are making loads of them, is to cook a couple more than you need and then crack one of them just before you think they'll be ready to check the cooked status of your batch of eggs. Remember that while you are checking, the other eggs are still cooking!

POACHED EGGS

Damnable poached eggs. There are more suggestions for cooking poached eggs than there are breeds of chook. I've tried them all, with mixed levels of success. After much trial and error I reckon the best is to fill a large, high-sided frying pan or braising pan with water and bring it to the boil. When it's bubbling, turn off the heat and carefully crack a couple of eggs into the water, making sure the egg slips into the water gently – use a ladle or cup. Then leave the egg for a few seconds over 3½ minutes for a soft, runny poached egg, or longer until it has reached the level of cooking you like. Use a slotted spoon to very gently lift out the egg.

I like my poached eggs on buttered toast with bacon and loads of black pepper. So does my son William. He has good taste!

FRIED EGGS

The trouble with fried eggs is that the bottom of the egg, nestled in spitting-hot oil and on a metal surface directly conducting heat, will cook more quickly than the top. This leaves you with three options – overcook the base of the egg so it becomes glassy, plasticky or even burnt in order to get a cooked top; put up with the undercooked top for a perfect base; or risk breaking the yolk of the egg by flipping it to create eggs 'sunnyside down', as they say in the States. The only other way is to spoon some fat from the pan over the egg while it's cooking, which is effective but can mean singed hands from fat spatters.

The best way to cook fried eggs that I've found is Heston Blumenthal's way. He suggests using a frying pan with a lid (ideally glass, so you can watch the egg). The idea is that this way the top of the egg gets cooked by the steam in the pan while the base fries.

I love fried eggs in a cheap white bread sandwich with butter and tomato sauce. This goes especially well with a hangover. Or try using hoisin sauce and some shredded spring onions instead. For some reason this combo always reminds me of Kylie Kwong, but that's weird because I've never been out drinking with her – or not that I can remember.

SCRAMBLED EGGS

I like my scrambled eggs creamy rather than bouncy. You can achieve this with loads of cream and butter, but don't. The far more virtuous alternative is to cook the eggs slowly over a low heat, stirring a lot. Basically this helps the proteins set without them clumping and thus making the eggs seem far, far creamier. Mix the eggs with a little bit of water before popping them in a pan greased with a little melted butter.

I love scrambled eggs with a dusting of fresh dill and some slices of cold smoked trout or hot smoked salmon.

OMELETTE

Mix 3 eggs with a splash of water. Season with salt and pepper. Pour into a small hot frying pan. Using a spatula, draw the eggs into the middle of the pan as they start to set. When the omelette becomes like folded crumpled sheets of almost-set eggs, leave the omelette alone and let the underside set. The top should look a bit runny still. Add any fillings you might want. Fold over one edge so the omelette becomes a half-moon shape. Drop some knobs of butter into the vacant side of the pan, heat it until it froths, then finish the omelette by spooning over the hot melted butter. Serve. The classic omelette is pale, but I like mine a little golden. Mushrooms, grated cheese, ham and soft herbs in any combination make perfect fillings.

PANCAKES

Mix 1 cup of flour with 1 egg. Now slowly whisk in 1½ cups of milk. Add a knob of melted butter, a pinch of salt and a little sugar. Leave to thicken in the fridge for half an hour before using.

MERINGUES

This is one of the simplest recipes of all. Just whisk 3 egg whites to soft peaks and then gradually beat in 1 cup of caster sugar until the combination looks glossy. Pipe or spoon the mixture onto a nonstick baking tray, or a tray lined with baking paper, and cook in a preheated 120°C oven for 1 hour. Then turn off the oven and leave the meringes to dry out for a bit. Sandwich together similar-sized meringues with whipped cream as the base for a fancy dessert, or break them up and mix with whipped cream, fresh berries and a little raspberry coulis for a take on Eton mess.

TIPS & TRICKS

- Adding a pinch of cream of tartar to the whites when they are frothy will help them plume and hold their peaks.

DESSERTS

It is a little-known fact that humans, like cows, have more than one stomach. They have four and I believe we have two – one for savoury food and the other for desserts. This explains why there is always room for pudding or a little piece of choccie after even the biggest feed. While the first stomach is full, the sweet stomach is still empty!

What is getting confusing for the body, however is, the shifting flavour profile of desserts. Homely desserts now often chase a fashionable salty edge to cut against the sweetness, whether it's a salty caramel with your sticky toffee pudding or a little sprinkle of good flake salt to make your chocolate tart really crackle and pop. You'll also find a little kick of salt really brings alive that pastry for a lemon tart or your apple crumble topping.

It's pretty obvious from looking at me that I think dessert 'matters', but my natural indolence – that's a sneaky hidden way of admitting I'm lazy – means that I seldom can be faffed making something too labour intensive. I'll leave that to restaurants with teams of chefs in the pastry section. That's why most of the desserts here are about delivering the maximum punch of flavour and texture for the minimum effort. Some are 'set and collect' dishes where the oven does the work, others are just the judicious pairing of ingredients to give you a pudding that seems like you've done far more hard graft than you actually have.

Of course no section on desserts would be complete without a little help in terms of what to serve with them. There are usually only two answers round our place – whipped cream or ice cream of some sort.

Getting the best whipped cream is simple. Cream whips because chilled fat forms crystals that helps the proteins to break free and allow the fat to reform around bubbles of air, thus trapping it. So the secret is to ensure that your cream is cool before whipping it. Also note that creams with a high fat content, like double cream, will whip faster but be less fluffy and stiffer. Conversely, a lower-fat pouring cream will take much longer to whip, but you'll get lots of volume. Finally the best, airiest results come from hard work with the hand whisk, which is another reason why it's a good idea to have children.

Things start getting more complex when it comes to ice creams and other frozen desserts such as granitas, sorbets, parfaits, semifreddo or shop-bought ice creams. Freezing liquids like fruit juices or strong coffee and then grating them up with a fork to make granitas can give a dish lovely contrast in terms of temperature, texture and flavour. It is dead easy too.

Ice creams are a little trickier. You'll find that most classic ice-cream recipes tend to revolve around a custard that is cooked out and then chilled before being churned. This causes two problems. Firstly, it takes time and hard work – that's why my favourite basic ice-cream recipe (right) doesn't need to be cooked and can be churned straight away! Secondly, as most homes don't have an ice-cream machine, I've included recipes for a couple of 'ice creams' in this book that don't require the use of any technology other than a processor and a freezer!

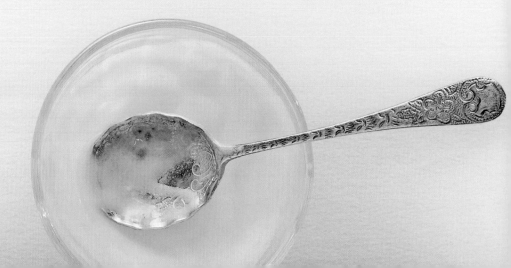

FAILSAFE QUICK ICE CREAM

2 eggs
165 g (¾ cup) caster sugar
500 ml (2 cups) plain cream
250 ml (1 cup) milk
1 teaspoon vanilla extract

Whisk the eggs until light and fluffy. Mix in
the sugar until it is completely blended. It
should look airy and pale yellow. Now whisk
in the cream, milk and vanilla until it's a lovely
velvety mess.

Pour the mixture into an ice-cream maker
and turn it into ice cream. Scrape out the
ice cream once it has set and freeze. Remember
to remove the ice cream 5 minutes before you
want to serve to help it soften.

*Note: This ice cream uses uncooked eggs,
so if this is a concern for you or for your
physician – or you don't have an ice-cream
machine – just buy a good commercial ice
cream instead. You can always jazz it up
easily, as you'll see over the page!*
Serves 6

TIPS & TRICKS

- Cooling the ice-cream mixture while it is
  moving is what makes for good ice cream.
  The quicker you freeze ice cream the
  smoother it will be. So for the best
  ice cream, making smaller batches is best.
  I should also note that while I am not a
  fan of splashing out dollars on swanky
  kitchen equipment, an ice-cream machine
  (along with a table top pizza oven and a
  kitchen thermometer) is one I couldn't live
  without, as making it without an ice-cream
  machine is too painstaking and never gives
  perfect results.

q ways with...
SHOP-BOUGHT ICE CREAM

Just because you don't have an ice cream machine doesn't mean you can't be creative by pimping some good-quality store-bought ice cream (like the caramelised peanut ice cream on page 178), adding a delicious simple sauce or combining familiar ingredients to create a dessert taste sensation that'll have your friends and guests 'oohing' and 'aahing' like they are at the dentist – but without the high-pitched drilling sounds. Basically, ready-made ice cream is a playground for the inner child in you – so go a little wild and experiment with ideas of your own as well!

SAUCES

In the world of sauce there are few things simpler than melting Mars bars to create a delicious fudgy chocolate sauce. Slice up 4 Mars bars (200 g) into small chunks. That allows for 12 g that will inevitably be lost (into your mouth) while cutting! Warm these chunks gently in a metal bowl over a pan of simmering water. The bowl must be bigger than the pan so it covers it. The water should not be so high that touches the bottom of the bowl. As the chocolate starts to melt, stir in 50 ml of cream. This will warm and thus further help the melting process – as well as giving the sauce a rich sheen. Yes, a little Kahlua, Bundy or cheap bourbon can be added, but do warm it before adding. And don't use too much; frankly it is far better to drink it than eat it! Pour the warm sauce over your ice cream of choice – vanilla, chocolate or raspberry ripple.

If the Mars bar sauce has suspiciously bogan overtones to you, then the juniper and cucumber notes of a traditional gin syrup are distinctly posh. To make this warm 250 ml (1 cup) of gin, 12 juniper berries (optional) and the green skin of half a long cucumber together in a pan. Mix in 220 g (1 cup) of caster sugar so it dissolves. Stir. Bring to the boil. Remove from

the heat and remove the cucumber skin. The syrup should be thick and sticky. Let it cool down a bit but while it is still warm stir in another 125 ml (½ cup) of gin bit by bit until your syrup has a smooth pouring consistency and a nice hit of gin. Place aside until you need it. For an interesting textural garnish take your skinned half cucumber and cut in half lengthways. Using a teaspoon scrape out the core of seeds from the cucumber's centre and discard these. Cut the firm remaining flesh into a small dice (2 mm). Pack this dice into a small bowl and cover with a little of the gin syrup. After an hour the syrup's sweetness will draw the water out of the cucumber, giving it that interesting texture. Drain before serving. Serve the gin syrup on a mix of vanilla ice cream and lemon sorbet. Decorate with the candied cucumber dice. For a further twist on a gin and tonic, take a small bottle of tonic and simmer it with the zest of half a lemon until reduced by half. Then freeze in a small plastic container. When serving blitz or scrape a sharp-edged spoon over the surface the top of the frozen tonic to create a tonic granita to further garnish the vanilla ice cream. There is something lovely about the icy crunch of the granita against the rich creaminess of the ice cream.

Ice cream also loves a salty caramel. For the perfect salty caramel sauce, please first invest in some good flake salt like Murray River pink salt or Maldon which is one of my few must-haves in the kitchen. I use it as a finishing salt to add both saltiness and also crunch to dishes just before they are served. First make a caramel by heating 1 cup of sugar with ¼ cup water in a high sided pan. Do not stir the caramel but carefully swirl the pan if needed as you take it to a rich golden colour. This is where things get interesting and as you add your next ingredients to the scoldingly-hot caramel expect it to foam up alarmingly so be careful. When the caramel cooks and bubbles its way to a rich

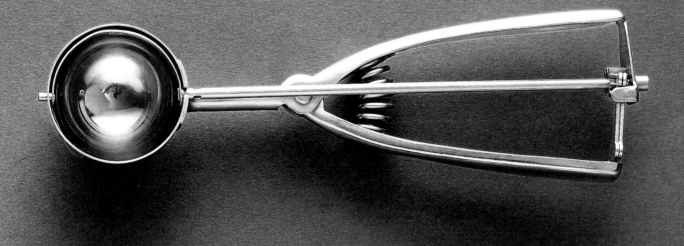

amber or bronze colour, carefully whisk in 60 g of butter cut into chunks. Keep the caramel over the heat while you do this. Then remove the pan from the heat and stir in ½ a cup of thick cream. Finally add a teaspoon of salt. Now leave your sauce to cool. Before serving, if the sauce is too thick to pour then warm it slightly. It thickens as it cools. Then taste the sauce and if it needs more salt – I reckon it will – stir in half a teaspoon of flake salt. This will give you some lovely diamonds of crunch. Serve with vanilla ice cream. If you want more add something appley as the tartness of the apples is the perfect foil to the caramel. Think baked apples (core and cook these for 25 minutes in an 180°C oven – for the first 15 minutes, cover in foil) or just diced apple stewed with a little water and spices like cinnamon.

MIXING IN

Stir 2 teaspoons almond essence through 1 litre of softened vanilla ice cream. Mix it in with a fork and return to the freezer before serving. Serve garnished with pan-browned almond slices for crunch. This is delicious with cherries or any other fresh, grilled or stewed stone fruit like plums, nectarines or even the peaches on page 189. To take this dish to yet another level add a drop or two of rosewater (to taste) to the stone fruit when cooking or spritz the plates with the tiniest spray of rosewater. Peaches, rosewater and almonds are a match made in heaven or a Persian harem garden.

It became a bit of a standing joke when I started writing recipes for the 'Taste' section of your favourite metro newspaper that pretty much any dessert left overs – stewed fruit, apple crumble, lemon delicious, chocolate ganache – could be stirred through ice cream to make it extra delicious and ripply. The key here is to soften the ice cream, then stir in your leftovers and re-freeze immediately. Eat as soon

as possible. Speed of eating is important because you want anything you stir through with crunch to maintain that texture. It will soften if you leave it in the ice cream too long!

Of course you can also do the Aussie playtime classic of smashing up chocolate bars to stir into the ice cream. The Violet Crumble is especially adept at filling this role. Just bash a couple in their unopened packaging once or twice with a rolling pin and add. I also like adding torn chunks of Cherry Ripe along with a swirl of fresh cherry syrup. Make this by placing 200 g of cherries in a large pan, mashing them to split them and so some juice spills out. Add 3 teaspoons caster sugar and a pinch of flake salt. Cook until the cherries go mushy. Then remove the pits. Strain, return to the clean pan and add a splash of vodka (1 tbsp). Cook to reduce to a syrup, cool and then swirl through chocolate or vanilla ice cream with or without the bits of Cherry Ripe. Adding shards of frozen dark chocolate is a sexy addition.

SUNDAES ANY DAY

The final arena for experimentation is what you plate with your quality shop-bought ice cream. Any fresh or poached fruit or nuts are always good but the iconoclasm of the dude food movement has seen many young chefs adding interesting textures to ice cream desserts whether it is crushed salty pretzels, breakfast cereals, popcorn – perhaps popped with rosemary, or a crushed flavoured ice.

The secret here is to take the idea of the classic tall glass knickerbocker glory and place layers that look visually exciting but also give your spoon a bit of an archaeological journey when you dig into it. When I've got chocoholic friends coming whose minds I want to play with I'll freeze 300 ml of strong espresso and make a thick sauce from 100 g of (cont.)

melted dark chocolate mixed with a prune purée made from a cup of pitted prunes cooked down with ½ a cup of booze like a dark sweet sherry, muscat or brandy and passed through a sieve. Then just before serving I'll sneak into the kitchen, blitz the frozen coffee and pop it back in the freezer and then layer four glasses with prune sauce at the bottom, then a handful of Coco Pops and then a large dollop of rich (and thus usually expensive!) shop-bought chocolate ice cream. I'll top this with whipped cream and garnish with a spoon of the coffee granita from the freezer. Grate over some more dark chocolate and serve immediately. The prunes, chocolate and coffee all go wonderfully together. If you want to add more layers think of using things like crushed pretzels, a rubble of crushed almonds or fresh blueberries. This is one of those sinful decadent desserts that require six Hail Marys or a 4 km run after eating!

I'm also a fan of using some form of salty crumble piled on the plate, layered with ice cream and fruits, or even just mounded under a delicate quenelle of store-bought vanilla just like a real chef would do. Like the salty caramel sauce, this works especially if there is some fruit being served with the ice cream as the saltiness balances both the richness of the ice cream and the sweetness of the fruit. For this reason there's usually a plastic container of salty oat crumble somewhere in the house. Making this is as simple as mixing a ¼ cup each of slivered almonds, rolled oats, plain flour and soft sugar with a teaspoon of salt. Now rub in 100g of cubed, chilled butter to make lumpy crumbs. Place these on a baking tray and bake in a preheated 180°C oven and watch them until they turn golden. As it keeps well it is not a bad idea to make double or triple the quantities as it is quite addictive. Oh, and add more salt if you want as the pleasure of this mix is in pushing the saline hit to the edge! The kids LOVE this!

If that's all too weird just spin the classic banana split but make it with sticky bananas. Cut three bananas into approximately 1 cm chunks and add to a small saucepan with 40 g of melted butter mixed with 40 g of brown sugar. Cook until the banana warms to a slippery state. To plate, in a glass or small bowl put the banana, then the ice cream and then the Mars bar sauce (previous page). Top with finely crushed, or chopped, salty roast peanuts. There's no need for a cherry on top but it is funny!!!

A good crumble has it all: rich, tangy but stickily comforting soft fruit and a nuggety, toasty crust that has all the appeal of freshly baked biscuits. For me the best crumbles are built around seasonal ingredients that are as much about their tartness as their sweetness. Apples, rhubarb, plums and apricots all leap to mind with the formers' winter seasonality making them especially attractive. But why be limited to just one fruit when you could be adding a foil to these familiar crumble fruits. Obviously adding blackberries to an apple crumble is a classic, but what about quince or pear in winter, or blueberries, raspberries, strawberries, cherries or apricots as the weather improves? Dried fruit can give your crumble a bit of a fillip. Plump sultanas are a natural mate for apples but you can also try adding in cranberries, dates or even dried figs. Basically the whole point of the crumble is that it's as unselective as a cheap $50 Kings Cross flop house when it comes to who it'll let slip under its covers. Just use what's cheap and available – and ensure your crumble is buttery, golden and loaded with crunch. Crunch is vital to crumbles. Think about adding macadamias to crumbles with pineapples or almonds to crumbles with stone fruit. If feeling wacky, try adding breakfast cereals like cornflakes or Weet-Bix.

APPLE AND RHUBARB CUSTARD CRUMBLE

3 apples (use Granny Smith or anything tart and crisp)

1 bunch rhubarb (500 g), trimmed and chopped into 4 cm lengths

2 tablespoons custard powder

20 g butter

125 ml (½ cup) apple juice

50 g brown sugar

2 teaspoons ground cinnamon

juice of ½ lemon

Crumble topping

75 g butter, chilled

75 g (⅓ cup firmly packed) soft brown sugar

100 g (1 cup) rolled oats

30 g plain flour

½ teaspoon ground allspice

good pinch of salt

30 g (¼ cup) crushed hazelnuts

30 g (¼ cup) walnut pieces

vanilla ice cream or double cream, to serve

Preheat the oven to 160°C.

To make the crumble topping, rub the butter into the sugar, oats, flour, allspice and salt. It should look like lumpy breadcrumbs. Add the nuts and toss them through the mixture.

Peel and core the apples and cut them into 1 cm thick wedges. Pour the custard powder into a clean plastic bag. Add the apples and rhubarb and toss lightly in the custard powder. Discard any powder that doesn't adhere.

Generously butter an ovenproof dish deep enough so that it will give you a nice thick seam of apple under the crumble. Pour the fruit in the dish. Sprinkle with the apple juice, brown sugar, cinnamon and lemon juice.

Cover the fruit with a thick blanket of the crumble mix. Bake in the oven for 1 hour, or until the fruit is easily pierced with a skewer. The crumble topping will have started to brown. Turn up the heat so the top turns golden and the filling starts bubbling out a little at the sides.

Remove from the oven. Rest for 5 minutes before serving with a large dollop of vanilla ice cream or double cream.

Serves 4

TIPS & TRICKS

- To speed things up, you can pre-cook the apple with the apple juice and cinnamon in a saucepan first. When the fruit is almost cooked, put the mixture into the buttered dish, sprinkle on 1 tablespoon custard powder, the lemon juice and the brown sugar. Top with the crumble. Cook in an 180°C oven for 25 minutes or until the topping is golden.

Why is it that sometimes we have such short memories? Every time I stumble back across a bowl of cornflakes with cold milk or a couple of soft-boiled eggs with soldiers I am reminded how close they are to perfection and how I should eat them more often. Bread and butter pudding with its soft heart and satiny custard sits in the same pigeon hole for me – something I always love when I catch up with it again. So hello, my old friend; It's been too long. Now, let's not be strangers!

BREAD AND BUTTER PUDDING

125 g (1 cup) sultanas

250 ml (1 cup) hot black tea

1 loaf 1-day-old white bread, thickly sliced

3 tablespoons butter, at room temperature, plus extra for greasing

6 eggs

170 g (¾ cup) caster sugar

300 ml double cream

300 ml milk

½ cup brown sugar for topping

cream, to serve

2 crisp green apples, to serve

lemon juice, for acidulating the apples

Preheat the oven to 180°C.

Soak the sultanas in the hot tea.

Butter a large oval baking dish.

Beat the eggs with the sugar until thick and pale. Beat in the cream and milk.

Spread the bread with the butter. Cut each slice of bread in half on the diagonal. Arrange half in the baking dish. Scatter over the drained sultanas. Pour over half the custard. Layer the rest of the bread with the points facing upwards so you get nice crisp bits. Pour over the remaining custard and allow to stand for at least 10 minutes. Ideally 20!

Sprinkle with brown sugar. Place the baking dish in a larger, ovenproof vessel. Pour boiling water to halfway up the sides of your baking dish. Bake for about 40 minutes, or until the custard is just set and the top is lightly brown.

Remove from the oven and serve with cream and batons of raw green apple tossed with lemon juice.

Serves 6–8

TIPS & TRICKS

- Swank up those sultanas and give this gentle, comfortable hug of a pudding a touch of sophistication by soaking the sultanas in brandy instead of tea. Warm 125 ml (½ cup) brandy, add the sultanas and leave to soak for at least 15 minutes. When you need the sultanas, remove them from the brandy and add them to the pudding. Reserve the brandy and add it to the mixing bowl when you are beating the cream and milk into the eggs.

- Try some customisation for a new spin on this old classic. Add seedless grapes, or the zest of a lemon or an orange. Spread the bread with a thin smear of jam, or make like Nigel Slater and use marmalade. If you decide to do this, think about soaking your sultanas in warmed whisky! Or how about sprinkling a cup of chocolate chips between the bread?

- Don't just be limited to using slightly stale white bread. If you have, or can buy, stale panettone, brioche, croissant or fruit bread, they all make a fine bread and butter pudding.

Every cookbook should have a lemon tart recipe, I am instructed. I'm not sure if that is a little-known parish by-law or a superstition, like how sailing ships always used to have naked women as their wooden figurehead to calm the sea, but I'm happy to abide by this lore – assuming the lemon tart is suitably tart like this one is, and that it can also come topped with plumes of meringue that I can bury my face in!

LEMON TART

4 lemons
375 g (1⅔ cups) caster sugar
6 eggs
300 ml pure cream
1 egg, lightly beaten
icing sugar, to serve

Pastry
250 g plain flour
70 g icing sugar
70 g caster sugar
120 g chilled unsalted butter, chopped into small cubes
3 egg yolks
20 ml thickened cream

To make the pastry, combine the flour, icing sugar and caster sugar in a food processor, then add the butter and pulse until the mixture resembles breadcrumbs. Add the egg yolks and cream and process until it forms a ball. Form the pastry into a disc, wrap in plastic wrap and refrigerate for 1 hour.

Roll the dough out on a floured surface to 5 mm thick. Gently place into a floured 28 cm round tart tin with a removable base, allowing the extra pastry to overhang the edges. Preheat the oven to 180°C.

Line the pastry with baking paper, fill with rice and blind bake for 20 minutes. Remove the paper and rice, brush with beaten egg and bake for a further 5 minutes until golden brown.

Remove the tart case from the oven and reduce the temperature to 150°C. Use a sharp knife to trim around the edges and remove excess pastry.

To make the filling, juice the lemons and strain the juice; you should have 250 ml (1 cup). Whiz the juice and sugar in a blender. Add the eggs and combine until the sugar has dissolved. Add the cream and mix well.

Pour the mixture into the tart shell and bake for 35 minutes or until the filling is just set.

Let cool to room temperature and dust with icing sugar to serve. If you want to be fancy, sprinkle the top with extra caster sugar and take to it with a blowtorch.

Serves 12–16

MARSHMALLOW MERINGUE TOPPING

6 eggwhites
330 g (1½ cup) caster sugar
½ teaspoon cream of tartar
1 teaspoon vanilla extract

To make the topping, place the eggwhites, sugar and cream of tartar in the top of a double boiler over medium heat. Whisk until the sugar dissolves and the mixture is warm to the touch (about 4 minutes). Remove from the heat, add the vanilla, and use electric beaters to whip for 6–7 minutes or until stiff peaks form. Immediately pipe or spread over the tart and either blowtorch or put under a hot grill until golden brown.

Brett Graham is quite frankly the best Australian-born chef working in the world today. The three Michelin stars he's earned in London for The Ledbury, and my old local, the Harewood Arms, prove it, albeit not as convincingly as this simple chocolate dessert he taught me when I was in London last year. It is one of the simplest and one of the cleverest bits of no-fail cooking I've seen for a while and it should become a recipe that's a valuable part of your culinary arsenal.

SLICE OF CHOCOLATE WITH
CARAMELISED PEANUT ICE CREAM

Base
30 g butter
150 g plain chocolate biscuits, crushed

Topping
400 ml cream
400 ml milk
10 egg yolks
75 g sugar
400 g best-quality chocolate (70% cocoa content)

Ice cream
80 g (⅓ cup) sugar
150 g (⅔ cup) salted roasted peanuts
pinch of sea salt
500 ml tub good-quality vanilla ice cream

20 g plain chocolate biscuits, crushed, to serve

To make the base, warm the butter in a small saucepan until it starts to smell a little toasty and reaches the 'brown butter' stage. Mix the butter into the well-crushed biscuits. Press the mixture firmly into a rectangular tin (approximately 30 cm x 12 cm), preferably with a removable base, until the biscuit base is smooth and even. Pop in the fridge to set.

To make the slice topping, bring the cream and milk just to the boil.

Whisk the yolks and sugar together in a bowl until the mixture is thick and pale.

Whisking continuously, gradually pour the hot milk mixture onto the yolk mixture, stirring until thick and smooth. Return the mixture to a clean saucepan and cook over low heat until the mixture reaches 84°. (Time to use that valuable thermometer I told you to buy 60 pages ago!)

Break the chocolate into small pieces. Pour the cream mixture over the chocolate and stir until the chocolate has melted and the mixture is smooth. Pour over the chocolate biscuit base and smooth the surface. Leave to set for a few hours in a cool place.

To make the ice cream, melt the sugar in a saucepan over a medium heat and cook for 3 minutes or until a golden caramel forms. Add the peanuts and the pinch of sea salt. Pour into a tray lined with baking paper and leave to cool.

Remove the ice cream from the freezer and let it soften a little. Roughly chop the peanut toffee and reserve a few pieces to decorate the plate. Fold the remainder into the ice cream.

To serve, cut the slice into 8 even pieces then put each slice on a plate with a small spoonful of the crushed biscuits and a scoop of the ice cream. Sprinkle with the reserved candied peanuts.

Serves 8

Some people laughed and scoffed when I suggested this dessert. They didn't understand that if Christine Manfield can lionise the Golden Gaytime then me championing the lime fizz and smooth vanilla-creaminess of a Lime Splice was equally valid. Sure, the cheesecake here can be as easily topped with fresh raspberries but my kids love the Willy Wonka chemistry of making the jelly and the sherbet that makes this dessert pop like a mouthful of sour worms! One other thing ... like me, it looks best with the light behind it.

LIME SPLICE CHEESECAKE

Crust
150 g sweet biscuits
4 tablespoons melted unsalted butter

Filling
500 g cream cheese, at room temperature
110 g (½ cup) caster sugar
2 teaspoons vanilla extract
3 teaspoons powdered gelatin
60 ml (¼ cup) boiling water
315 g (1 cup) condensed milk

Lime Jelly
1 packet (80 g) lime jelly crystals

Lime Wizz Fizz
1 packet lime jelly crystals
30 g (¼ cup) icing sugar
7 teaspoons citric acid

zest of 2 limes and thin slices of lime, to garnish

Line the base and side of a 20 cm springform tin with baking paper.

To make the crust, finely grind the biscuits in a food processor, add the butter and blend to form moist sandy crumbs. Press the crumb mixture evenly over the bottom of the prepared tin.

To make the filling, beat the cream cheese, sugar and vanilla in an electric mixer until smooth and creamy.

Dissolve the gelatin in the hot water and set aside to cool. Fold the gelatin through the cream cheese mixture. Add the condensed milk and continue beating until smooth.

Pour the filling into the cooled crust and place in fridge to set for 3–4 hours.

Make the lime jelly according to the packet directions, using half the amount of water required, so that your jelly is double strength and extra springy. Set in a shallow tray in about a 1 cm layer. When set, cut into small cubes and use to decorate all over the top of the cake.

Make the lime wizz fizz by combining all the ingredients. Sprinkle over the top of the jelly. Arrange 3 slices of fresh twisted lime on top, cut the cake into slices and serve.

Serves 8

This treacle tart is a brilliantly simple peasant dessert to make at home. It's another dish that is there like mortar between the bricks of my early life. The trick here is to make sure that the filling is thick enough so the surface can go chewy but the inside remains rich and… well… treacly!

TREACLE TART

1 large sheet of store-bought shortcrust pastry

55 g (⅔ cup) fresh breadcrumbs (brown breadcrumbs work best)

250 g golden syrup (the paler the better; I like Tate and Lyle if you can get it)

zest and strained juice of ½ lemon

double cream or crème fraîche, to serve

Preheat the oven to 180°C. Line a 23 cm flan tin or ovenproof pie dish with the pastry sheets, trimming excess pastry from around the edge of the dish. Line the pastry case with a sheet of baking paper weighed down with uncooked rice. Blind bake for 8 minutes. Remove the paper and rice.

Pop the pastry case back in the oven until golden (about 5 minutes). Put the breadcrumbs on a baking tray and bake for 5 minutes. Stir, then dry in the oven for a further 4 minutes.

Warm the golden syrup. Mix the syrup with the crumbs and lemon juice. Fill the pastry case evenly with the mixture and bake for 30 minutes.

Serve with double cream or crème fraîche.

Serves 6

Raw apricots can often be a little floury and so I reckon the best way to eat them is how they serve them in the magical Indian city of Hyderabad. There, apricots are cooked with spices and sugar to make a dark, sweet dollop called khubani ka meetha. *That dish was the inspiration for this recipe which uses fresh apricots and omits dates. It results in a fresher, lighter version of the original. The combination of apricot and cardamom is a wee bit mind-blowing given the simplicity of the pairing!*

POACHED APRICOTS WITH CREAM

1.5 kg just-ripe apricots (about 16), blemish free
1 cup (220 g) sugar
1.5 litres (6 cups) water

12 cardamon pods
75 g (2/3 cup) flaked almonds
300 ml double cream

Wash and gently dry the apricots. Pick a wide pan that will hold the apricots in one layer.

Place the sugar and water in the pan and stir over low heat until the sugar dissolves, then increase the heat to medium. Crush the cardamom pods and add them to the syrup. Gently slip the apricots into the liquid. If necessary, add extra water so the apricots float. Increase the heat and gently poach the apricots at a simmer for about 4 minutes or until softened. Then immediately remove the apricots with a slotted spoon to a separate bowl. They will continue to cook, so it's better to take them out too early than too late!

Reduce the remaining syrup by a third or until it becomes thick, but not treacly. Strain the syrup and discard the cardamom pods and seeds. Set the syrup aside.

Toast the almonds, tossing them in a frying pan. Keep them moving and watch carefully that they don't burn.

Divide the apricots among the bowls. Drizzle on the syrup. Sprinkle with almonds and serve with a big dollop of double cream.

Serves 4–6

TIPS & TRICKS

- If there are any leftover apricots, remove their stones, mix them with the remaining syrup and stir the mixture through very slightly softened vanilla ice cream to make a delicious apricot ripple.

I love meringue, I love cream, I love berries. Together these flavours are as summery as those memories of sizzling your beach-wet bum cheeks on the searing hot vinyl of the family sedan. I wanted to pull these flavours together into a dessert that had a more intense riot of texture than the usual pavlova or Eton mess. That's where the idea of using another love – albeit one long-forgotten like a childhood sweetheart, jelly – came in. Jelly's firm but voluptuous springiness does give this dessert a nursery-playfulness but its sweetness is balanced by the acid presence of the fresh strawberry slushie. And both work wonderfully against the soft clouds of cream and the crunch and chew of meringues. This is one of those 'clean plate' desserts, but beware of the sugar rush that follows!

MATT'S MESS

4 egg whites, at room temperature

a pinch of salt

220 g (1 cup) caster sugar, plus extra if needed

1 packet (80 g) raspberry jelly crystals

500 g strawberries

1 ripe peach, sliced

juice of 1 lemon

300 ml cream, chilled

100 g slivered almonds, toasted

Preheat the oven to 120°C.

Using a beater on high speed, whisk the egg whites and the salt to soft peaks. Reduce the speed to medium and slowly add the sugar in a fine stream to ensure it gets properly incorporated into the meringue.

When you've added all the sugar, keep beating for a couple of minutes until the meringue looks thick and glossy. Check that the sugar is incorporated properly by rubbing the meringue foam between your fingers; if you feel any graininess, it needs more beating.

Lightly grease a couple of baking trays. Line with baking paper. Dollop the meringue onto the trays in generous dessertspoonfuls, leaving space between them to allow for spreading. Try to keep the dollops the same shape and size.

Pop in the oven for 20 minutes or until the meringues turn golden and are crisp on the outside. Then turn off the oven and leave the meringues in there to dry out. Leave the oven door slightly ajar if you can.

Hull the strawberries and blitz them with the sliced peach and half the lemon juice. Taste the purée. If it needs sweetening, add a little caster sugar. Then taste and add more lemon if required. Pour the purée into a small plastic container and pop in the freezer for 4 hours or until frozen.

Make the jelly as per the packet instructions, but use half the boiling water specified. Set the jelly in a small slice tray or flat-bottomed plastic container so when it is poured in the jelly is 1 cm deep and level. (Check this before you make the jelly by using the same amount of (cold!) water that you'll be using for the jelly until you find the perfect container. Pour out the water and dry the container before using it for the jelly.)

Remove the strawberry slush from the freezer. If it has frozen solid, give it a blitz in a food processor or blender to break it up. Cut the jelly into 1 cm cubes. Start buiding your dessert with a layer of slush, then meringue and whipped cream followed by the jelly, more cream and slush, then top with meringue and garnish with toasted slivered almonds.

TIPS & TRICKS

- For a more tropical (and more expensive) spin on this dessert that references your typical pavlova, dump the jelly and the strawberry slush. Instead arrange the cubed flesh of mango cheeks on each plate and slosh the juice and pulp of a passionfruit over the creamy seam of each meringue. Fresh!

Peaches, rosewater and almonds – these are the aromatic flavours that fire the imagination with images from Scheherazade – like a scratch 'n' sniff One Thousand and One Nights. *To take the dish to another level, when you serve the roast peach, spritz the plate with a little mist of rosewater. Of course we're in Australia, not a sultan's palace in Mosul, so forget the perfume and the fresh peaches and make this recipe with that post-war Aussie favourite – canned peaches. The most noble of canned fruit – after the pineapple ring.*

CANNED PEACHES WITH ALMOND CRUMBLE

6 plain (digestive) biscuits
110 g slivered blanched almonds
2 egg whites
110 g (½ cup) caster sugar
½ teaspoon vanilla extract

30 g butter, softened, for greasing
8 tinned peach halves (or use
4 ripe peaches, halved)
1 litre vanilla ice cream, to serve

Preheat the oven to 180°C.

Crush the biscuits with the almonds.

Whisk the egg whites until stiff, then keep beating and slowly pour in the sugar. Continue whisking until the mixture is white and glossy. Fold the almond and crumb mixture and the vanilla extract into the whisked egg whites.

Grease a baking tray with the butter and place the peach halves, cut side up, on the tray. Top each peach with a dollop of the almond mixture, making sure it fills the stone cavity.

Roast in the oven for about 20 minutes or until the topping is set and golden. Serve with vanilla ice cream.

Serves 4

TIPS & TRICKS

- If using fresh peaches that aren't ripe, you can pop them in the oven, untopped, for 10 minutes. Then top and cook for the remaining 20 minutes.

For some people travel broadens the mind; for me it tends to broaden the waistline. This recipe was given to me by a wonderful nonna I met in Greve last time I took my wife to Italy on one of our annual hand-swinging excursions. I've changed it slightly but it is still obscenely rich so a little goes a long way – sadly that's the tart and not me!

TUSCAN CHOCOLATE TART

200 g dark chocolate
(70% cocoa content)

100 g butter

4 eggs, separated

1 tablespoon rice flour
(or potato starch)

200 g icing sugar

70 g (½ cup) hazelnuts,
toasted and skins removed

extra icing sugar, to serve

fresh raspberries, to serve

crème fraîche, to serve

Preheat the oven to 150°C. Grease a 25 cm diameter ovenproof tart plate or metal flan tin. Line the bottom with baking paper.

Melt the chocolate and the butter together in a metal bowl over a pan of simmering water. Stir well to combine.

Whisk the egg yolks with the rice flour and icing sugar to form a stiff batter. Stir in the chocolate and butter mixture.

Whisk the egg whites until stiff, then delicately fold them into the chocolate mixture, lifting from the bottom of the bowl to the top using a thin-bladed silicon or plastic spatula if you have one.

Pour the chocolate mixture into the prepared tin and joggle the tin so the mixture spreads evenly. Sprinkle the hazelnuts evenly over the tart and bake for 20 minutes. The tart should still be fudgy in the middle.

When cooked, remove and leave to cool in a safe place.

Sieve a fine dusting of icing sugar over the finished tart. Slice and serve with fresh raspberries and crème fraîche on the side.

Serves 8

TIPS & TRICKS

- Even though I've suggested rice flour here (because it's a lot easier to find), the texture of this cake is better with potato starch.

Sometimes I dream about food. It an occupational hazard of my job and usually it's a good dream. But not this time. Not about this dessert. Doing this book I dreamt about this recipe getting me into terrible trouble – and it did! The next time I made it my butter was too cold and it wouldn't cream properly with the sugar. Disaster! I hope that was the moment that my dream was foretelling. If, however you hear of me being found dead in my office, ask if there were little custardy footprints around the body. If there were, it's the delicious wot done me in!

LIME AND PASSIONFRUIT DELICIOUS

3 passionfruit
2 tablespoons softened butter, plus extra for greasing
110 g (½ cup) caster sugar

2 eggs, separated
2 tablespoons plain flour
zest and juice of 1 lime
250 ml (1 cup) milk

Preheat the oven to 180°C. Generously butter a deep oven dish.

Using a sieve, strain the seeds out of the passionfruit pulp then free the remaining juice from the seeds using a wooden spoon.

Cream the butter and sugar together gradually using a hand whisk until the mixture is light, pale and fluffy. Add the egg yolks.

Mix the flour, lime zest and juice and passionfruit juice into the creamed butter.

Stir in the milk until a batter forms.

Beat the egg whites to stiff peaks. Gently fold about a quarter of the whites into the egg, butter and flour mixture with a sharp-edged metal spoon, then fold in the rest.

Pour the mixture into the prepared oven dish and put the oven dish into a baking dish.

Fill the baking dish with boiling water to come halfway up the delicious dish. Bake the delicious dish in this water bath for 30 minutes or until it is golden-topped and the bottom of the dish is full of rich, tangy custard.

Serve with cream or vanilla ice cream.

Serves 4–6

I have a dirty little secret about rice pudding. I like it left over the next morning, cut in a cold slice, and then fried in butter. This, like redheads, is now something that I have given up for the sake of my health – not that it stops me occasionally day-dreaming. About the rice pudding, not the redheads, obviously … although … stop it! Bad Matt!

OK, so that secret wasn't as dirty as it could have been, but then I'm a pretty vanilla sort of guy – a bit like this rice pudding. Vanilla it might be, but it's the sort of saucy under-the-covers vanilla that sends a sinful shiver down your spine when you taste the hidden depths of its sensual silky-smoothness. Grrrrr!

BAKED RICE PUDDING

500 ml (2 cups) milk
500 ml (2 cups) water
110 g (½ cup) sugar
1 vanilla pod, or 1 teaspoon vanilla extract

3 eggs, beaten
185 g (1 cup) arborio rice
jam of your choice, to serve
cream, to serve

Preheat the oven to 170°C.

Combine the milk, water and sugar (and the vanilla pod, if using) in a saucepan. Heat gently, stirring, until the sugar dissolves. Don't allow the mixture to boil.

Remove from the heat. Split the vanilla pod along its length and scrape out all the tiny seeds. Add the seeds to the milk and discard the pod. Or, if using vanilla extract, add it now. Stir in the eggs and rice, then pour the mixture into a greased large baking dish and bake for 1¼ hours, or until golden and just set.

Serve with a dollop of jam and some cream.

Serves 6–8

Sometimes when my wife is going through the accounts she questions some of my expenditure – the trips to eat at fancy restaurants overseas, the bar tabs spotted with expensive cocktails. I used to tell her it is all about 'benchmarking' but since coming up with this dessert I tell her it's all in the name of research. I saw pear and bourbon used wonderfully in cocktails in Buenos Aires and New York. They inspired this recipe. Yeah, she didn't buy that argument either! Still, this is a wonderful twist on the old vanilla, saffron or red wine poached pear we've all seen a million times. Not that I should denigrate those classic recipes. Saffron-poached pears with a custard scented with lavender flowers was my no-fail 'second date' dish – well, I cooked it for the woman I love when I started seeing her and I haven't had a second date since. To make lavender custard, throw a handful of clean lavender flowers into warm milk to infuse off the heat for 5 minutes before you reheat it to pour on your egg yolks to make the custard. It's a very simple process – just be careful not to over-steep or overheat the lavender as you want the delicate aromatics rather than the harsher oils that higher temperatures release.

BOURBON-POACHED PEARS WITH MAPLE PECANS

6 pears
250 ml (1 cup) cheap bourbon, plus extra bourbon for finishing
220 g (1 cup) sugar
1 vanilla pod
juice of ½ lemon

1 litre (4 cups) water
25 g (¼ cup) pecans
125 ml (½ cup) maple syrup
250 ml (1 cup) cream

To cook the pears, choose a saucepan that will snugly fit six of the pears standing up.

Fill the saucepan with the bourbon, sugar, vanilla pod, lemon juice, and 750 ml (3 cups) water. Pop on the heat and stir so the sugar dissolves.

Peel the pears but leave on the stalks. Turn each pear over to show its bum and use a teaspoon to remove the base and scoop out the core and seeds while leaving the pear whole.

Place the pears in the saucepan and top up with water so they are submerged.

Simmer the pears until tender. The length of time depends on how ripe the pears are, but leave yourself an hour as some supermarket pears are as hard as a Gorbals' grandmother. The pears are done when they can be pierced with a wooden skewer – a perfectly poached pear can be eaten with the gentle pressure of a spoon.

While the pears are cooking, make the candied pecans. Heat the maple syrup over medium heat in a small saucepan. The syrup will bubble, foam and reduce.

When the maple syrup is reduced by half, throw the pecans in and give them a toss to coat. Using a slotted spoon, scoop the pecans out onto a baking sheet lined with baking paper. Leave the pecans to cool.

Once the pears are cooked, remove them to a warm bowl. To make the bourbon syrup, place 2 cups of the pear cooking liquid back on the heat and reduce to a syrup. (Throw the rest away.) Stir in 2 tablespoons of bourbon. Taste. Add more if you like your bikie juice. The bourbon should be there but not too loud and strident – a bit like the best sort of security at an inner-city nightclub.

To serve, place a pear in each bowl and drizzle with the bourbon syrup. Pull apart some of the sticky maple-toffeed pecans and place in the syrup around the pear. Finish the plate with a dollop of the whipped cream. The pears can be served cold, hot or warm.

Serves 6

TIPS & TRICKS

- To make a vanilla pear cream to accompany the dessert, peel and juice a pear. If you don't have a juicer, grate the pear and squeeze out the juice with clean fingers. Remove the vanilla pod from the poaching syrup and scrape its seeds into the cream along with two tablespoon of the fresh pear juice.

Zabaglione is a delicious warm custardy foam that is a standard fallback dessert in my house – especially when friends drop over and end up staying for dinner. What's great is that it uses familiar ingredients you almost always have to hand and is equally delicious made with sweet dessert wine or sherry if you don't have marsala. It's also incredibly versatile. Here I've paired it with mango and champagne because I like the celebratory nature, and the foamy theatre, of the combination but it also works spooned simply – like a sweet, warm blanket of custardy fog – over loads of different biscuits, berries or poached or fresh fruits.

ZABAGLIONE, MANGO AND CHAMPAGNE

2 ripe mangoes
3 tablespoons caster sugar
6 egg yolks
125 ml (½ cup) marsala
zest of 1 lemon

750 ml bottle champagne or sparkling wine
12 macadamia nuts, smashed
3 cantucci biscuits, smashed

Cut the cheeks off the mango. Score the flesh north to south and east to west. Pop the cheeks by pushing the skin side inward so the outside skin of the cheek goes from convex to concave and the mango flesh pops out like blunt orange skyscrapers. Cut off this flesh and cut it into cubes. Place in four tall glasses.

Keeping in mind that your mixture is going to froth up a lot, pick a decent-sized glass or metal mixing bowl that fits snugly over a saucepan.

Now pour some hot water into the saucepan. Do not put in too much, as the bowl's base must not touch the water when placed over the saucepan. Steam from this water will gently heat the bowl and the whisked eggs will gently cook. If the bowl touches the water, you risk the eggs scrambling.

Whisk the sugar and eggs together in your bowl. Use an electric beater on high speed if you have one. When the eggs and sugar go creamy and pale, place the bowl over your steaming water.

Use an oven mitt or a clean dry tea towel to steady the bowl, as you don't want to get a nasty steam burn.

Continue whisking but at a slower speed until the mixture is foamy and a paler yellow colour. Keep the egg mixture moving to prevent it from cooking on the hot edges of the bowl.

Now steadily add 3 tablespoons marsala and lemon zest, while still whisking. I like the flavour of marsala, but you should add it gently until it reaches a flavour that you like. It's OK to add less than suggested.

The zabaglione is ready when the mixture falls in ribbons from the whisk or your whisk leaves a pattern on the surface of the foam – should take about 7 minutes. For a firmer foam, cook and whisk longer until soft peaks form.

At the table, pour a good splash of champagne onto the cut cubes of mango in each glass. It will foam crazily. When it dies down, spoon on the fresh zabaglione. Sprinkle with a few crushed macadamias and cantucci.

Serves 4

TIPS & TRICKS

- Let's face it – that bottle of marsala is probably just going to sit in the cupboard unused until the next time you make zabaglione. So make it lots. Give your 'zabag' a French twist by using those thin, crisp cat's tongue biscuits or go all Italian with sugar-topped savoiardi sponge finger biscuits for dunking. Or just be all Aussie and roughly crumble Anzac biscuits as a base to pour the foam over. This is great served with grilled apricots or on your plums.

TEATIME

I love the warm fuzzy feeling that comes from baking, but that is nothing like the joy of the warm, homely cake-shop aromas that waft through the house. Oh, and the sheer pleasure of eating the results. That's why I hope these recipes for simple, crowd-pleasing biscuits, show-stopping cakes and other sweet stuff will become the most stained pages in your copy of this book. So let's start with cake …

But first, some basics:

BASIC CAKEMAKING TIPS

- Make one basic error and you can destroy the whole cake.

- OK, sorry, that last tip was a little scary. The rest are far more supportive and encouraging.

- Always warm your oven by turning it on before you start the recipe so it is at the right temperature when you want to pop the cake in.

  - Measure everything out before you start cooking. You don't want to be scrabbling for your scales at a vital point in the cooking process. It will also help ensure that everything is at room temperature when you start cooking.

    - Having your eggs at room temperature makes for better aeration.

      - Oh, and room temperature butter will cream far more properly. You see, nothing else is too scary about cake making, is it?

        - Line your cake tins with baking paper when making heavier cakes and wetter mixtures. The batter for a sponge is lighter and airier, so just greasing the tin with butter and then flouring it will be enough to stop it sticking.

- Make the baking paper stick to the tin by lightly spraying the tin with oil first. In this case you don't need to use butter as it won't flavour the cake as it will when directly in contact with the batter.

- A whole range of factors will affect how long it takes your cake to cook. OK, I admit that this unknown quantity is a bit terrifying, but fear not, as there are ways around it …

- There are simple ways to tell if a cake is cooked. If the surface of the cake shimmers or wobbles slightly in the middle, it needs longer in the oven. Or stick a wooden skewer into the middle of the cake and if it comes out with cake on it, it needs longer. When it comes out clean the cake is cooked. Alternatively, lightly press a finger into the centre of the cake and if the cake springs back it's cooked. Phew! Easy!

- When spreading icing or jam on the bottom layer of a sponge, dollop the mixture in the middle and smooth outwards to the edges. Keep dolloping into the middle and spreading out until the face of the bottom cake is covered.

- When piping cream or icing, do the fancy edges first and then work into the centre.

- The tricky thing about baking is that you always seem to have the wrong old cake tin. Basically if your cake tin is larger than the 20 cm ones suggested here you can use them, but note that the cakes will cook more quickly.

- When adding chocolate to a mixture, always make sure it is melted and warm, or else it will seize. One of Adriano's key baking rules is 'chocolate warm, cream cold'.

HOW TO MAKE BUTTER

But before we bake, let's have some fun and make some butter because you can't have teatime without a slab of golden buttery goodness!

All you need to make butter is any leftover cream, sour cream or crème fraîche and flake salt, just make sure that it's cold.

Use a hand whisk, hand beater or electric mixer to beat the cream steadily. It will whip and then it will start to separate as the milky white buttermilk parts ways from the yellow butterfat particles.

Drain off the buttermilk and reserve it for use in pancakes or scones.

Keep beating until the fat starts forming into yellow popcorn-sized nuggets. Continue to regularly drain off the buttermilk as the cream lets go of it.

Pop the butter nuggets into a colander and wash them with iced water. Continue to wash the butter, squeezing it together lightly until all the remaining buttermilk is washed away. When the water poured over the emerging butter starts running clear and no longer looks cloudy, the butter is ready.

No buttermilk should be seeping out of the butter that's left behind and the butter you have should be creamy with a rich, glossy texture that's silky, not waxy. Form the butter into a pat and sprinkle it with flake salt.

Now make toast and smugly enjoy your own handmade butter melting into a nice piece of sourdough.

NOTE: Your yield of butter will depend on the fat content of the cream you are using and how much cream you are churning. But basically a litre of 35% cream will yield about 300 g butter. Use the butter quickly on toast or in your cooking and baking as it will not keep as long as commercial butter.

TAKING YOUR HOME BUTTER-MAKING TO THE NEXT LEVEL

Once you've made this 'resurrection' butter, you may well find yourself bitten by the butter bug, and you aren't alone! Artisan Aussie butter is all the rage in Australia's swankier restaurants. Pierre Issa, who is the butter whizz behind the Pepe Saya butter that has been popping up in cool Sydney restaurants, says the secret to making butter is using a good, heavy, thick farmhouse cream. He also lets the separated butterfat sit with the iced water on it for 20 minutes before kneading out the remaining buttermilk.

When making butter by hand, Naomi Ingleton of Victoria's Myrtleford Butter Factory likes to squidge butter under cold running water to 'wash' it. She has a simple tip for making cultured cream, which is perfect for turning into butter rather than just going the lazy route and using sour cream or crème fraîche. Basically you add 1 teaspoon of active natural yoghurt to 1 litre of cream, warmed to body temperature, and leave it overnight. This slightly sours the cream before it is churned. Souring the cream like this is important because it creates good bacteria that produce an aroma compound called diacetyl. This adds to the buttery flavour when the cultured cream is churned.

Naomi's final tip is somewhat more basic – if using a mixer to churn the cream, cover the bowl with a clean tea towel otherwise you'll splash buttermilk everywhere when it starts to separate out!

PERFECT RASPBERRY JAM

2 kg clean raspberries
1.75 kg sugar
½ lemon
glass jars (with metal lids) – enough to hold 6 cups
of jam (ideally 250 g jars are best)

Pick through the fruit, removing stalks, leaves and bad raspberries.

Squeeze the juice of the lemon half into a small bowl. Reserve the juiced half.

Wash the jam jars and metal lids in hot, soapy water until spotless and rinse well under hot water. Place jars on a baking tray that allows some space between them. Heat in the oven at 100°C for 25 minutes. Place the lids in a pan of water and bring to the boil. Simmer for 5 minutes. Place on a clean rack to dry.

Place the raspberries in your largest heavy-based pan (or, if you have one, nan's old wide-mouthed copper jam-making pan). Make sure it is spotless.

Add the sugar and lemon juice, place on high heat and start stirring with a long-handled wooden spoon. Ensure the mixture never stays in contact with the pan's bottom or edges for too long, or the fruit will stick and the jam will burn. The fruit will break down and release its juice, and the sugar will dissolve. Add the juiced lemon half.

Bring the mixture to the boil, stirring all the time. Keep the jam at a rolling boiling but not so overheated that it foams out of the pan.

After about 15 minutes you'll notice that the jam starts to smell a little cooked, and that it resists your wooden spoon as the liquid evaporates. Remove the lemon half. Watch how the jam behaves on the edge of your wooden spoon. Early on, it will run cleanly off. As it gets to the perfect setting point the mixture will roll down slowly, form little dollops and look a bit jellified. When that happens, it's ready.

Carefully ladle the jam into the jars (still on the tray) to fill them just past their shoulders. Screw on lids. Allow to cool, then wipe cooled jars clean.

Makes enough to fill 10–12 x 250 ml jars

TIPS & TRICKS

- If you make small batches the jam will retain more colour and the flavour will be truer.

LIME MARMALADE

I find lime marmalade goes brilliantly with sourdough toast, can be used as a glaze on pork and also sits nicely with the creamy saltiness of good feta – which I know sounds a bit weird – but it tastes great. The secret of good lime marmalade is the limes. Pick limes that have plump, perfect skins and feel heavy for their size. Old limes will make for leathery chunks in your marmalade.

22 limes (2 kg)
2 kg sugar

Soak the limes in warm water for 3 hours.

Sterilise more jars and lids than you think you'll need (see Perfect Raspberry Jam).

Dry and juice the limes. Put the juice aside.

Using a sharp knife, cut the limes into quarters and cut off the top. Slice the skins of the limes thinly. Place the slivers of skin into a large, wide-mouthed, heavy-bottomed pan. Pour in half the juice. Top up with water to cover the skins.

Simmer until the skins are tender. This will take at least an hour.

When the skins are cooked, mix the sugar and the remaining juice into the skins and the liquid they now sit in. Stir until the sugar dissolves. Bring the mixture to the boil and let it bubble away, stirring all the time with a wooden spoon, until the liquid starts to gel. This will take about 20 minutes. You'll notice that the marmalade starts to smell a little cooked, and that it resists your wooden spoon as the liquid evaporates. Watch how the marmalade behaves on the edge of your wooden spoon. Early on, it will run cleanly off. As it gets to the perfect setting point the mixture will roll down slowly, form little dollops and look a bit jellified. When that happens, it's ready.

Carefully ladle the marmalade into the jars to fill them just past the shoulders. Screw on lids. Allow to cool, then wipe cooled jars clean.

Makes enough to fill 14 x 250 ml jars

CRUMPETS

15 g dry yeast
½ cup warm water
500 ml skim milk, warmed to body temperature
1 teaspoon caster sugar
500 g plain flour
pinch of bicarbonate of soda
1 teaspoon salt

Add the yeast to the warm water in a bowl. Add the warmed milk to the yeast mixture, stir in the sugar and leave to stand for 10 minutes.

Mix the flour and salt in a large bowl and make a well in the centre. Little by little, pour the yeasty milk into the middle of the flour. Using a wooden spoon, mix into a smooth batter. Cover with a tea towel and stand in a warm place for an hour. The batter will be bubbly, light and somewhat elastic.

Mix the bicarbonate of soda and salt in a tablespoon of water and stir it into the batter.

Heat a flat-bottomed griddle or heavy frying pan and grease it with butter.

Grease four egg rings (or crumpet rings if you are that way inclined – yes, they do exist) and place the rings on the griddle or pan. Pour about 2 tablespoons of batter into each ring and cook for 4 minutes. The batter shouldn't totally fill up the rings because it will rise a little during cooking. Little bubbles will appear and burst on the surface. Ease off each egg ring and flip the crumpet to cook on the other side until golden brown.

Clean the rings and repeat, greasing them between batches.

Eat the crumpets warm with golden syrup or jam and butter.

Makes about 30

TIPS & TRICKS

• For a savoury Welsh-accented breakfast – well, crempogs are originally Welsh after all – serve crumpets with thinly sliced leeks, sweated in butter with some grated nutmeg. Serve with poached eggs and/or a slice of crumbly blue cheese.

Every so often I have quite a good idea. In 2011 this was persuading Sydney's dark lord of the sweet kitchen, Adriano Zumbo, to teach me how to cook the perfect sponge and chocolate cake. Admittedly, there was something rather funny about asking the cake-making equivalent of a rocket scientist to solve a Year Six maths problem, but the result is two sure-fire cakes that anyone can make even if the only time they've previously used cake tins was as makeshift cymbals on the kitchen floor.

As Adriano is a pastry chef you'll notice that the next two recipes have measurements that read like a complicated maths equation, but then top pastry chefs like Adriano and Rosio Sanchez (my banana bread queen) are like the children of an unlikely coupling between a Nobel-winning chemist and Salvador Dali.

Bear this in mind when baking: these are not recipes but chemical formulae and as such it's important to pay close attention to the process and the exact quantities. The pastry kitchen is not the place for cavalier cooking – not if you want to get spectacular results. Cavalier cooking belongs back in the pasta section where the recipes have far great tolerances! Having said that, making the chocolate curls for this cake is about the most fun you can have with your clothes on. (Do let me know if it is even more fun with them off!)

So, time to bake!

This chocolate cake is like a chocoholic's dream – light moist chocolate cake, covered AND filled with chocolate icing and then smothered in curls of chocolate. This is jolly good news as the icing covers any problems that might occur with your cake and the curls cover any problems that might occur with smoothly applying the icing!!!

CHOCOLATE CAKE

200 g plain flour

24 g cocoa powder

1 teaspoon bicarbonate of soda

½ teaspoon baking powder

½ teaspoon salt

64 g unsalted butter, at room temperature

320 g caster sugar

2 eggs, beaten

144 g sour cream

200 ml hot water

500 g dark chocolate (70% cocoa content), to decorate

Frosting

150 g chocolate (use one with 70% cocoa content, the best you can afford), melted

440 g butter, at room temperature

250 g (2 cups) icing sugar

2–3 tablespoons milk

Preheat the oven to 170°C. Spray two 20 cm cake tins with oil and line the base and sides with baking paper.

Sieve together the flour, cocoa powder, bicarbonate of soda, baking powder and salt.

Put the butter and sugar in a food processor or electric mixer and process or beat until crumbly. Then, with the motor or beaters still going, add the eggs a little at a time until incorporated. Add the sour cream and mix.

Keep the machine going and sprinkle in the sieved flour and cocoa mixture. Add the hot water to help activate the bicarbonate of soda. Mix just until combined. Kids plus beaters equals good times – assuming you've remembered to remove the beaters from the base.

It will look scarily liquid, but pour it equally into the two cake tins and bake for about 25–30 minutes or until a skewer inserted into the centre comes out clean.

When cooked, remove the cakes from the tins, gently turning them out onto a cooling rack.

To make the frosting, melt the chocolate in the microwave on low power. Use 1-minute bursts and stir gently with a rubber spatula after each burst, until the chocolate is melted and smooth.

Cream the butter and sugar until pale and fluffy.

Then add the melted chocolate. The chocolate must be warm or it will stiffen and become grainy. Mix in enough milk to help loosen the mixture.

Trim the tops of the cakes if they are domed, so they are flat on both the top and the bottom.

Place one cake, top side up, on a flat board. Cover the top and sides with some of the frosting.

Pop the other cake upside down on the top of the first iced cake. Cover the top and sides of this with more of the frosting. Using smooth strokes and a flat-bladed knife, smooth the icing round the side. The frosting will mound up at the top edges of the cake, so smooth the top from the sides inwards. It doesn't need to be too neat as we'll be covering it with chocolate shavings. Just make sure all the cake is covered.

Melt the 500 g decorating chocolate in the microwave. Using long stokes with a flat palette knife, spread the chocolate in a long stripe on a cold surface (such as a marble slab) with long strokes. Spread it to about 1 mm thick. It should be very thin so when you shave it you get thin curls to decorate the cake.

With the palette knife, move the top layer of the spread chocolate around to help with cooling. When the chocolate is semi-set but still soft, draw a sharp cook's knife in quick, confident long strokes at an angle across the chocolate stripe so you shave up curls.

Using a skewer or toothpick (so your body heat doesn't melt the chocolate), gently lift the curls and shards and sprinkle all over the frosted cake so they cover it. Press them in a little if need be. If pressing them in with your hands, do so quickly and carefully so the curls don't melt.

If this is too much palaver you could just cover the cake with grated chocolate, but it won't looked nearly as good.

Serves 8–10

CHOCOLATE CAKE

SPONGE CAKE

SPONGE CAKE

butter, softened, for greasing
6 eggs
185 g caster sugar
165 g plain flour, plus extra for dusting
seeds scraped from ½ vanilla pod (see Tips and Tricks)
zest of 1 lemon
icing sugar, for dusting

Jam filling
300 g fresh or thawed frozen raspberries
25 g sugar
4 g pectin

Cream filling
250 ml cream (35% butterfat)
seeds scraped from 1 vanilla pod
25 g caster sugar

Preheat the oven to 170°C. Using well-softened butter and a pastry brush, grease two 20 cm cake tins. The butter needs to still be creamy in consistency. Dust the tin with flour.

Warm a mixing bowl either over a flame if it is metal or with warm water if it is glass, ceramic or plastic. This is especially necessary on a cold day.

Roughly mix the eggs with a fork and pour them into the warmed mixing bowl. With an electric mixer on slow speed, whisk in the sugar until combined. Then turn the speed up to medium. Leave the eggs and sugar alone for a while with the mixer going, as the eggs need time to develop strength. Whisk too fast and they'll puff up quickly but they might collapse later.

Sieve the flour onto a long sheet of baking paper. This removes lumps and helps the flour not to recompress, hence making it easier to fold into the eggs.

Continue beating the eggs and sugar until the mixture is thick and glossy. Mix in the scraped vanilla seeds and the lemon zest.

The mixture is ready when it is at about the soft peak stage and it falls from the whisk in thick, slow ribbons. Note that if in doubt, slightly under-mixing is better than over-mixing.

Remove the bowl from the machine. Sprinkle half the flour onto the eggs and fold in using a plastic or silicon spatula. When folding, the technique is to slice and scrape around the outside of the bowl, lifting the mixture and folding it into the centre. This should be a slow, methodical movement. Make sure you get your spatula into the well at the centre of the bowl as the flour tends to hide here.

When the first batch of flour is combined, add the rest. Remember that every time you fold you knock a little bit of air out of the eggs, and it is this air that gives the sponge its lightness. (This is all far harder when Adriano is standing next to you watching your technique and voicing his concerns for any rough handling of his eggs.) Don't be hesitant, be confident and sure – just like when you are shop-lifting.

Fill the two tins with equal quantities of the mixture, leaving space at the top of the tin for the sponge to rise.

Bake for 20–25 minutes or until the cakes are golden and set and a skewer comes out clean. Alternatively, lightly press a finger into the centre of the cake and if the cake springs back it's cooked. For those with a thermometer, the cake is ready when the core temperature has reached about 88°C.

While the cake is cooking, make the fillings.

To make the jam filling, mash or blitz the raspberries, then pass them through a sieve so you get a fine purée. You should end up with about 400 g purée. Heat this purée with the sugar, sprinkling in the pectin as you gently mix. Bring the fruit to an enthusiastic boil, then remove from the heat when the fruit starts to gel and coats the back of a wooden spoon. Put the raspberry jam to one side to set and cool. (Using warm jam will risk melting your cream).

To make the cream filling, lightly whisk the cream, vanilla seeds and the sugar together until firm but still soft.

When the cakes are cooked, remove them from the oven, let them rest for 5 minutes, then turn out onto a wire rack. Rest them upside down, as the base will become the top and you don't want wire marks on your cake's top. When the cakes are cool, use a bread knife to trim off any bits of crusty sponge that may have risen over the edge of the tin like love handles over the top of tight hipster jeans.

Place one cake bottom-side down and dress the top with the jam and the cream. Mix up the jam a bit before you start spooning it on as it might have started to gel. Start in the centre and spread the jam outwards to the edges. You can apply the cream artistically using a piping bag, or just dollop it on. Either way it will still taste great.

Now gently top with the other sponge, base up. Dust thickly with icing sugar and serve with a nice cup of tea.

Serves 10–12

TIPS & TRICKS

- Adriano dresses his sponges with a dark brown dust made from ground heavily roasted vanilla beans, which have a taste between coffee and wood smoke. This vanilla, 'taken to another level' as Adriano describes it, kicks against the sweetness of the icing sugar. To get this smoky vanilla dust, roast a couple of used vanilla pods until they blacken and dry. Then blitz them in a spice grinder before use.

- If you can't get your hands on vanilla pods or can't be bothered making the jam, just use good-quality shop-bought alternatives. One teaspoon of vanilla extract is equivalent to 1 vanilla pod.

Recipes travel. This orange cake comes from the Middle East via the wonderful Claudia Roden and then to me via a country farmhouse kitchen in the rural west of Victoria that's home to one of the best cooks I know. My old flatmate Jen introduced me to baking biscuits and her fingerprints (and her culinary sensibilities) echo to me through this book. This gluten-free cake is great to bake during winter when oranges are cheap and you need a little sunshine in your life! You can have it for tea or serve it for dessert.

JEN'S ORANGE CAKE

2 oranges, washed
250 g slivered almonds
8 dried apricots
220 g (1 cup) caster sugar
5 eggs
1 teaspoon baking powder

Syrup
1 orange, extra
110 g (½ cup) caster sugar
125 ml (½ cup) water

icing sugar, for dusting
double cream or Greek yoghurt,
to serve

Preheat the oven to 150°C. Grease a 22 cm round cake tin and line the base and side with baking paper. Lining is very important as otherwise your cake might stick and the middle drop out.

Place the oranges in a plastic bag and microwave on high for 12 minutes. Do not seal the bag tightly and take care as you remove them from the microwave, as they will be very hot and steam will escape from the bag when opened. Cool the oranges enough to cut in half and remove any pips.

Roughly chop the almonds by pulsing them a couple of times in a food processor.

Place the oranges, skin and all, in the food processor with the almonds and apricots and chop finely. Add the caster sugar, whiz for a couple of seconds, then add the eggs and baking powder. Whiz for 5–10 seconds, then pour the mixture into the tin. Cook for 1 hour or until a skewer comes out clean when tested. Leave the cake to cool in the tin, then turn out onto a wire rack.

Make the orange syrup while the cake is cooling. Zest and juice the extra orange (you should have around 125 ml (½ cup) orange juice). In a small saucepan over medium heat, combine the juice, zest, sugar and water. Stir until the sugar dissolves. Increase the heat and boil for 10 minutes without stirring. Take off the heat and allow to cool.

Serve the cake dusted with icing sugar and with double cream or Greek yoghurt and the orange syrup on the side.

Serves 12–16

TIPS & TRICKS

- For a twist, ice with a cream-cheese icing (as for a carrot cake) and decorate with little chunks of dried apricots soaked in warm Grand Marnier and candied pistachios.

Compared to most of my recipes, this one does seem like a lot of palaver and yes, it does take hours to make and prepare, and yes it is also true that all these steps may not be necessary. Having said that this is my mother's recipe and I'm just too scared to fiddle with it! My only areas of extemporisation are with the dried fruit and the booze you should use. For this I follow the time-honoured tradition of 'what's in the cupboard'. Basically pantries always seem to be full of packs of dried fruit, pastas, chutneys and jams that are mostly used, meaning there are scrabbly bits that need to be used up. I can't do much about the chutneys and jams here, but this fruit cake sorts out those dribs and drabs of currants, sultanas, dried apricots, prunes or dates. It also help finish up that tin of black treacle you bought for making the Boston baked beans (see page 160) as well as that annoying quarter bottle of booze that's cluttering up the cupboard.

MY MUM'S FRUIT CAKE RECIPE

125 ml (½ cup) sweet sherry, brandy, rum or whisky

zest and juice of 1 orange

250 g (1½ cups) seedless raisins

250 g (1½ cups) sultanas

150 g currants

250 g mystery dried fruit, such as dried apricots, prunes or dates, or a mix of the three, cut into little fingernail-sized pieces

225 g butter, at room temperature

225 g (1 cup firmly packed) dark brown sugar

2 tablespoons black treacle

4 eggs, at room temperature

275 g plain flour

¼ teaspoon bicarbonate of soda

1 teaspoon ground cinnamon

1 teaspoon ground mixed spice

1 teaspoon salt

150 g (⅔ cup) glace cherries – the expensive real ones, not the fake jellies, please!

110 g (⅔ cup) whole blanched almonds

Ideally, the day before you bake you should prepare your fruit. Warm the booze and the orange juice on the stove. Add the raisins, sultanas, currants and your mystery dried fruit. Throw in the zest. Warm through then pour the lot into a plastic or ceramic bowl. Leave them to soak overnight until they plump up and get all squishy.

Prepare a 23 cm round or a 20 cm square tin cake tin by buttering the base and sides. Cut a piece of baking paper to the exact size to line the base of the tin. You can line the sides as well if you can be bothered. If you are a devil-may-care risk taker ... don't! But that sounds a little cavalier to me.

Now take five sheets from a good-quality family newspaper – any respected metro tabloid like the *Herald Sun*, *Daily Telegraph*, *Courier Mail* or *Adelaide Advertiser* will do – and place the tin in the middle of them. Lift up the newspaper and wrap it tightly around the sides of the tin, securing it with about 1 metre of string. This is to insulate the cake so it cooks evenly. Trim the excess edges off the paper so just a small collar remains above the top of the tin.

Preheat the oven to 150°C.

In a large metal or ceramic mixing bowl and using a whisk or an electric mixer, cream the room-temperature butter and sugar together for at least 5 minutes, or until the result is pale, fluffy and largely increased in volume. Now beat in the treacle in a thin dribble.

 CONTINUED

CONTINUED ...

Using a fork, roughly mix the room-temperature eggs together so the yolks break and the whites are well marbled. Slowly beat in the egg bit by bit. First add about one-sixth of the egg. Beat it in so it's fully incorporated. Now add some more egg and beat it in properly. And so on. After you've added about two-thirds of the eggs, beat in about 1 tablespoon flour. This should stop the creamed butter and eggs curdling. Now beat in the rest of the eggs in two batches.

Phew, almost there. Next sieve the flour, bicarbonate of soda, spices and salt into the egg mixture. Add the soaked (and drained) fruit, the cherries and half the almonds. Stir together with a wooden spoon.

Fill the cake tin with the mixture and smooth out the top. Now make a pattern on the top with the remaining almonds. Cover the top with foil and bake on an oven tray for 90 minutes.

Now reduce the temperature to 140°C, remove the foil and cook for a further 90 minutes.

Depending on your oven, the cake may now be cooked. Check it by piercing with a skewer. If the skewer comes out clean, it is definitely cooked. If it has a lot of cake mix stuck to it, then it needs another 30 minutes. If it has a little bit of cake on it – and you like your fruit cake a little sludgy in the middle – just check it again closer to the edge. If it's set there (and basically the skewer comes out clean) then take the cake out now.

Leave to cool in the tin. Then remove and wrap in baking paper and then a layer of foil (or see the tip below). Store in an airtight cake tin or plastic box. Try to avoid cutting it for a week or two so the cake can mature.

Serves 8–12

TIPS & TRICKS

- If you are more of an online/i-Pad app sort of newspaper reader, then you can always place your cake in a tray of sand in the oven to insulate it instead of wrapping the tin in newspaper.

- Maturing a fruit cake is a skill all of its own. I like to mature mine for 4–6 weeks. Grab some plastic wrap, a sheet of muslin big enough to wrap the cake and the bottle of booze you used to soak the dried fruit. Soak the muslin in the booze and squeeze out the excess. Pull out a large length of plastic wrap. Lay the booze-soaked muslin on top. Place the cake in the middle of the muslin. Brush half a glass of your booze onto the top of your cake. Now lift the side of the muslin so it covers all sides of the cake. Secure the plastic wrap around it. Now wrap in another layer of plastic wrap and then a layer of foil. Place in an airtight plastic box or cake tin. Open every week, brush with more booze and reseal. Eat after 4–6 weeks.

THE 14 GOLDEN RULES of SCONE MAKING

Scones are the sure mark of the amazing kitchen skills of the older generation. Don't believe me? Then check out all this culinary lore you need to take in to make perfect scones. You'll need these when you turn the page.

1. Follow the recipe! This is basic stuff but especially important with scones, which need a lot of whichever raising agent you are using to ensure that they are light and puffy, high and handsome.

2. Or don't follow the recipe – well, follow it a bit, but instead of milk use fizzy lemonade for lighter scones or cream for richer scones.

3. Don't overwork the dough. In fact don't think of scone mix as a dough at all, but instead as ingredients that are no more than gently pulled together.

4. In fact rather than mixing the ingredients together, use a technique which is called 'cutting them together'. Use a flat-bladed knife or palette knife and cut it (or pull it) through your ingredients after you add the 'wet ingredients' so they are just barely incorporated.

5. Don't overwork the dough! Roll the dough out once only, and wield your rolling pin very lightly. Alternatively, you can gently press out the mix on the floured surface with the heel of your hand. About 3 cm thick is good.

6. Only lightly flour your work surface to press out the dough, as you want to avoid incorporating extra flour into your mixture.

7. Just a reminder: don't overwork the dough or your scones will turn out rubbery – or even worse, bullety and hard. Yuk!

8. The mixture should be moist, and while it should come out of the mixing bowl clean, expect it to leave your fingers a little sticky. Scone mix is far wetter than a dough – in fact somewhere between a batter and a dough.

9. Cut out your scones cleanly using only downwards pressure. Twisting the cutter can impair the rise. I like the impact of using a fluted cutter – which also means you can't twist it! If you don't have a cutter, just use a straight-edged glass or a kid's plastic beaker.

10. Pack the scones close together on the baking tray so they will support each other as they rise, rather than spread out. If they fuse together, don't worry as they can easily be torn apart.

11. As this is quite a light dough, it will cook quickly, so put the scones at the top of the oven where it's hottest – assuming your oven isn't fan forced. A fan-forced oven tends to help equalise temperatures across the oven – although you'll know where in your oven is hottest better than me.

12. Make scones the day you need 'em. They taste far better warm and they'll perfume the house beautifully.

13. If you want your scones to have a soft top, brush with milk 7 minutes into the cooking time. Or you can wrap them in a clean tea towel as soon as they come from the oven.

14. Never ever give only 13 golden rules for fear of bad baking karma.

CONTINUED

If you ever intend to embark as a contestant on the good ship MasterChef, there are a few things you need to know. To whit: 1) never skimp on the gravy; 2) only wear a hat if you want to be a national figure of derision; and 3) be very afraid of anything that comes from the country. Especially if that's a challenge involving the sort of baked goods that make up a judging class at the agricultural show at Deniliquin, Dumbleyung, Dubbo or Dalby.

Forget the 'croquembouche' and the V8 cake – few recipes ever caused more trouble on MasterChef than the scones in the CWA challenge in series two. But also, perhaps coincidentally, no recipe was more downloaded from series one than Gary's recipe for date scones.

In the sixties, seventies and eighties, scones were your nan's, the ones served for those genteel cream teas up in the hills, or Flo's pumpkin scones that went some way to distracting the populace from the shenanigans of her husband, Queensland Premier Sir Joh Bjelke Petersen. Yet Australia's love affair with scones now seems like something from an era of black and white movies, dating back to a time where generations of 'new' Australians were pilloried at school for what was in their lunch box – whether they were Greek, Indian or Italian.

Thankfully over the last decade this has started to change. It is wonderful that nowadays Aussie kids of all cultural backgrounds spend their cooking time making stir-fries or gnocchi and eating salami sandwiches, but there is also a sense that some of the old Anglo-Celtic ways have been left behind. The great thing about being part of a multicultural society is that you get to embrace other culinary cultures, but you also get to hang on to your own. With this in mind – and the education of the next wave of aspiring MasterChef contestants – it seemed like it was time to address 'Everything You Need to Know About Making Scones'.

SCONES

600 g (4 cups) self-raising flour
pinch of salt
40 g chilled butter, chopped

310 ml (1¼ cups) full-cream milk
125 ml (½ cup) cream, plus extra
for brushing

Preheat the oven to 230°C. Lightly butter a baking tray.

Place the flour, salt and butter into a bowl. Gently rub the butter into the flour, lightly lifting the mixture as you go to get air into it – I said gently and lightly!

When you've rubbed in all the butter, make a well in the centre and pour in the milk and cream. Mix with a flat-bladed knife, cutting the mixture together so that you barely pull it together.

Turn out on to a floured surface, flatten with the heel of your hand to about 3 cm and cut out the scones, using up all the dough. I use a very old, much beaten-up cutter 5.5 cm in diameter.

Place the scones close together on the baking tray.

Brush the tops of the scones with a little more cream and then place the tray in the very hot oven. Cook for 12–15 minutes. The scones are ready when they feel firm (not wet and squishy) when squeezed in the middle.

You can always try one to make sure they are perfect before you pull them from the oven – cook's treat!

Makes 12

First up, let me say that contrary to what has been said in the media this book IS NOT just a flimsy excuse for me to taste test thirty different chocolate brownie recipes. It just sort of worked out that way…

Now we all know that chocolate brownies are a bit of a lunchbox treat but they also have a very real currency in the playground black market. I think the current exchange rate here is one chocolate brownie = one large temporary cobra tattoo and your favourite footy card or five sparkly 'Stika-Lulu' water stickers. As such they are the perfect thing to bake for teaching your little ones the machinations of capitalism and the art of making a deal. But I think they can also do more!

CLASSIC CHOCOLATE BROWNIE

200 g good-quality dark chocolate
120 g unsalted butter, chopped
1 teaspoon vanilla extract
200 g brown sugar
2 eggs
150 g plain flour

1 teaspoon baking powder
½ teaspoon salt
100 g of bling – such as white chocolate, toasted whole almonds or walnuts
flake salt

Preheat the oven to 170°C.

Melt the chocolate with the butter and vanilla. Do this in the microwave, or in a metal bowl set over a smaller saucepan of boiling water, ensuring the base of the bowl does not touch the water. Stir until smooth. (Glove up and mind the steam if you use the saucepan method.) When smooth, remove from the heat. Stir in the sugar until it has dissolved into the chocolate. Now whisk in first one egg and then the next.

Mix the flour, baking powder and salt together. Sift a little of this mixture onto the chocolate mixture and fold it in. Keep going until all the flour is incorporated. Now it's time to add the bling!

Butter a low-sided metal slice tray and line with a sheet of baking paper, extending it beyond the long sides of the tray to act as a sling to lift the brown out of the tin.

Spoon the mixture into the tin and sprinkle with a few grains of flake salt. Bake for 25–30 minutes, which means the brownie will have risen, the top will look shiny and cracked in places and if you jab it with a skewer in the middle it will still come out a bit sticky and fudgy. Cook longer if it's still sludgy and wet.

Remove from the oven and leave to cool in the tin. Cut into squares and eat.

Serves 8

TIPS & TRICKS

- I'm torn between these classic brownies and the sultry and rather exotic malty lure of Tehan's Fabulous Brownies, aka The 'Other' Brownie. To make these, melt 310 g butter and 250 g grated dark chocolate in a saucepan. When melted, add 370 g (2 cups) brown sugar and 5 eggs. Then add 185 g (1¼ cups) plain flour, ¼ teaspoon baking powder, 60 g cocoa and mix. Lastly add 1 cup malt powder (aka Horlicks) and 170 g (1 cup) chocolate chips. Pour into a low-sided metal slice tray lined with baking paper. Bake for 50 minutes at 160°C.

Why do we try to limit the brownie's potential by sentencing it to always be consumed with little more than a cup of tea or glass of milk? Surely when the lights go out and the airtight lid is popped, with a slight burp back on the plastic brownie box, don't they start dreaming of being more… perhaps of even being… a fully fledged dessert. Now I am sure this sort of radical thinking is frowned on by the more conservative brownies who disapprove of such brownie activism but here we embrace change. Here we think that a brownie can very easily make the perfect centrepiece for any number of sexy desserts – and suddenly that tray of brownies you baked gets a second life. A glamorous second life swathed in rose petals and the crunch of almonds and partnered up with the easiest and quickest sorbet known to man or woman.

PIMP YOUR BROWNIE WITH CHEAT'S RASPBERRY ICE CREAM

400 g frozen raspberries
1 eggwhite
100 g sugar

50 g almond slivers
100 g white or dark chocolate
1 unsprayed red rose

Blitz 300 g of the frozen raspberries in a blender or food processor so they look like red crumbs.

Whisk the eggwhite until white and foamy but not peaky. Pour in the sugar and keep whisking. Add the raspberry bits and keep whisking for another 3 minutes. The mix will look deliciously pink and suitably airy.

Scrape into a 1 litre plastic container and pop in the freezer until it freezes. Due to the air incorporated in the mixture, this will take at least 2 hours.

Before serving, chill your plates. Toast the almonds shards in a dry pan until golden, then allow to cool. Cut six beautiful rectangles of brownie.

Finally get everyone sitting down. Blitz the remaining 100 g frozen raspberries and draw a line of this frozen raspberry powder across each plate. Place a brownie at the end of each line. Put a neat quenelle of raspberry ice cream on each one. Using a clean potato peeler, shave curls of chocolate along the line of frozen raspberry powder. Sprinkle the line with almonds and three rose petals. Serve and eat immediately.

Serves 6

MORE BROWNIE PIMPING IDEAS

- For the total chocoholic, why not serve your brownie with a slick of rich chocolate ganache and a dollop of chocolate mousse? For the chocolate mousse, melt 125 g good-quality chocolate, then blend it with 4 egg yolks. In a separate bowl, beat 4 eggwhites to stiff peaks and fold into the chocolate mixture. Pour into a bowl and leave to set in the fridge. For a more adult mousse, mix in a little warmed Frangelico or Tia Maria into the melted chocolate before folding in the fluffy whites.

- To make the chocolate ganache, warm 200 g cream and then pour it over 200 g broken-up chocolate to melt it. Stir in a double boiler (or in a bowl resting over simmering water) until combined and glossy. Add more cream if you want a pouring sauce. Go all exotic and flavour the cream with alcohol (Tia Maria, rum, etc) or infuse it with vanilla, ginger or even chilli while warming it and before pouring on the chocolate.

CLASSIC CHOCOLATE BROWNIE WITH CHEAT'S RASPBERRY ICE CREAM

Houston, Texas. 1993. I eat my first banana bread. It is toasted, slathered with cream cheese that has softened slightly with the heat of the bread and a shimmering emerald rubble of green chilli jelly. It confirms that banana bread is always better warm, but the search for the perfect recipe has been long.

It ended at the doorstep of the world's number 1 restaurant, Noma in Copenhagen, which is about as far from bananas as you can get. You see the thing is their top pastry chef here is from Chicago, and Rosio Sanchez cut her teeth as a kid by making banana bread. Needless to say it's good, very good – as you are about to find out.

BTW in this country please can I commend to you Andrew's banana bread at the Sonoma Bakery in Sydney and Justin's banana bread at Perth's West End Deli. If you have another banana bread you'd like to add, send me a tweet at @mattscravat with the hashtag #bananabread.

ROSIO'S BANANA BREAD

500 g walnuts
450 g sugar
40 g honey
milk, as needed
200 g butter

408 g plain flour (or tipo 00 if you can find it)
12 g bicarbonate of soda
1 teaspoon salt
3 eggs
700 g super-ripe bananas

Preheat the oven to 160°C.

If you prefer more crust to your cake, then Rosio recommends using one shallow baking tin. If you want a more cake-like banana bread, then the mixture should be cooked in two deep loaf tins. Butter the tin(s) and line the base(s) with baking paper.

Blanch the walnuts in boiling water three times to remove all the bitterness.

Blitz the walnuts with 50 g of sugar and the honey. Add enough milk so that the mixture blends easily and is moistened. Set the nuts aside. (Making this recipe without these ingredients works just fine, but the nuts add another depth of flavour.)

Make browned butter by heating the butter in a saucepan over a medium heat, stirring constantly with a whisk. Once it has reached a beautiful colour and a nutty smell, remove it from the heat and into a bowl that is sitting over ice to stop the cooking. You'll need 154 g of this browned butter.

Put the flour, bicarbonate of soda and salt into a bowl and set aside.

Whisk the eggs with the remaining sugar until the mixture is slightly paler. Mix in the bananas until fully incorporated. Next mix in the dry ingredients and then the brown butter, but do so slowly so that it is absorbed properly into the rest of the mixture. Finally stir in the nut mixture.

Pop in the oven for about 45 minutes. The exact time depends on the oven. The cake is cooked when a skewer inserted into the centre comes out clean.

Makes 2 large loaves, so give one to a friend

TIPS & TRICKS

- Feel free to spice up this recipe or add other things like shredded coconut or spices.

- Note that any nuts should be crushed so they are super fine and blended into the bread so the flavour is fully incorporated without adding much texture.

There always seems to be too much banana bread in a loaf, and so following on from my thinking on brownies (see pages 218–219) I wondered if it too could take its place as a dessert. The answer, of course, was a resounding yes! Especially as banana bread goes a little chewy when grilled or toasted. Good times!

If you want to step things up a little bit – both in terms of how your banana bread looks in the lunch box and also on the dessert plate – you could bake your banana bread mixture in mini muffin tins. Serve these warm from the oven or, if you've baked in the morning, re-warm in the microwave with a quick 30-second blitz just before serving as a dessert.

To serve, warm your chosen squares of banana bread by giving them a 30-second burst in the microwave. Pour some rum butterscotch on a serving plate. Place a square of the banana bread to paddle in it. Pop a scoop of the incredibly virtuous banana ice cream on top, along with some walnuts and a dollop of cream.

DOLL UP YOUR BANANA BREAD

SPICED RUM BUTTERSCOTCH

100 g (½ cup) brown sugar
125 g butter
125 ml (½ cup) cream
5 cloves
60 ml (¼ cup) rum

To serve
300 ml whipped cream
110 g walnuts

To make the spiced rum butterscotch, heat the brown sugar and butter together until the mixture starts to bubble. Add the cream, taking care as it may spatter, the cloves and half the rum and stir to mix. Cook gently to infuse all the flavours. Just before serving, mix in the remaining rum and remove the cloves.

TOO-SIMPLE, TOO-PURE BANANA ICE CREAM

2 very black, over ripe bananas, peeled, cut in thirds and frozen

To make the ice cream, blitz the pieces of frozen banana in a processor and magically it will come together like the world's most virtuous ice cream, ready to quenelle. Preserve the banana ice cream's cool in the freezer until needed. (Note: the bananas need to be really black or else the ice cream will be tannic and mucousy.)

TIPS & TRICKS
- Feel free to use peanuts instead of walnuts, and/or to add something fruity – perhaps plumped mandarin warmed in a little Cointreau and sugar, or just cubes of fresh mango, depending on the season.

I absolutely hate muffins – nasty, sawdusty excuses for cakes that have 'worthy', 'healthy' and 'con' written all over them. They promise so much when you read 'apple and cinnamon' or 'plump blueberry' but rather than some ethereal cloud of egg-bound flour overloaded with the succulent pop of fruit, what almost always appears is something stodgy, dense and about as appealing as a mud-snowball. Still, as they are one of Australia's three most-demanded recipes – alongside banana bread and brownies – it is beholden to me to try and ~~cash in~~ help reverse this trend. These muffins aren't bad – brilliant compared to most muffins, even – and the tang of loads of raspberry, the saltiness of the white chocolate and the crunch of the sugar crust all help. The muffin itself is good and crumbly too!

WHITE CHOCOLATE AND RASPBERRY MUFFINS

300 g (2 cups) self-raising flour
185 g (1 cup) brown sugar
2 large eggs
125 ml (½ cup) canola oil
185 ml (¾ cup) buttermilk

1 teaspoon vanilla extract
250 g (1 cup) white chocolate chips
300 g frozen or fresh raspberries
2 tablespoons raw sugar,
for topping

Preheat the oven to 170°C.

Line a 12-hole standard muffin tin or a six-hole large (Texas) muffin tin with paper cases.

Mix the flour with the brown sugar in a large bowl.

Whisk the eggs with the oil, buttermilk and vanilla in another bowl. Gently stir into the flour mixture until just combined. The mixture will be thick and slightly lumpy. Do not overmix, or your muffins will be tough.

Fold through the white chocolate chips and raspberries. Spoon into the muffin cases, filling them to about three-quarters full. Sprinkle raw sugar over the top. Bake for 20–25 minutes, until a skewer inserted in the centre of a muffin comes out clean. Remove from the oven, leave the muffins in the tin for a few minutes then remove them and cool on wire racks.

Makes 12 regular muffins or 6 large muffins

TIPS & TRICKS

- If you yearn for some crunch, add 50 g roughly smashed-up macadamias to your muffin mix.

- To make your own buttermilk, simply mix 185 ml (¾ cup) milk with 1 teaspoon lemon juice or vinegar.

- The 1 cup choc chips to 300 g fruit ratio works for other combos too – try dark choc and blueberries or milk chocolate and strawberries.

You know red velvet isn't just for smoking jackets, the heavy drapes in your billiard room or your gold-crested bedroom slippers. No, it is also for making cupcakes! Yes, I know cupcakes are all very last decade but these ones reference the American part of my cultural background and also have a bit of naughtiness about them with all that billowing white icing hiding a passionate red heart; a bit like an angel wearing saucy red lingerie under their shimmering white raiment. Also in this world where we are constantly being made to make choices – muffins or cupcakes, vampires or werewolves, seersucker or tweed – it's nice to echo the same red and white theme across the muffin and cupcake recipes here. For me cupcakes always win.

RED VELVET CUPCAKES WITH MARSHMALLOW FROSTING

300 g (2 cups) plain flour
60 g (½ cup) cocoa powder
1 teaspoon bicarbonate of soda
315 g (1½ cups) caster sugar
250 ml (1 cup) buttermilk
200 g unsalted butter, melted
2 eggs, lightly whisked
1 tablespoon white vinegar

1 teaspoon vanilla extract
1 tablespoon red food colouring

Marshmallow Frosting
3 eggwhites
165 g (¾ cup) caster sugar
¼ teaspoon cream of tartar
½ teaspoon vanilla extract

Preheat the oven to 170°C.

Line sixteen 80 ml (⅓ cup) capacity muffin holes with paper cases. Sift the flour, cocoa powder and bicarbonate of soda into a bowl. Stir through the sugar. Whisk the buttermilk, butter, eggs, vinegar and vanilla in a large jug until combined. Make a well in the centre of the flour mixture. Add the buttermilk mixture and stir until just combined. Stir in the food colouring.

Divide the mixture among the lined tins, filling them about three-quarters full. Bake for 20 minutes or until a skewer inserted into the centres comes out clean. Transfer to a wire rack to cool completely.

To make the frosting, place the eggwhites, sugar and cream of tartar in the top of a double boiler over medium heat. Whisk until the sugar dissolves, and the mixture is warm to the touch – about 3 minutes. Remove from the heat, add the vanilla, and use electric beaters to whip for 6–7 minutes or until stiff peaks form. Immediately pipe or spread over the cupcakes.

Makes 16

TIPS & TRICKS
- To make your own buttermilk, simply mix 250 ml (1 cup) milk with 1 teaspoon lemon juice or vinegar.

4 ways with...
BISCUITS

COCONUT BISCUITS

This easy-to-remember, never-fail recipe arrived with the wife as a sort of dowry. It could almost be the perfect biscuit, with a good friable crunch. Pull some out of the oven a little earlier and they'll be deliciously chewier.

90 g (1 cup) desiccated coconut
150 g (1 cup) self-raising flour
220 g (1 cup) sugar
1 egg
125 g butter, melted

Preheat the oven to 180°C.

Mix the dry ingredients together. Stir in the egg, then the butter. Work everything together with your fingers.

Form walnut-sized nuggets with your hands. They'll feel a little greasy, but resist the temptation to add more flour. Arrange on an ungreased baking tray, allowing lots of room for them to spread. Bake for 10 minutes. Allow to sit on the trays for a couple of minutes then transfer to a wire rack to cool.

Makes 30 small biscuits

BROWN SUGAR CRUNCHIES

I find these biscuits ridiculously addictive. I also love that you can store the sugared dough-logs (wrapped in baking paper) in the freezer. Cut cold and use as needed when you have drop-ins for tea.

185 g butter
150 g (¾ cup) light brown sugar, plus extra for sprinkling
300 g (2 cups) plain flour
pinch of salt

Preheat the oven to 180°C.

Cream the butter and sugar together, ideally in an electric mixer. Add the flour and salt and mix into a firm dough. Knead dough together and then form into two rolls, about 4 cm in diameter.

Sprinkle brown sugar on baking paper. Roll the dough up in the paper so it gets coated in the sugar. Rest in the fridge until needed (it should be firm).

Unwrap and slice into 5 mm discs. Arrange on a lined baking tray and cook for 15–25 minutes or until the brown sugar around the edges colours. The time needed will depend on how cool the dough is.

Allow to sit on the trays for a couple of minutes then transfer to a wire rack to cool.

Makes 30 small biscuits

THE MOTHER-IN-LAW'S SHORTBREAD

This recipe actually originally comes from one of Australia's shortbread legends, Jane Robbie, aka Jane Robinson, but as my mother-in-law Jude gave me the recipe, tradition and sucking-up demand that I must name it after her.

250 g butter
125 g sugar
375 g (2½ cups) plain flour
60 g cornflour
pinch of salt
caster sugar, for sprinkling

Preheat the oven to 170°C.

Cream the butter and sugar using an electric mixer until pale and fluffy.

Sift in the plain flour, cornflour and salt and mix until well combined. Turn out onto a lightly floured bench and knead until smooth. This will take about 3 minutes and 27 seconds (approx).

The mixture can be made into individual biscuits or into the traditional large round shape. For individual biscuits, roll the dough to the desired thickness and cut into the desired shapes. Let the kids play with the scraps – good times! Prick with a fork, sprinkle with caster sugar and place on a greased baking tray.

Alternatively, shape the dough into a round on a piece of baking paper (this makes it easier to transfer onto the baking tray) and score with eight equidistant dividing lines. Press a connecting thumbprint pattern evenly all around the edge. Prick with a fork, sprinkle with caster sugar and place on a baking tray.

Bake for 20 minutes. Allow to sit on the trays for a couple of minutes then transfer to a wire rack to cool.

Makes 25 small biscuits or 1 large round

ANZAC BISCUITS

Anzac Day provides an opportunity for some culinary remembrance.

100 g (1 cup) rolled oats
65 g (¾ cup) desiccated coconut
165 g (¾ cup) sugar
150 g (1 cup) plain flour
125 g butter
2 tablespoons golden syrup
1 teaspoon bicarbonate of soda
2 tablespoons boiling water

Preheat the oven to 150°C. Line a baking tray with greaseproof paper.

In a large bowl, mix together the rolled oats, coconut, sugar and flour.

Put the butter and golden syrup in a small saucepan over low heat and stir until melted and combined.

Mix the bicarbonate of soda with the boiling water and add to the butter mixture. Pour the butter mixture into the dry ingredients and stir until completely combined.

Roll heaped tablespoons of the mixture into balls between damp hands and place on a greased baking tray. Leave plenty of space between them, as they will spread. Press down slightly and bake for 15–20 minutes or until golden. Remove the tray from the oven. Allow them to sit on the trays for a couple of minutes then transfer to a wire rack to cool.

Makes 30 small biscuits

JEANETTE'S COCONUT DATE SLICE

125 g (1 cup) pitted dried dates
125 g (½ cup) sugar
90 g butter

120 g (4 cups) Rice Bubbles
175 g (2 cups) desiccated coconut

In a large, heavy-bottomed saucepan, slowly simmer together the dates, sugar and butter until the dates are soft and mushy (about 15 minutes). You can chop the dates first, but it is not necessary. When it is done, the cooked mush will taste fudgy. Do not cook too long or too hot or the caramel may burn, become bitter or set so hard it will turn into a binding agent strong enough to crack the teeth of a carthorse.

Add the Rice Bubbles. Stir in well, then press into an 18–20 cm square cake tin lined with baking paper so the mixture is 3–4 cm thick. Put in the refrigerator for 2 hours.

Cut into 25 cubes and roll in coconut.

Hate dates? Then melt four Mars bars with 125g of butter and then mix that through the Rice Bubbles instead. Decorate with drizzles of melted chocolate on top – if you can be bothered.

Makes 25

One of the perks of taking a bus up the Hume Highway is a certain bus driver on the Euroa line and the slices that her mother-in-law makes. The topping is more like a thick, nutty glaze than an icing so feel free to increase the quantity of topping by, say, 25 per cent if you want an extra-generous covering on the slice. This is another of the recipes in this book that you must make no matter what!

BUS DRIVER'S MOTHER-IN-LAW'S SLICE

Base
90 g butter, melted
120 g (½ cup firmly packed) brown sugar
150 g (1 cup) plain flour
70 g (½ cup) packaged ground almonds

Almond Topping
125 g butter, chopped
95 g (¼ cup) honey
200 g (1 ½ cups) slivered almonds

Preheat the oven to 170°C.

Combine the base ingredients and mix well. If the base seems floury, add a little extra melted butter. Press into a greased 18 cm x 32 cm lamington or slice tray. (If you do not have a tray this size, use a smaller tray rather than a larger one. This is a fairly thin slice, and the mixture may not be enough to cover a larger tray.)

Bake for 12 minutes or until lightly browned. Remove from the oven, but leave the oven on while the slice is cooling and make the almond topping. Combine the butter and honey in a small, heavy-based saucepan and stir over heat until the butter is melted. Simmer, uncovered, for about 3 minutes or until mixture is a light caramel colour. Stir in the nuts.

Spread the base with the hot topping and bake for about 15 minutes or until golden brown. Cool in the tray then cut into squares.

Makes 15

MUST DOS WHEN SLICE BAKING

- Always have a pot of tea on the go.

- Grease the baking tin with butter and line it with baking paper.

- All spoon measurements are for a spoon levelled off with a knife, not a heaped spoon – unless otherwise specified.

- Cup measurements are for loosely filled cups rather than 'packed' cups – unless otherwise specified.

- Note that some recipes use different tin sizes, which is undoubtedly a conspiracy by cake tin manufacturers. Generally though, so long as the surface area of your tin is about the same as the one given, you should be right. Just keep an eye on the slice when it is cooking, because the different dimensions can alter your cooking times slightly.

- When in doubt, cool in the tin.

- If you like any of these recipes, pass them on to your friends.

RATIO RANTS

Nowhere are ratios more important that in the kitchen. Every recipe broken down to its purest form becomes an easy-to-remember ratio. The ratios here are largely measured around weight rather than volume as weight is a more reliable standard measure.

BASIC PASTRY

The recipe: 2 parts flour, 1 part butter

Kneading together two parts of plain flour with one part of fat will make a very basic pie pastry. Remember that the secret to great pastry is gently rubbing the flour and butter together, then pulling the dough gently together and not working it too much or it will become tough. Leaving lumps of butter in the dough will make for a lovely flaky pastry. For a richer pastry, try '3-2-1 pastry' using three parts flour, two parts butter and one part water – adding a little lemon juice to your water before using will improve the pastry.

TIPS & TRICKS

- Always use cold ingredients. Ice-cold butter, iced water and cold equipment give the best results. If you've got hot hands, use a food processor to combine the ingredients.

- Wrap your pastry, formed into a disk, in cling film and pop it in the fridge to rest and chill for about 30 minutes before rolling. You don't want the fat to melt as this is what will make the pastry light.

- Once you've rolled it out and laid it in the pie dish, rest it for about 30 minutes before baking it, to stop it contracting while cooking.

SAVOURY CUSTARD PIE FILLING

The recipe: Equal parts cream, milk and egg

Use this as the basis for any set savoury custards, such as the filling for a tart. Or think of an asparagus and tarragon custard with chicken, or a pot of Japanese chawanmushi custard full of mushrooms with dashi and a dash of soy replacing the milk.

To make, whisk together 100 g of cream, 100 g milk and 100 g egg. Season with salt and any other seasonings you want to use. For a quiche or tart, bake in a blind-baked pastry case. For a savoury custard, cook in the oven in a water bath until set.

WHITE SAUCE OR VELOUTÉ

The recipe: 6 parts flour, 4 parts butter, 30 parts milk

Blend 60 g of plain flour into 40 g of melted butter to make a roux, or thickening agent. Add milk to make a white sauce (aka béchamel). Add stock to make a velouté, which is a great sauce base or velvety gravy.

The flour in this roux can swell to bind up to 10 times its volume of liquid, but the more that you cook out the flour and butter mix, the less thickening power it will have. A browned roux will add some nutty deliciousness to your velouté. It also works as the base soup for a chowder.

TIPS & TRICKS

- Add 10 parts grated cheese such as cheddar or parmesan to your white sauce to make cheese sauce.

- You can infuse your milk with aromatics like nutmeg, bay leaf, cloves or onions to give your white sauces some more complexity.

SWEET PASTRY

The recipe: 3 parts flour, 2 parts butter, 1 part water, 1/3 part sugar

- For a simple sweet pastry, just use your fingertips to combine 300 g of flour with 200 g of butter, rubbing the butter in until the mixture resembles breadcrumbs. Mix in 35 g of sugar and then add 100 ml of water to pull the dough together. Flatten your pastry into a disc, wrap in cling film and pop in the fridge for about 30 minutes to rest and chill it before you roll it out. You don't want the fat to melt as this is what will make the pastry light. Once rested, roll it out, use it to line a pie dish, then rest it again to stop it contracting while cooking.

CUSTARD

The recipe: 4 parts milk/cream, 1 part sugar, 1 part egg yolks

Whether to pour on your apple pie or chill to turn into ice cream, this custard ratio is always there for you! Just simmer 400 g of milk and/or cream with a split vanilla pod. Then remove from the heat, scrape the vanilla seeds into the milk and leave to infuse and cool a little. Whisk 100 g of sugar and 100 g of egg yolks together until they are frothy. Now pour the warm (but not hot) milk over the egg mixture while whisking. Return this combo to the pan and stir over a gentle heat until it thickens to a spoon-coating consistency. Serve as is with dessert, or if using it for ice cream, strain into a bowl set over iced water to cool.

TIPS & TRICKS

- To make crème brûlée from this custard, preheat the oven to 170°C. Into the oven place a high-sided baking tray half-filled with warm water. Pour the custard into ramekins. Place them in this water bath to bake for 30 minutes or until just set. Test them by inserting a knife into the custard – if it comes out clean, the custard is ready. Then remove, dust the tops with sugar and brûlée under a ridiculously hot grill or use a kitchen blowtorch.

VANILLA PANNACOTTA

The recipe: 300 ml milk, 600 ml cream, 150 g sugar, 4 teaspoons gelatine

Bring 300 ml of milk just to the boil with a vanilla pod in it. Spoon a good splash of the warm milk into a cup and mix in 4 teaspoons of powdered gelatine so it dissolves. Leave to stand. Remove the vanilla pod from the milk and scrape the seeds into the milk. Add 600 ml of cream to the milk and bring to a simmer. Stir in 150 g of sugar until dissolved. Stir in the gelatin mixture. Pour the mixture into individual oiled moulds and place in the fridge to set for 4–6 hours.

TIPS & TRICKS

- If your pannacottas prove tricky to turn out, first run a knife around the edge of the mould to ease the surface tension. If that fails, place the moulds into a bath of hot water to melt the sticky edges slightly.

CHOCOLATE MOUSSE

The recipe: 125 g chocolate, 4 eggs

Melt 125 g of good chocolate and then blend with 4 egg yolks. Beat the whites up to stiff peaks and fold into the chocolate mixture. Pour into a bowl and leave to set in the fridge. Serve with stewed apricots or tart berries and whipped cream.

THANKS

Publisher, wordsmith and muse Mary Small, for just being practically perfect in every way, and simply 'getting it'. Ellie Smith, for her humour and for pushing me. Mark Roper, for being a good friend, a fantastic travelling companion and the most unflappable and happy photographer ever put on this planet. Style queen and über-cook Caroline Velik, for finally agreeing to work with me and for making the food in this book look so very good. Jamie Humby, Fiona Rigg, Peta Gray and Marnie Rowe for their cooking – and Marnie for her brutal but most valued honesty about the recipes that needed to be dropped. That's why there's no dodgy chickpea soup in this book – the world thanks you! Pauline Haas, for typesetting that went well beyond the call, and Kirby Armstrong, for delivering a design that manages to make my words look a lot more approachable than they are. The whole team at Pan Macmillan, in particular Joybelle McIntosh, who is both a paragon of fashion and the reason I ended up at Pan – if she hadn't posted my Spag Bol recipe from the *Herald Sun* up on the notice board, who knows if they would have ever signed me!

Along my decade-long road of recipe writing I have had many mentors and guides but I'd especially like to thank the amazing Valli Little and her team, Kylie Walker, Kate Murdoch (and Ollie) and the teams at both *Delicious* magazine and at *Taste*, including John McGourty and visual wizard Steve Moorhouse. *Taste* editor Jana Frawley has been especially influential using both the carrot and the stick in shaping much of my current approach to recipe writing – I owe her a huge debt of gratitude. She is responsible for much of what is good here, and absolutely none of what is bad!

The last ten years or so have been made all the more satisfying by the wisdom and long-term friendship of my three editors at NewsLifeMedia: Trudi Jenkins, Sally Feldman and Danielle Opperman. They have inspired me (not surprising), continued to employ me (surprising) and even occasionally forgiven me for late copy (even more surprising!). My life is made all the sweeter by having these collaborators and others who understand where I live and work far better than I do – people like Fiona Nilsson, Nicole Sheffield, Sarah Nicholson, Caroline Roessler; and Sandra Hook, Tim Sligo and Alan Oakley, who got me on board at News Ltd. Also my other great photographic collaborator, Catherine Sutherland.

Inspiration and wisdom doesn't just come from those I work with, and I'd also like to acknowledge the dizzying amount of light-bulb moments and knowledge shared by so many chefs and cooks both here and overseas – some are represented in the book, such as Maggie Beer, Adriano Zumbo, Rick Stein, Heston Blumenthal, David Chang, Darren Purchese, Brett Graham and Rosio Sanchez, but so many aren't and to them I say thank you.

Specifically those cooks who have championed a simpler style of fresh, flavour-packed cooking that I have slavishly devoured, from Margaret Fulton onwards and including Donna Hay, Jill Dupleix, Karen Martini, Maggie Beer, Bill Granger, Sophia Young – and Valli Little and Caroline Velik obviously. I have also drawn massive inspiration from spending time listening to great chefs like Massimo Bottura, Rene Redzepi, Gaultiero Marchesi, Antonio Carluccio, Stephanie Alexander, Wylie Dufresne, Shane Osborn, Philippa Sibley, Paul Wilson, Mario Batali, David Thompson, Ben Shewry, Brett Graham, Andrew McConnell, Christine Manfield, Thomas Keller and Michel Roux. And hats off to my fellow food writers, both in Australia and overseas, who continue to inspire, excite and to make people think more about the food they eat.

I'd like to thank all those friends (and friends of friends) who have been willing to share their recipes and ideas with me. Foremost is my old housemate Jen 'Ryan' and my mother-in-law, Jude. I've tried to mention those others where relevant but my salami guru Emi di Fasio warrants a special mention.

Thank you to my children, Jono, Will and Sadie, who are far better critics than I could ever be, and my wife Emma, who is my favourite cook in the world. I love you, thank you. I know I've always said I married you for your gnocchi but there was so much more!

Having spent the last 15 years thinking often and occasionally deeply about food, much of that has been fired by all the *MasterChef* contestants that I have had the pleasure of working with, and of course, Gary and George, who are constant weather vanes and a living, breathing brains trust when it comes to advice on cooking just about anything! Thank you boys, for everything.

Finally, a huge thankyou to my other family: the beautiful and extremely smart Henrie Stride, Mark Klemens and all at Profile Talent Management, my legal eagles David Vodicka and Yasmin Naghavi, moneyman

INDEX

A Plum book
First published in 2012 by
Pan Macmillan Australia Pty Limited
Level 25, 1 Market Street,
Sydney, NSW 2000, Australia

Level 1, 15–19 Claremont Street,
South Yarra, Victoria 3141, Australia

A CIP catalogue record for this book is available from the
National Library of Australia.

Photography by Mark Roper
Designed by Kirby Armstrong
Food preparation by Marnie Rowe, Jamie Humby, Fiona Rigg and Peta Gray
Styling by Caroline Velik
Typeset by Pauline Haas
Edited by Susie Ashworth and Janine Flew
Indexed by Jo Rudd

Colour reproduction by Splitting Image, Clayton, Victoria
Printed and bound in China by 1010 Printing International Limited

Front cover: Lemon tart with marshmallow meringue topping (page 177)

Versions of the recipes on the following pages appeared originally
in *Delicious* magazine: 17, 18, 32, 92, 130, 157

Versions of the recipes on the following pages appeared originally in the
Taste section of the *Herald Sun*, *Daily Telegraph*, *Courier Mail*, *The
Adelaide Advertiser*, *Sunday Times* and *The Mercury*: 2–3, 4, 9, 10,
23, 26, 29, 42, 43, 45, 52, 54, 55, 60, 62, 65, 68, 71, 74, 79, 83, 84, 86,
88–89 90, 96, 98–101, 104, 105, 106, 107, 110, 111, 112, 114, 116, 120,
121, 123, 124, 127, 136, 138, 142, 144, 147, 150, 152, 155, 157, 158,
159, 162, 163, 164, 165, 166, 172, 178, 183, 184, 186–189, 190, 196,
202, 203, 210, 216, 234, 235